JOURNAL

OF THE

WATERLOO CAMPAIGN

JOURNAL

OF THE

WATERLOO CAMPAIGN

KEPT THROUGHOUT THE CAMPAIGN OF 1815

BY THE LATE
GENERAL CAVALIÉ MERCER
COMMANDING THE 9TH BRIGADE ROYAL ARTILLERY

IN TWO VOLUMES
VOL. I.

WILLIAM BLACKWOOD AND SONS
EDINBURGH AND LONDON
MDCCCLXX

PREFACE.

THIS work—the 'Journal of the Campaign of 1815'—was written by my father in its present form about forty years ago, from rough notes jotted down every evening after the scenes and events of the day were over. It has no pretension to be an account of the military operations of the war, but merely a diary of the writer's own impressions—what he saw and felt while with the army, from the first landing in Belgium to the final embarkation for England. Of the great battle, no other description than that of the part taken in it by his own troop of Horse Artillery, or those corps in his immediate vicinity, is given; but from its very nature as a diary, the tedium of out-quarters, the fatigues of the march, and the hardships of the bivouac, are made present, as it were, to the reader. My father having been a very good amateur artist, was much struck, of course, by new and picturesque scenes, consequently has described them *con amore*, and in considerable detail. The author himself belonged to a military race; all his family were either in the army or navy. He was the second son of General Mercer of the Royal Engineers, who, after serving on Sir H. Clinton's staff during the American War of Independence, was more than twenty years commanding engineer in the West of England, where his honourable character procured him many friends. My father (also a general officer at the time of his death) was born in 1783, and passing as usual through the Military Academy at Woolwich, obtained a commission in the Royal Artillery at sixteen, and was sent to Ireland at the time of the Rebellion. In 1808 he went to the river Plate to join Whitelock's unfortunate expedition, and covered the retreat from Buenos Ayres. This proved a most unhappy affair for him; for having been in South America, he was prevented from partaking in the glorious campaigns of the Peninsula, and only saw foreign service again in the campaign of

Waterloo. After the peace, he was placed upon half-pay. In 1824 he was ordered to Canada, having the brevet rank of major (I should have noticed that at Waterloo he only held the rank of second captain, although commanding a troop —Sir Alex. Dickson, whose troop it was, being otherwise employed). In 1837, being then a lieutenant-colonel, he was again sent to North America, and commanded the artillery in Nova Scotia at the time when the Maine boundary-line threatened to terminate in a war between this country and the United States. He subsequently commanded the garrison at Dover, after which he retired from active service, although, being colonel-commandant of the 9th Brigade of Royal Artillery, he was never placed on the retired list. From that time to the period of his death, at the advanced age of eighty-five, he continued to reside at Cowley Cottage, near Exeter.

Another addition to the numerous books which have been published about Waterloo will hardly seem out of place at a time when the subject has been revived both here and in France. It would seem that men's interest in this great "World Battle" is as strong now as fifty years ago; and although this little contribution will not elucidate any of the questions that are agitated, still (as far as memory serves) it is the first account of the campaign given to the world by an artillery officer, and may add another stone to the cairn raised to the glory of the British army and its immortal chief. At any rate, the surviving veterans of this stirring epoch will rejoice to go again over the scenes of their younger days; while the lovers of peace will congratulate themselves on the cessation of such strife between two noble nations, whose last (and may it continue to be the last) hostile *rencontre* took place upon the plain of Waterloo.

CAVALIÉ A. MERCER.

Tripoli, Syria.

CONTENTS OF THE FIRST VOLUME.

CHAPTER I.

Preparations for Departure—Reports of Fugitives—Embarkation and Departure—The Voyage—Off the Coast—First View of Ostend—Aspect of the Coast—Ostend Harbour—Its Dangers—Unceremonious Landing of Dragoon Horses, . . 1

CHAPTER II.

Confusion at Landing—Scene on Shore—Difficulties—Confusion on the Beach—A Catastrophe—The Town by Night—Difficulties of the March—Night Quarters—A Pleasant Change—Return to Ostend—Waiting to Start—Costumes of the Natives—Scenes in the Town—A Wreck—Fearful Scene—Impressions of Ostend, ... 14

CHAPTER III.

Change of Scenery—Arrival at Ghistel—Our Quarters there—Again on the March—Arrival at Bruges—Our Hotel—First Impressions of Bruges—Present and Past—The Stadthouse and Cathedral—Mass in the Cathedral—The Worshippers—The Ramparts—Dinner, ... 32

CHAPTER IV.

Eccloo—Arrival at Ghent—Our Quarters there—My Host—My Quarters—Louis XVIII. and his Court—French Officers—Marshal Marmont—French Deserters—Ghent—Street Architecture—The Place D'Armes—Flemish Postilions—View from the Citadel—The Corn-Market—The Hôtel de Ville—Meat and Vegetable Markets—General Order and Cleanliness—A Suppressed Monastery—The Cathedral—A Royal Mass—Domestic Architecture—An Interior—Comfortable Quarters—Numbers of Priests—Costumes—Character of the People—Immorality—German and English Cavalry, . 46

CHAPTER V.

Again on the March—The Pays de Waes—Lokern—A Village Curé—Dendermonde—My Quarters at St Gille—View from my Windows—Kindness of the Natives—A Flemish Farmhouse—Fertility of the Land—At Dinner—Our Host—Attachment to Napoleon—Peace and War—Flemish Teams—Cattle and Sheep—Dendermonde, ... 78

CHAPTER VI.

Excursion to Alost—Aspect of the Place—We Lose our Way—Again on the Move—Parting with my Hostess—A Last Breakfast—On the March—Change of Scenery—Views from the Hills—Beauty of the Country—Arrival at Strytem—The Chateau—Our Quarters there—Comfortless Prospect—Family Portraits—Choosing our Quarters—A Private Chapel—Increasing Comfort—Our Mess-Room—Karl—His History—His Acquirements—An Interruption—The Maire and his Following—A Garde-Champêtre—A Scene—M. L'Adjoint's Speech—Our Answer to it—I am peremptory—The Deputation in a Fright—The Mayor in Safe Keeping—Petit Jean—A Sleepless Night, . . . 100

CHAPTER VII.

Occupations at Strytem—Our Fare—The Country round Strytem—Beauty of the Scenery—Rich Cultivation—The Flemish Farmers—Farming Establishments—Execrable Roads—Drunkenness—Frog-Concerts—Draining the Moat—Result of the Experiment—The Duc de Berri—His Brutality—A Dog-Chase—Disposition of the Troops—Visitors from England—The Duc de Berri again—Artillery at Waterloo—Our Equipment—Our Organisation, ... 138

CONTENTS. xi

CHAPTER VIII.

My Difficulties—Plundering—The Duke and the Rocket Troop—
Ride to Ninove—Ninove—The great Monastery—A ruined
Convent—Liederkerke—Aspect of the Country—A Character—The Lord of Gaesbeke—The Chateau de Gaesbeke—
My Reception—The Marquis D'Acornati—Interior of the
Chateau : its desolate Aspect—The Kitchen—The Grounds :
their Beauty—Variety of Views—History of the Chateau—
Career of its Owner—His Singularities—His Mode of Life
—Visits to the Grounds, ... 163

CHAPTER IX.

Visit to Hal—Return to Strytem—Start for Brussels—First View
of Brussels—Its Internal Aspect—The Park—The Ramparts—The Hôtel de Ville—The Cathedral—The Bruxellaises—The Allée-Vert—Prince D'Aremberg—A Mistake—
Anticipations of the Campaign, ... 194

CHAPTER X.

Cavalry Review—The Duc de Berri again—His Unceremonious
Reception—The Duke and Blucher—Dinner after the Review—Strytem again—New Species of Game—Change of
Quarters—A Death—Visit from our Host—Our Landlord
—A Spy—Approaching Departure, . . . 212

CHAPTER XI.

Order to Advance—Preparations—Farewell to Strytem—On the
March—News from Brussels—Halt at Enghien—Doubts as
to my Route—Uncertainties—Braine le Comte—Still without Orders—Beauty of the Scenery—We are left alone—
Sounds of Distant Battle—Pressing on—Nivelle—Excitement in the Town—Signs of Battle—Fugitives from the
Field—A Wounded Highlander—Belgian Gasconading, . 230

CHAPTER XII.

At Quatre Bras—Our Bivouac—Morning after the Battle—Our
Position—The Battle-Field—Position of the French—Skirmishing—An Alarm—The Retreat—Aspect of the Field—

A Memento of Battle—Alone on the Field—Inactivity of the Enemy—Their Advance—Orders and Counter-Orders—Napoleon—A 'Storm—Our Danger—Our Narrow Escape—Our Retreat—Arrival at Genappe—The Enemy again—In Action with them—The Rocket Brigade—An Eccentric Missile—Panic among the Brunswickers—Take up Position—Rejoin the Army—Bivouac for the Night—Discomforts—Comfortless Night—Speculations as to the Morrow—A Godsend,   253

CHAPTER XIII.

Morning of Battle—Survey of the Field — Alarm of Battle—Commencement of the Battle—Orders at last—Take up Position—The Field of Battle—View from our Position—Our own Position — We open Fire — Our first Casualty—An Alarmed Doctor—Death of Captain Bolton—A Wounded Horse—A Cavalry Charge—Our Situation—Advance of Cavalry — Dangerous Mistake — New Position—The Brunswickers — Danger of Panic—Advance of Cavalry—Their Retreat—Our first Death—Skirmishers—Attack Renewed—Effect of our Fire—The Cavalry again Repulsed—A Narrow Escape—A third Attack and Repulse—The Duke—Heavy Fire—Fearful Losses—Further Escapes—A Remonstrance—Our Losses—Victory—Arrival of Prussians—The Field by Moonlight—The Prussian Bivouac—Moonlight Thoughts,   291

CHAPTER XIV.

Preparing to Move—The Field by Morning—The Wounded—The French Wounded—An Ingrate—A Grenadier à Cheval—A Welcome Feast—Visitors from Brussels—Visit to Hougoumont—A Contrast—Garden of the Chateau—A Striking Oration—A Noble Enemy—A Keepsake—A Recognition—On the March—A Comfortable Bivouac—Resume our March—Block before Nivelles—Reception in the Town—Aspect of the Town—Arrival of Prisoners—We get on at last—Belgic Infantry—Our Bivouac—Rejoin the Army—The Greys and Highlanders—Aspect of the Country—We Cross the Frontier—Our first Night in France, ...   338

JOURNAL

OF THE

WATERLOO CAMPAIGN.

CHAPTER I.

THE return of Napoleon from Elba, though a surprise to many, was far from being so to those who, well aware of his restless disposition, his insatiable ambition, and the enthusiastic attachment of the French soldiery to his person and fortunes, had scarcely expected that he would have remained so long as he actually did without some new attempt at disturbing the general peace.

The steps taken on this occasion by the different European Powers—their preparations for a renewal of the bloody scenes so lately ended—are out of my province. They belong to the historian, and not to the simple journalist, whose affair it is to confine himself strictly to those transactions in which he was himself a participator; or at most to glance at those more general subjects, merely to give connection to his narrative and make it better understood.

At the time the news of this extraordinary event arrived, the troop of horse-artillery which I commanded was stationed at Colchester; and the reductions necessary to put us on a peace-establishment had already commenced, when the order arrived for our being immediately equipped again for foreign service. To do this effectually, another troop, then in the same barracks, was broken up, and we got the picked horses of both, thus making it the finest troop in the service; and such diligence was used, that although our equipment fell little short of a complete reorganisation, Major Sir A. Fraser, commanding the horse-artillery in Colchester, was enabled to report on the third day that the troop was ready to march at a moment's warning.

Meantime the town of Colchester (situated as it is on the great road from Harwich to London) presented a scene of bustle and anxiety seldom equalled—couriers passing to and fro incessantly, and numerous travellers, foreign and English, arriving day and night from the Continent, many travelling in breathless haste, as if fearful, even here, of Napoleon's emissaries.

The reports spread by these fugitives were various and contradictory, as might be expected.

According to some, Louis XVIII. had been arrested in Paris; according to others, he had sought refuge in the Pays Bas; and again, it was asserted that his Majesty was at Ostend, awaiting permission to pass the sea and return to his old and secure quarters in England.

In the midst of all this, on the 8th April, the post brought our order to march forthwith to Harwich, there to embark for Ostend— an order received with unfeigned joy by officers and men, all eager to plunge into danger and bloodshed, all hoping to obtain glory and distinction.

On the morning of the 9th, the troop paraded at half-past seven o'clock with as much regularity and as quietly as if only going to a field-day; not a man either absent or intoxicated, and every part of the guns and appointments in the most perfect order. At eight, the hour named in orders, we marched off the parade. The weather was fine, the scenery, as we skirted the beautiful banks of the Stour, charming, and the occasion exhilarating.

Near Manningtree we halted a short time to feed our horses, and then, pursuing our route, arrived at Harwich about three o'clock in the afternoon. Here we found the transports — the Adventure, Philarea, and Salus, in which last I embarked — awaiting us; but the tide being unfavourable, although we immediately commenced operations, we only succeeded in embarking the horses of one division and those of the officers; the remainder were therefore put up in the barracks for the night. As might be expected, the little town of Harwich presented a most animated spectacle. Its narrow streets of modest houses, with brick trottoirs, were crowded with soldiers—some, all over dust, just arrived; some, who had already been a day or two in the place, comparatively at home, lounging about in undress; others, about to embark, hurrying along to the beach with baggage and stores; sailors marketing, or rolling about half-seas-over; country-people bringing in vegetables and the like, and towns-people idling at their windows, or in groups at corners of the streets — in short, the usual picture incident on such occasions.

The morning of the 10th was foggy, which

much retarded us, since it was necessary to embark the horses in flats to be taken off to the transports, not easily found in the fog. However, by noon all were on board, and without any serious accident, although a sailor was somewhat hurt in endeavouring to recover a horse that had fallen overboard. In the afternoon our guns, carriages, &c., were embarked; but as the wind blew right into the harbour, the agent would not attempt to get out, and we adjourned to Mr Bull's comfortable house (the Three Cups), there to pass our last evening in England in the enjoyment of a good dinner, and perhaps for the last time to sleep in good beds.

About two P.M. on the 11th, a light breeze from the N.W. induced our agent to get under way, and we repaired on board our respective ships with every prospect of a good and speedy passage. In this, however, we were disappointed, for the breeze dying away as the sun went down, we anchored, by signal, at the harbour's mouth, just as it got dark.

The evening was splendid. A clear sky studded with myriads of stars overhead, and below a calm unruffled sea, reflecting on its glassy surface the lights of the distant town, the low murmuring sounds from which, and the rippling of the water under the ships' bows, were the only interruptions to the solemn stillness that prevailed after the people had retired to their berths. In our more immediate neighbourhood stretched out the long, low, sandy tract, on the seaward extremity of which the dark masses of Landguard fort could just be distinguished.

With daybreak on the morning of the 12th came a favourable wind, though light, and again we took up our anchors and proceeded to sea. For some distance, after clearing the harbour, our course lay along the Suffolk coast, and so near in that objects on shore were plainly discernible. To us, who had long been stationed at Woodbridge, only a few miles inland, this was highly interesting. We knew every village, every copse, every knoll—nay, almost every tree. There were the houses in which we had so oft been hospitably entertained; there were the sheep-walks on which we had so often manœuvred; and there in the distance, as we passed the mouth of the Deben, our glasses showed us the very barrack on the hill, with its tiled roofs illumined by the noontide sun. About Bawdsey we left the coast, and steered straight over, with a light but favourable wind: the low sandy shores of Suffolk soon sank beneath the horizon. At noon fell in with a fleet of colliers bound for the river, and soon after saw the Sunk-Sand Light; when, as the wind had died away and the tide was setting us towards the bank, we anchored until the flood-tide. During the night a light breeze right aft, and smooth water, enabled us to make good progress; but towards morning (13th) the wind had very considerably increased, and although the coast was not in sight, we were sensible of its neighbourhood from the number of curious heavy-looking boats plying round us in all directions, having the foremast, with its huge lug-sail, stuck right up in the bow, or rather inclining over it. From one of these boats we soon procured a pilot —a little sturdy fellow, with a full, good-humoured countenance, and his breast decorated with a silver medal bearing the impress of an anchor, like our porters' tickets, the badge of his calling.

The poor fellow was hardly on deck ere he was surrounded and assailed by innumerable questions —"Where is Buonaparte?" "Where is the French army?" "What are the English about?" "Has there been any fighting?" &c. &c. Of this he understood or heard only the word "Buonaparte," and therefore to all kept repeating, "Il est capôte," accompanied by a significant motion of the hand across the throat, at the same time showing much anxiety to get rid of his tormentors and proceed to business, which he did with such earnestness as soon gave us to understand there must be more than ordinary difficulty in entering the port of Ostend. The first and principal care was the getting up a hawser and coiling it on deck, the use of which we were soon to learn.

Meanwhile we had been approaching the coast, which, though still invisible, the pilot informed us was not distant. The first intimation of the truth of this was the appearance of the church tower and lofty lighthouse of Ostend; and we had brought about half their height above the horizon before land began to show itself, which it did in a number of isolated and rounded yellow hummocks, and at the same time the houses of the town became distinctly visible. With that impatience and excessive curiosity always felt upon approaching for the first time a strange land, especially under the present interesting state of things, all our glasses were directed to the coast, which we were rapidly nearing and hoped soon to reach, when, to our great disappointment, the pilot ordered the vessel to be hove to, and we found that the tide would not permit our running for the port before two P.M. Numbers of ships, brigs, and schooners were lying-to as well as ourselves, and others continually arriving.

Nothing, certainly, could be more repulsive than the appearance of the coast — sand-hills as far as the eye could reach, broken only by the grey and lugubrious works and buildings of Ostend, and further west by the spires of Mittelkerke and Nieuport, peering above the sandhills. The day, too, was one little calculated to enliven the scene. A fresh breeze and cloudy sky; the sea black, rough, and chilly; the land all under one uniform cold grey tint, presenting scarcely any relief of light and shadow, consequently no feature. Upon reconnoitring it, however, closer, we found that this forbidding exterior was only an outer coating to a lovely gem. Through the openings between the sandhills could be seen a rich level country, of the liveliest verdure, studded with villages and farms interspersed amongst avenues of trees and small patches of wood. An occasional gleam of sunshine breaking out and illumining it, communicated to it a dreamy appearance that was very pleasing, and tended to revive our spirits, drooping from the gloomy aspect of the coast.

A black-looking mass of timber rising from the

waters off the entrance of the harbour, and which we understood to be a fort, now became the principal object of our attention. As the tide rises the depth of water is announced by different flags hoisted on this fort; and we were delighted when at last that (a red one) indicating the necessary depth for our ship was hoisted, and we bore up for the harbour mouth.

The harbour of Ostend is an artificial one, formed by *jetées* of piles projecting as far as low-water mark. The right, on entering, is merely a row of piles running along in front of the works of the town; but on the left is a long mole or *jetée*, on the extremity of which is a small fort. Behind this mole, to the north-east, the shore curving inwards forms a bight, presenting an extent of flat sandy beach on which the water is never more than a few feet deep, even at the highest tides. A tremendous surf breaks on this whenever it blows from the westward. As the flood-tide sets past the harbour mouth with great rapidity, a vessel attempting to enter with a westerly wind is in danger of being swept beyond it and thrown on the beach just mentioned. And this we now discovered was the cause of the anxiety displayed by our pilot, and for which we could not before account. In approaching the harbour, we steered as if going to run the ship ashore on the broad stone glacis of the town, which extended into the water all along the sea-front. Even with this precaution we were drifted so much to leeward that, instead of shooting into the harbour, we went bump upon the *jetée*.* The poor pilot raved and jumped about like a madman, but there still was method in his madness; and now we discovered the use of the hawser he had coiled upon deck, for passing the end of this to the Belgic soldiers, who upon the shock immediately ran out of their guard-room, the vessel was saved from swinging round (as she otherwise would have done) and falling ashore on the beach beyond, stern foremost, and soon dragged within the influence of the current setting up the harbour.

Our attention, before engaged by our perilous situation, was now directed to new and exhilarating objects on the other side, where the works of the town arose immediately from the sands. These were crowded with spectators, and, being Sunday, all in their best; so that the sun, just peeping out as we shot along, imparted to the scene quite an

* The port of Ostend is what people usually term a "dry harbour." It is dry at low tide, but the flood brings in about 16 or 18 feet water.

air of gaiety; and to us it was also a novel one. I remember being mightily struck with the head-dress of the women, so different from what we had been accustomed to see at home, and the comparison was certainly not in favour of my fair compatriots. With these the fashionable coiffure was a large low *poke*-bonnet, which I had always fancied very becoming; but there is no describing how this sunk into meanness and deformity in a moment when I cast my eyes on the elegantly tapering, high-crowned straws of the *belles* on the rampart, encircled sometimes with two, and even three, rows of gay ribbon or artificial flowers. These gave them such a lofty commanding air, and withal was so light and graceful. But bonnets were not allowed long to occupy my attention. Followed by a crowd of other craft of all sorts and sizes, we shot rapidly along towards that part of the harbour where a dense assemblage of shipping filled up its whole breadth, and forbade further progress, so that one wondered what was to become of the numerous vessels in our wake. The mystery was soon explained, for each having attained the point, turning her prow to the town, ran bump on the sands, and there stuck fast. Those immediately above us had just arrived, and from them a regiment of Light Dragoons was in the act of disembarking by throwing the horses overboard, and then hauling them ashore by a long rope attached to their head-collars. What a scene! What hallooing, shouting, vociferating, and plunging! The poor horses did not appear much gratified by their sudden transition from the warm hold to a cold bath.

CHAPTER II.

Our keel had scarcely touched the sand ere we were abruptly boarded by a naval officer (Captain Hill) with a gang of sailors, who, *sans cérémonie*, instantly commenced hoisting our horses out, and throwing them, as well as our saddlery, &c., overboard, without ever giving time for making any disposition to receive or secure the one or the other. To my remonstrance his answer was, "I can't help it, sir; the Duke's *orders are positive that no delay is to take place in landing the troops as they arrive, and the ships sent back again; so you must be out of her before dark.*" It was then about three P.M.; and I thought this a most uncomfortable arrangement.

The scramble and confusion that ensued baffle all description. Bundles of harness went over the side in rapid succession, as well as horses. In vain we urged the loss and damage that must

accrue from such a proceeding. "Can't help it—
no business of mine—Duke's orders are positive,"
&c. &c., was our only answer. Meantime the ebb
had begun to diminish the depth of water along-
side, and enabled us to send parties overboard
and to the beach to collect and carry our things
ashore, as well as to haul and secure the horses.
The same operation commenced from the other
vessels as they arrived, and the bustle and noise
were inconceivable. The Dragoons and our men
(some nearly, others quite, naked) were dashing
in and out of the water, struggling with the
affrighted horses, or securing their wet accoutre-
ments as best they could. Some of the former
were saddling their dripping horses, and others
mounting and marching off in small parties. Dis-
consolate-looking groups of women and children
were to be seen here and there sitting on their
poor duds, or roaming about in search of their
husbands, or mayhap of a stray child, all clamour-
ing, lamenting, and materially increasing the
babel-like confusion, amidst which Erin's brogue
was everywhere predominant. Irish beggars
swarm everywhere and in all quarters of the
globe. Even here they pestered us to death, and
one young bare-legged rascal, when he found his
whining and cant unavailing, suddenly changing

his tone, tried to excite our liberality by a dirty joke on the Flemish pronunciation of their word horse (*pferd*). Add to all this crowds of people from the town idling about—some as spectators, others watching for windfalls; some bringing cakes, beer, &c., for sale, others teazing the officers with various offers of service, and these not always of the most respectable kind.

It was not without difficulty that I succeeded at last in impressing upon Captain Hill the necessity of leaving our guns and ammunition-waggons, &c., on board for the night—otherwise his furious zeal would have turned all out to stand on the wet sand or be washed away. Meantime, although we were on shore, we were without orders what to do next. Not an officer, either of the staff, the garrison, nor even of our own corps, came near us. Night approached, and with it bad weather evidently. Our poor shivering horses and heaps of wet harness could not remain on the sands much longer, when the flood began to make again; and it was necessary to look about and see what could be done. With this intent, therefore, leaving the officers to collect their divisions, I got one of my horses saddled and rode into the town. Here was the same bustle (although not the same confusion) as on the sands. The streets were thronged with British officers, and the quays with guns, waggons, horses, baggage, &c.

One would hardly expect to meet with any delay in finding the commandant of a fortress, yet such was my case; and it was not until after long and repeated inquiry that I discovered Lieutenant-Colonel Gregory, 44th Regiment, to be that personage, and found his residence. From him, however, I could obtain nothing. He seemed hardly to have expected the compliment of reporting our arrival, and stated that he had no other orders but that the troops of every arm should march for Ghent the moment they landed, without halting a single day in Ostend.

Strange to say, neither I nor the Colonel recollected there was such a person in Ostend as an Assistant-Quartermaster-General, who should be referred to on such an occasion. Yet this was the case; and that officer, instead of attending the debarkation of the troops, or making himself acquainted with the arrivals, kept out of sight altogether. Baffled at all points, I was returning to the sands when I met Major Drummond on the Quai Impérial, and related my story. He had been here some time, and was consequently acquainted with the locale. His advice was to march to Ghystelle (a village about six miles from

Ostend), and after putting up there for the night, to return and disembark my guns, &c., in the morning. Whilst speaking, however, some one (I forget who) came up with the agreeable information that Ghystelle was already fully occupied by the 16th Dragoons. He, however, gave me directions for some large sheds about a mile off, where his own horses had passed the preceding night. This was some consolation; so riding off immediately to reconnoitre the place and the road to it, I returned to the beach just as it got dark; and a most miserable scene of confusion I there found. Our saddles, harness, baggage, &c., were still strewed about the sand, and these the flood, which was now making, threatened soon to submerge. *Pour surcroit de malheur*, the rain came down in torrents, and a storm, which had been brewing up the whole afternoon, now burst over us most furiously. The lightning was quite tremendous, whilst a hurricane, howling horribly through the rigging of the ships, was only exceeded in noise by the loud explosions and rattling of the incessant claps of thunder.

Our people, meantime, blinded by the lightning, had borrowed some lanterns from the ship, and were busily employed searching for the numerous articles still missing. The obscurity, however, between the vivid flashes was such that we were only enabled to keep together by repeatedly calling to each other, and it was not without difficulty and great watchfulness that we escaped being caught by the tide, which flowed rapidly in over the flat sands. At length, having collected as many of our things as was possible, and saddled our horses (some two or three of which had escaped altogether), we began our march for the sheds a little after midnight, with a farrier and another dismounted man carrying lanterns at the head of our column. The rain continued pouring, but flashes of lightning occurred now only at intervals, and the more subdued rolling of the thunder told us that it was passing away in the distance. Our route lay through the town, to gain which we found some advanced ditch to be crossed by a very frail wooden bridge. Half the column, perhaps, might have cleared this, when "crack" down it went, precipitating all who were on it at the moment into the mud below, and completely cutting off those in the rear. Here was a dilemma. Ignorant of the localities, and without a guide, how was the rear of the column to join us, or how were the people in the ditch, with their horses, to be extricated? Luckily none were hurt seriously, and the depth was not great—

not more, perhaps, than six or eight feet; but that was enough to baffle all our attempts at extricating the horses. Some Belgic soldiers of a neighbouring guard, of which we were not aware, fortunately heard us, and came to our assistance; and one of them, crossing the ditch, undertook to guide the rear of our column and those below to another gate, whilst one accompanied us to the Quai Impérial, where, after waiting a while, we were at length assembled, drenched with rain and starving of cold and hunger. The Quai was silent and dark; the only light gleamed dimly through the wet from a miserable lamp over the door of a café, in which people were still moving; and the only sounds that broke the stillness of the quarter were the splashing of the rain and the clattering of our steel scabbards and horses' feet as we moved dejectedly on—winding our way through unknown avenues (for in the dark I found it impossible to recognise the narrow streets through which I had so hurriedly passed in the afternoon), occasionally illuminated by a solitary lamp, the feeble light of which, however, was somewhat increased by reflection on the wet pavement. After following for some time this devious course, I began to fear I had missed the road, when again we stumbled upon a Belgic guard, by whose direction and guidance we at length reached the outer barrier. Here we again came to a standstill, the officer in charge refusing to let us out. Some altercation ensued: I forget the particulars, but it ended in his opening the gate.

Once clear of the town, we hoped soon to reach our lodging; but had scarcely advanced a hundred yards ere we found that result was more distant than we had fancied, and that patience was still requisite. The rain had rendered the fat soil so slippery that our horses could scarcely keep their legs, and the road running along the narrow summit of a dyke, with ditches on each side, rendered precaution and slow movement imperative. Every moment the fall of some horse impeded the column; our lanterns went out; and after wandering a considerable time, we at length ascertained, by knocking up the people at a house by the wayside, that we had overshot our mark, and it was not until two in the morning that we succeeded in finding the sheds. These were immensely long buildings attached to some sawmills, for what use I know not, unless to store planks, &c., for they were now empty; but they were admirably adapted to our purpose, since we could range all our horses along one side, whilst the men occupied the other, in one of them. A quantity of hay, and some straw, left by our predecessors, was a valuable acquisition to man and beast under such circumstances. All our enjoyments are the effect of contrast. It would be considered miserable enough to be obliged to pass the night under such equivocal shelter as these sheds afforded, and that, too, in wet clothes; yet did we now, after twelve hours of harassing work and exposure to the weather, look upon them as palaces, and, having cared for our poor beasts as far as circumstances would permit, proceeded to prepare for that repose so necessary and so longed for.

I was already ensconced in some hay, when Lieutenant Leathes, who had been reconnoitring, brought intelligence that the people were still up in an adjoining miller's house, and that they were willing to give us shelter until morning. Thither, therefore, we repaired; and being ushered into the kitchen, quite a pattern of neatness, found the good woman and one of her men already busy making a fire and preparing some coffee for us—unlooked-for luxury! To this kindness she added the offer of two beds, which were eagerly and thankfully accepted by Lieutenants Ingleby and Bell. For my part, I preferred not pulling off my wet clothes and putting them on again in the morning, and therefore declined. Spite of our fatigue, we were all so refreshed by the coffee, that a pleasant hour was passed chatting to our kind hostess and joking with her man Coché, a sort of good-humoured, half-witted Caliban. At last sleep began to weigh heavily on our eyelids. The lady retired to her chamber, Coché hid himself somewhere, and, sinking back in our old-fashioned high-backed chairs, we were soon unconscious of everything.

14*th*.—Awoke from my slumbers just as the grey dawn began to render objects visible in the kitchen. My companions still slept soundly, so without disturbing them I quietly explored my way to the door, and soon found myself in a pretty little garden, ornamented and intersected by high hedges or walls of verdure, the young leaves of which, scarcely yet fully developed, were of the brightest green. These screens, effectually protecting the beds, in which many an early flower already blossomed, I thought delightful. It was the first time I had seen these *brise-vents*, or hornbeam hedges, which I subsequently found so common. The air of the morning was delicious, and my clothes having dried during my repose, I again felt comfortable and happy as I sauntered about the garden, enjoying the morning song of the little birds, with which the whole neighbourhood resounded. I could have stayed for ever in this tranquil and, as I then thought it, lovely retreat. By-and-by my companions turned out, and we lost no time in getting again under way in order to reach the gates of Ostend as soon as they opened.

Sass, or Schlickens, where we had passed the night, is the port of the Bruges canal, and hence the Treckschuyt from Ostend for that city takes its departure. It cannot be called a village, there being only a few small houses connected with the canal business, and some saw-mills and others worked by wind. Surrounded by marsh, it is a dreary comfortless place, although this was hidden from me in the early morning by the verdant screens in the miller's garden.

Our road back to the town, now we had daylight, appeared very short, and, having dried considerably, was not so slippery as last night. The gates were not yet opened when we arrived; a crowd of workmen of different kinds had already assembled and were waiting for admission, as were we, for a few minutes. At last they opened, and we proceeded to the harbour in search of our ship. The Quais, beach, &c., were thronged as on the day before, and we added to the bustle in disembarking our guns and carriages, &c. This was completed by eleven o'clock, and we were ready to march forward; but the commissariat detained us waiting the issue of our rations until three P.M.— four mortal hours, considering our eagerness to get on and explore this new country, and the bore of being confined to one spot, since it was impossible to wander about the town, seeing that we could not calculate the moment when these gentry might find it convenient to supply us. Of our horses two were still missing, as were some saddle-bags and a number of smaller articles; and this is not to be wondered at when the scandalous manner in which they were thrown overboard, the badness of the weather, the darkness of the night, together with the ebbing and flowing of the tide, are taken into consideration.

The appearance, too, of the troop was vexatious in the extreme. Our noble horses, yesterday morning so sleek and spirited, now stood with drooping heads and rough staring coats, plainly indicating the mischief they had sustained in being taken from a hot hold, plunged into cold water, and then exposed for more than seven hours on an open beach to such a tempest of wind and rain as that we experienced last night.

Here was a practical illustration of the folly of grooming and pampering military horses, destined as they are to such exposures and privations. As for our men, they looked jaded, their clothes all soiled with mud and wet, the sabres rusty, and the bear-skins of their helmets flattened down by the rain. Still, however, they displayed the same spirit and alacrity as that which has always been a characteristic of the horse-artillery, more particularly of G troop.

Whilst thus awaiting our rations, we had ample leisure to look about us, and amuse ourselves with the varied groups collected on the quay and the novelty of the scene. To be sure, the principal of these were English, and mostly soldiers too. Some were drinking at the doors of the cabarets, knapsacks on their backs, and prepared to start; others already in movement, escorting baggage; near us a battery of field-artillery parked, with their horses picketed in a long line along the rear of the carriages, quietly eating their corn out of hair nosebags, which ever and anon they would toss in the air, the better to get at the few remaining grains of their food; gunners and drivers lying about ready to fall in or mount at the shortest notice. Here they had passed the night, and the remains of their fires were still

COSTUMES OF THE NATIVES. 27

glowing in some rudely-constructed fireplaces of loose stones or bricks. Such objects were familiar to our eyes, but they were intermixed with others which were not. These were the Flemish peasantry, with their heavy countenances, walking by the side of their long, narrow waggons, and guiding their noble horses with admirable dexterity through the throng by long reins of small (very small) cord passing through holes in the clumsy highly-ornamental collars or haims. Long blue smock-frocks, decorated with embroidery in coloured worsted about the breast and shoulders; their skulls ensconced in night-caps, red or white; many with long thick queues—and all in clumsy wooden shoes. Women, with hard weather-beaten features, in long-eared caps, enormous gold pendants in their ears, a small cross on the breast, suspended from the scraggy neck by a strip of black velvet, thick petticoats, giving great swell to the hip, and from their shortness exhibiting a pair of stout understanders cased in coarse blue stockings and terminating in heavy *sabots*, enriched about the instep by a rabbit's skin clumped about in all directions. From time to time a patrol of the gendarmerie, in plain blue uniforms, with large white grenades on the skirts and the ends of their valises, broad belts, and high, stiff, well-polished boots, passed quietly through the assembled crowds; their quick inquiring eyes cast searchingly about as they moved leisurely along. At the corner of the quay was a group of boatmen (not much differing in outward appearance from our own of the same class) listlessly reclining on the pavement, or lounging up and down with folded arms, amusing themselves with the bustling anxiety of a score of soldiers' wives, who, loaded with children or bundles, their ample grey or faded red cloaks flying out loosely behind them, struggled through all impediments opposed to their progress with an activity, perseverance, and volubility which seemed highly diverting to the mariners, many of whom, in broken English, were bantering these amazons, or exchanging coarse jokes with them; at which play, however, —the ladies being mostly from the Green Isle— the gentlemen came off second best.

Such were the scenes we contemplated, when a loud cry of dismay suddenly pervaded the crowd, and all simultaneously rushed to the ramparts. I followed this movement. The morning, though somewhat overcast, had been fine, and the wind moderate; but as the day advanced, and the flood-tide set in, the south-westerly breeze had gradually increased to a gale. On reaching the rampart, I immediately observed that the flat shore to the northward, as far as the eye could reach, was covered with a sheet of white foam from the tremendous surf breaking on it; whilst the spray, rising in clouds and borne along before the blast, involved the whole neighbourhood in a thick salt mist. Nothing could be more savage and wild than the appearance of the coast. In the offing, numerous vessels under small sail were running for the harbour. One small brig had missed, and before assistance could be given, had been whirled round the *jetée*, and cast broadside on amongst the breakers. Her situation was truly awful. The surf broke over her in a frightful manner, sending its spray higher than her masts, and causing her to roll from side to side until her yards dipped in the water, and induced a belief every moment that she must roll over. Every now and then a huge wave, larger than its predecessor, would raise her bodily, and then, rapidly receding, suddenly let her fall again on the ground with a concussion that made the masts bend and vibrate like fishing-rods, and seemed to threaten instant annihilation. Of her sails, some were torn to rags, and others, flying loose, flapped and fluttered with a noise that was audible from the rampart, despite the roaring of the surf. The people on board appeared in great agitation, and kept shouting to those on shore for assistance, which they were unable to give. Intense anxiety pervaded the assembled multitude as the shattered vessel alternately rose to view or was buried in a sea of foam. Numbers ran down to the sands opposite to her; and from them she could not have been twenty yards distant, yet could they not afford the despairing crew the slightest aid. Whilst thus attending in breathless expectation the horrid catastrophe, the return of our quartermaster with the rations summoned us unwillingly from the rampart to commence our march. We afterwards learnt that a boat from the harbour had succeeded in saving the crew (she had no troops on board); but the unfortunate pilot who thus gallantly risked his own life for them was killed by the boat rising suddenly under the vessel's counter as he stood in the bow, which dashed his brains out.

Of Ostend I have little to say, my whole time and mind being fully occupied during the few hours of my stay in it. The impression it made on me was a dismal one. Narrow dirty streets; gloomy, old-fashioned, low, mean houses; the whole surrounded by marsh, sand-hills, or sea; and that sea, from its muddy colour, detracting nought from the lugubrious effect of the scene. Of the fortifications I saw still less than of the town; yet, from what little I did see, it would appear that Ostend depends more upon water than earth or stone—its great protection consisting in the facility of inundating the neighbouring marshes. On the Blanckenberg side, situated upon an eminence (I think of sand), we had a glimpse of Fort Napoleon, and working parties were busy constructing a redoubt among the sand-hills toward Nieuport. We had no leisure, however, to visit either.

CHAPTER III.

RIGHT glad were we to find ourselves at last *en route* from this dismal place. In passing through the streets towards the barrier, soon after leaving the quays, we found that we had likewise left all the bustle, crowd, and confusion behind us. Few people were moving about in any of them, and some were totally deserted. The prospect which presented itself on issuing from the gates was as *triste* and repulsive as can well be conceived. In front and to the left marsh! marsh! for miles, and looking black, dreary, and pestilential; the distance obscured by a red haze, occasioned by the clouds of sand blown inland by the gale from a range of sand and sand-hills (the *dûnes*) extending all along the coast. A straight, ill-paved, and muddy road, running away in long perspective between two wide ditches filled with stagnant, stinking water, bordered here and there by a few stunted willows bending to the blast, and their usual cold colour rendered still more cold by thus exposing the whitish backs of their young leaves. Such was the scene, in which our column (men, horses, and carriages, soiled, and looking miserable; the mounted gunners leaning to windward, with one hand generally upraised holding on their helmets; the limber-gunners sitting sideways, turning their backs to the gale) formed an appropriate accompaniment, as it proceeded slowly along the causeway. About half-way to Ghystelles,* at a barrier, we were rejoiced at finding the horses that had escaped from us on the sands. The man said they had been there all night.

After traversing these marshes for about five or six miles, we entered on a country almost as flat, but of a very different character, highly cultivated and well wooded. The road became an avenue, whilst the adjoining fields were interspersed everywhere with patches of copsewood, and rows of tufted bushes serving here and there as boundaries in place of hedges; the scenery, of course, much more pleasing, although not seen to advantage under the still gloomy, overcast sky.

It was late when we reached Ghistel, the ap-

* *Ghistel*, according to the map of Maillart, &c.

pearance of which, however, was consolatory, and promised some comfort.

Before we could seek that, a troublesome task still remained to be performed. Our men could not understand their billets, some of which were on isolated farms a mile or two from the village; neither could they inquire their way. It therefore became necessary for us to accompany and see them safely housed ere we could resign ourselves to the enjoyments of our auberge. In the village itself they were soon put up, for many of the people spoke or understood a little English.

At length, as night set in, our business was finished, and we all assembled at our auberge, which, though humble, was delightfully clean, and to us, after last night's adventure, appeared luxurious. No less so was the excellent dinner to which we soon sat down; whilst doing justice to which we could not help laughing at its spread, for it was composed, not of solid joints, &c. &c., but of an immense multitude and variety of little dishes of stews and all sorts of nameless (to us) things. A bottle of good port would have rendered us superlatively happy, but that was not to be thought of in Ghistel; so having amused ourselves, and puzzled the neat, pretty, black-eyed girl who officiated as *garçon* by our inquiries for this our national, but by her unheard-of, beverage, we were fain to make ourselves comfortable, and pass the evening in social chat over the poor, thin, though well-flavoured liquor that the house afforded. Some of our number, to be sure, were unreasonable enough to grumble, and one actually got the stomach-ache, but whether from the wine or last night's wetting it is difficult to say, though he swore it was the former.

I shall not easily forget my delight on retiring, when I found a most clean, enticing bed prepared for me, in a pretty little room, the window of which looked into a quiet well-kept garden. The enormous pillow at first took me aback. Such a thing! It seemed to occupy half the bed. I, however, soon made acquaintance with it, and enjoyed a most delicious sleep. The first steps in a new country are to me always a source of pleasurable sensations. Everything one sees is striking, interesting, and makes a lasting impression. This evening and its enjoyments will long remain a bright spot in my memory.

15*th*. A fine, mild, grey morning. Our people paraded in much better order, and very much higher spirits, than yesterday, and all seemed pleased with their entertainment. The novelty amused them, and every one had some tale to relate of last night's adventures. Their hosts had generally been very kind to them, and allowed them to take as much forage for their horses as they chose. The poor animals, therefore, had passed the night equally well. In marching out of Ghistel, I noticed many houses of a superior description to the rustic dwellings which alone I saw last night. Some of these had much the appearance of stage scenery, having façades painted to represent pilasters, urns, wreaths, festoons, &c. &c., all in very childish taste. These, no doubt, were the villas or *lusthausen* of the Ostend citizens.

Our march to Bruges (about twelve miles) was through a country perfectly flat, but rich and highly cultivated; and from the numerous little woods, farms, and substantial villages—added, again, to the charm of novelty—it was far from uninteresting.

About noon we entered the city by a fine, broad, airy street, rendered pleasing by the intermixture of foliage with its picturesque buildings, and swarming with people. By-and-by we came to narrower streets and more antiquated-looking houses; winding our way amongst which, we at last reached the cavalry barrack, situated in a narrow, dirty back lane at the further extremity of the town—a large, heavy, inelegant mass of masonry, more like some old storehouse than a barrack. Here, in the extensive yard, we parked our guns, and put our men into the barrack, the rooms of which were large, lofty, and vaulted, but extremely filthy, so that our people had to regret the clean comfortable billets and kind hospitality which they would have enjoyed amongst the inhabitants. A range of ruinous wooden sheds, extending along two sides of the yard, served as stabling, and received all our horses.

Having arranged affairs at the barrack, and called on Sir F. Lyons, the British commandant, we betook ourselves to our billet at the Hôtel de Commerce, which, however, we had some difficulty in finding. As this was the first large hotel we had been in, it had the recommendation of novelty, and everything in it became subject of curiosity. The large dreary hall; the comfortless bar adjoining, and separated from it by an immense window or glazed partition, so unlike the cheerful snug-looking bar of an English inn; the equally comfortless and gloomy saloon behind it, into which we were shown; the squalid, dirty appearance of the domestics (men or boys), in filthy cotton jackets and *bonnets de nuit*,—all served to chill one on first entering. Our arrival, followed by orderlies and servants carrying portmanteaus, &c. &c., caused a sensation in the establishment, every member of which, not excepting the *chêf*, was assembled to greet us in the hall. For some minutes a scene of bustle ensued, which ended in mounting the stairs to inspect our dormitories. These contrasted strangely with the vast apartments below. From the head of the staircase a long corridor ran right and left the whole length of the house, off which a number of doors opened into as many little cells, each barely large enough to contain bed, chair, and a small table. The beds (without curtains) were very homely, but quite clean, the furniture and utensils of the commonest kind. The attendants, having shown us our rooms, withdrew, and with the sound of their departing footsteps ended the bustle of the day. When I again stepped out on the gallery, the stillness of the place astonished me—hall, staircase, bar, all deserted; not a soul to be seen, nor a sound heard except that of my own tread over the creaking floor; no ringing of bells; no calls for chambermaid, boots, or waiter; no running to and fro;—in short, the place appeared altogether abandoned, and I hastened into the street to lounge away the time until dinner, of which, however, I had my misgivings.

Bruges is a highly interesting town at all times; but after being shut out from the Continent so many years, the novelty of everything one saw enhanced this interest amazingly. My ramble led me through streets of lofty, whimsically constructed houses, the upper parts of which sometimes projected in the manner one frequently sees in our old midland towns, the projections decorated with drop-balls on fretwork; immense windows sometimes occupied the whole front of each floor; ample portals, the lofty folding doors of which were occasionally studded with iron, like those of a fortress or dungeon; gables, with high pointed roofs, presented almost everywhere to the street; chimneys of bizarre and fantastic forms, and surmounted by a finish of semicircular tiles rising pyramidally over each other; here and there towers or turrets with high conical roofs;—such were the architectural peculiarities that attracted my attention. The long streets running in wavy lines, and of unequal breadth, between these grotesque buildings, exhibited specimens of costume as novel, and frequently not less grotesque, which, intermingling with the scarlet and blue uniforms of our soldiers, very much heightened the picturesque effect. It was only in the principal thoroughfares and business parts of the town that all this animation was met with. In those quarters principally inhabited by the richer citizens the streets were as dull, solitary, and scrupulously clean as it is possible to conceive. In these I frequently found myself the only animated being visible—not a loiterer at a door, not even a head at a window. Many of even the best houses appeared absolutely uninhabited. Could this have always been the case? Was this the state of things when Bruges was the central mart for the whole Pays bas, and saw merchants from every nation in Europe crowding to its fairs in search of its linen and woollen cloth, and of the naval stores and rich productions of India continually arriving from the north, the Venetian and other Italian States, when the splendid dress and magnificent palaces of its citizens were sufficient to excite the indignation and envy of a queen? Surely not. These grass-grown streets, now so solitary, then exhibited very different scenes. Many a plumed and portly burgher then trod their pavement, and many a fair bejewelled dame graced the numerous windows of its palaces, now so silent. This decay and depopulation dates from the moment when these wealthy merchants arrogantly resisted their sovereign, Maximilian, who, aided by Antwerp and Amsterdam, shut up its port of Sluys, and thus, diverting its commerce into other channels, inflicted on it that punishment the effects of which are so perceptible even after a lapse of more than 300 years. From these melancholy monuments of fallen grandeur, and the deathlike silence of these deserted streets, I suddenly emerged into the midst of bustle in the Grand Place, where crowds of peasantry were assembled apparently for the sole purpose of buying and selling little earthen pots of a peculiar form (*terrines*), the number of which, disposed in long rows on the ground, really surprised me. The Stadthouse stands in this place. It has a lofty square tower, surmounted by another of nearly equal height of an octagonal form. This certainly possesses no beauty, but the singularity of the construction attracts notice. From the Place I wandered to the *Cathédrale*,[*] the very lofty spire of which, I am told, serves as a landmark for vessels approaching Ostend, though certainly I do not recollect having seen it there. It is even *said* by some to be visible from the *banks of the Thames*—a pretty long view! Entering the temple, I found the garish light of broad day exchanged for a mysterious twilight,

[*] The Church of Notre Dame ceased to be a cathedral 1801, when it was united to the diocese of Ghent.

and the busy hum of high market for a solemn silence, scarcely interrupted by the light step of some veiled female (of males only a few, very old men, were there) as she glided to the spot chosen for her devotions, where, rapidly crossing herself, she sank on her knees before a shrine in some side chapel. At the high altar, priests in embroidered robes were celebrating mass with a solemnity which rendered still more ridiculous their repeated genuflexions, the extinction from time to time of a taper, and the removal of a crucifix from one end of the altar to another, only to bring it back the next moment, whilst ever and anon they would bow, cross themselves, and bow again.

The nave of the church was not spoilt, as ours are, by pews. A number of plain chairs were assembled round the pillars, and these served the worshippers to kneel upon—that is, the men, for the women invariably sank on the pavement in most picturesque attitudes. Of the latter, most seemed in earnest; but with the former, a duty was hurried through, in which the heart had evidently little or no concern. Some certainly placed both knees on the chairs, and, leaning over the backs with clasped hands, kept their eyes steadily on the altar, whilst the rapid motion of their lips betrayed the hurried manner in which they prayed. Others, however, with one knee only on the chair, and the body half-turned, gazed about them whilst mumbling over their daily portion of prayer. People were continually coming in and going out, which seemed to disturb no one, but rather served as amusement to the gazers just mentioned. However lukewarm the frequenters of the temple might evince themselves, yet was there something very impressive in the scene. In a pictorial point of view it was most interesting, for the building is a fine Gothic structure, and the interior of these always affords picturesque scenery, even without such accessories as those furnished by the various kneeling groups, more particularly of females. Some good pictures I saw, but did not like to stop and examine them. A striking feature in this church are the colossal statues of the Apostles perched upon shelves, one to each column of the nave: the effect is not good. The pulpit, and staircase leading up to it, are a most elaborate and ingenious example of sculpture in wood. The impression on me was one of wonder at the inexhaustible patience of the artist. Sauntering about the church, near the great door I stumbled upon something not unlike a sentry-box; it was a confessional! In this sat a sleek-looking priest, head resting on his left hand, and the ear inclined to a little grated aperture in one side, through which a female on her knees, and shrouded in a black veil, poured out her heart in a loud whisper. The holy man received the communication with becoming gravity, though it was easy to divine, by a short perusal of his countenance, that he was receiving nothing but commonplace, or at best no very important, intelligence. Everything in this religion appears most childish mummery;—what more so than this? Leaving Notre Dame, I sought the ramparts. These no longer exist in a military sense, but the high grassy mounds which remain, being planted with trees, serve at once as a pretty promenade, and diversify the views of the city from without. The moat in most places still remains green—almost as the meadows—with aquatic plants. Some of the ancient gateways, also, are still there to tell a tale of other times. These, with their sombre grey towers, roofed with tile, are eminently picturesque, and harmonise well with the other buildings of the town. These towers, with high conical roofs, which one meets almost everywhere throughout the Continent, particularly in this country, form a characteristic feature, distinguishing its scenery from that of the British Islands, where the ruins of ancient castles have almost invariably their round or square towers terminated by a castellated parapet and flat roof. True it is that the Irish round-towers have such roofs; but they are low, and form a very small portion in the general aspect of the building: as also those solitary square towers seen along the Scottish Border, and sprinkled here and there over the soil of Ireland—the dwellings or keeps of petty chieftains—were also surmounted by high, but not conical roofs.

Tired of rambling about the streets, I returned to our hotel, where, to my surprise, an excellent dinner awaited me, exceedingly well served, and the attendants (who had made themselves clean) very active and obliging. Among these a boy of fifteen or sixteen was a perfect beauty—so much so as to excite universal admiration. Nor must I forget another beauty of a far different kind—some very old and genuine cognac. It was quite a liqueur; and we were so pleased with it, that each secured a small stock to carry forward with him. In short, we went to bed in better humour with the Hôtel de Commerce.

CHAPTER IV.

16*th.* Marched through a country very similar to that of yesterday — that is, flat rich soil, highly cultivated, very populous, and diversified with patches of wood, &c.—to Eccloo (*chêf lieu du canton*), a neat little village consisting of two broad streets forming a sort of place at the point of union, where we parked our guns, despite the objections of the inhabitants, who were woefully afraid of an explosion. The Duke of Wellington, *en route* to Ostend, passed as we were forming up, and scrutinised us pretty closely, but said nothing, although I afterwards learned that it was positively against orders to park ammunition of any kind in a village.

The landlord of the only auberge was so very insolent that we formed a mess for the day in one of our billets, our own servants cooking for us. The fare was not sumptuous, but, *en revanche*, very cheap, consisting entirely of our rations. My own billet here was in the house of a widow, who kept a hardware shop—humble, but, as usual in this country, a pattern of cleanliness. Returning from the mess, I joined the old lady and her daughter in their little parlour behind the shop, and two or three neighbours coming in, the conversation became animated. The subject was the return of Napoleon and the probable consequences. According to their ideas, our cause was hopeless. Last year our hostess had lodged an officer of Cossacks, whom she described as a most gentlemanly man.

17*th*. The same description of country accompanied us to Ghent. At the large village of Lovendeghem the road joined the canal ; and here we obtained the first view of this celebrated city, the birthplace of Charles V., and the scene of so many interesting events in the history of the middle ages, forming, with its numerous towers, a fine termination to the long vista of the canal.

Nearer the coast the trees had been small and somewhat stunted ; indeed, most of the woods we had seen were merely coppice. Here, however, they assumed a different character, being of large size and great luxuriance, giving a much higher interest to the landscape as they bordered the fine meadows lying along either side of the canal, on the bank of which our road lay. The scenery now became further enriched and enlivened by the frequent occurrence of country-seats, generally of brick, and embowered in foliage; a lawn stretching down to the canal, and terminated by a terrace with a low parapet-wall and a summer-house at one end of it. The only boat, however, we met, was the packet going to Bruges; and the road itself was so solitary that, had not our eyes convinced us to the contrary, we should never have imagined ourselves approaching so rich and populous a city.

About two P.M. we reached the canal harbour, separated from the city by a handsome *barrière* (*grille*) or iron railing in imitation of spears, the shafts painted light blue, with gilded blades. A small building, with the word "*Octroi*" in large letters over the door, stood on one side of the gate by which we now entered the capital of Flanders, and immediately found ourselves in a fine broad street, with large and stately houses on either side. Yet the very first impression was that of disappointment. The street was lonely, almost deserted, and nearly every second house exhibited a board bearing a notice in French and Flemish that it was to sell or let—"Maison à louer,"

"Huys zu heuer," or "Maison à vendre," &c. &c. Curious it is that two languages should be indispensably necessary; but such seems to be the case here, for I observed that all proclamations and public notices of any kind were invariably in French and Flemish. We proceeded some way through the same sort of quiet and (apparently) depopulated region; but at last, crossing a broad canal, or, may be, one of the several rivers which here unite, we came at once into the very heart of bustle, business, fine shops, and crowds of people, continuing on nearly a mile, through all which we at last reached the cavalry barracks (our destination), quite at the further extremity of the town, near the Barrière de Bruxelles, where we parked our guns and put up our horses; but there was no room for the men, consequently they were billeted.* Nothing could be more inconvenient than this arrangement, though I believe it could not be helped, the place being already crowded with troops, English and French—for this was the headquarters of Louis XVIII.'s phantom of an army. Upon ascertaining the situation of our billets, too, we found things still worse, these being generally in the Quartier de Bruge, a distance of nearly one and a half miles from the barrack, and some still farther off—one detachment

* M'Donald's troop had arrived ten days before us.

being billeted at La Barqué, a cabaret on the canal harbour, and another at some village still farther off. A serious inconvenience this for horse-soldiers, whose duties required them to be so continually at the barrack, and most harassing when it is recollected that the distance from barrier to barrier is reckoned three miles—the whole distance over an execrable pavement. It was not without some trouble that I succeeded in finding my own billet in Bruge Straet, a respectable house, but nowise remarkable either for size or architecture. My host, a stout cheerful-looking old gentleman, whose bearing and dress bespoke the opulent citizen, met me in the gateway, and with great cordiality (recognising my billet) ushered me into a large room by the side of the brick-paved entry, announcing it as mine during my stay, at the same time offering me the use of his whole establishment, particularly of his cook. This last I accepted with pleasure, having arranged with my officers that our mess should be in my quarter, wherever that might be. Meantime, my baggage-cart having been drawn up the narrow yard and the horses dismissed, the great gates reclosed, and the bustle of arrival subsided, everything sank into silence—a silence as predominating in the street without as within the house.

MY QUARTERS.

My apartment was a large, lofty, long room, running back from the street, towards which two high windows admitted such insufficient light that even in fine weather it was particularly gloomy. At the farther end two folding-doors cut off a portion of its length, and this was fitted up as a bed-chamber—dark enough. The furniture of the *salle* consisted of a few common chairs and a large table covered with oil-cloth. The floor was without carpet, as the windows were without either blinds or curtains. How the rest of the house might have been fitted up I am ignorant, having seen no more of its interior than the kitchen, which opened into the yard, and that was certainly the neatest and cleanest I ever saw, with its red floor and red stoves and highly-polished brass pans, &c. &c. Nor did I ever see much more of the inhabitants; for, with the exception of two females in the kitchen, the house seemed deserted. A man-servant certainly assisted at our dinner, but we rarely saw even him at any other time. Not a voice—not a foot-fall—not a sound of any kind, unless emanating from ourselves, ever disturbed the death-like silence that reigned through this establishment. Mine host was, I believe, a merchant, and went out every morning to his business, whence he returned not until the evening, at least as far as I could ascertain. I saw nothing more of him from my first reception until I called to take leave and thank him for his attentions and hospitality. These consisted in the assistance of his servants and the use of his beer-cask, on which we drew for our daily supply.

During the seven days we remained in Ghent, our time was so occupied by duties that there was little leisure to look about us. Twice every day it was necessary to be at the barracks, so that a very great portion of my time was spent in walking backward and forward between them and Bruge Straet.

Amongst other duties it fell to our lot to furnish a guard of honour to Louis XVIII., then residing in Ghent, his own troops having been sent to Alost to make room for the British, which were continually passing through. Our subalterns were very well pleased with this arrangement, for the duty was nothing. They found an excellent table, and passed their time very agreeably with the young men of the *garde du corps*, some of whom were always in attendance. Many of these were mere boys, and the anteroom of his most Christian Majesty frequently exhibited bolstering matches and other amusements, savouring strongly of the boarding-school; however, they were good-natured, and always most attentive to the comforts of the officer on guard. The royal stud was in the barrack stables, and consisted principally of grey horses, eighteen or twenty of which had been purchased in England at a sale of *cast horses* from the Scots Greys.

We frequently met French officers of all ranks, and formed acquaintance with many gentlemanly, well-informed men. At the Lion d'Or and Hôtel de Flandre we found there was a table-d'hôte every night at 8 o'clock, and, by way of passing the evening, usually resorted to one or the other for supper. Here we were sure of meeting many Frenchmen, and as the same people were generally constant attendants, we became intimate, and discussed the merits of our national troops respectively over our wine or *ponche*. It was the first time most of them had had an opportunity of inspecting British troops closely, though many had often met them in the field; and they were very curious in their inquiries into the organisation, government, and equipment of our army. Although allowing all due credit to the bravery displayed by our troops in the Peninsula, and the talents of our General (the Duke), yet were they unanimous in their belief that neither would avail in the approaching conflict, and that we must succumb before their idol and his grand army; for though these gentlemen had deserted Napoleon to follow the fortunes of Louis XVIII., it was evident they still revered the former. Their admiration of our troops, particularly of the cavalry, was very great; but they expressed astonishment at seeing so few decorations. It was in vain we asserted that medals were rarely given in the British army, and then only to commanding officers, &c. They shook their heads, appeared incredulous, and asked, " Where are the troops that fought in Spain?" There might have been something more than mere curiosity in all this. There might have been an anxiety to ascertain whether their countrymen were about to cope with veterans or young soldiers. It might have been thrown out as a lure, to provoke information relative to the present employment of those veteran bands. Moreover, I shrewdly suspected many of these gentlemen were actually spies. Amongst others who had followed Louis XVIII. was Marmont. I think it was the day after our arrival, passing over the open space near the Place d'Armes, by the river, I saw a French general officer exercising a horse in the *manège,* and learnt with astonishment that this was Marmont; for the man in question had *two* good arms—whereas, for years past, I had, in common with most people in England, looked upon it as a fact that he had left one at Salamanca. French deserters, both officers and privates, were daily coming in; it was said they deserted by hundreds. Be that as it may, I one day saw a column of thirty march up to the Bureau des Logemens. They were in a most miserable plight—all in rags — and apparently half-starved. All these deserters, as well as the rest, were forwarded without delay to Alost. The Commissaire des Logemens told me that, after the departure of the French troops to Alost, there still remained more than 300 of his Majesty's immediate followers for whom it was necessary to provide in Ghent.

The huzzars of the K. G. Legion, stationed about Detto, and toward the frontier, frequently sent intelligence of hostile movements; but except this, we were in perfect ignorance of the positions either of our own or the French army. Regiments arrived from England, halted a night, and were off again we knew not where.

Meantime we lived well, and saw as much of the place as our scanty time would permit. The markets were most abundantly supplied with everything, and very cheap; so that with the assistance of our *bourgmestre's* cook we kept an excellent table at a moderate rate. As for our horses, although they had exhibited symptoms of having felt their exposure on the sands at Ostend when we first arrived, yet rest and good forage soon restored their original appearance, and we began to get tired of Ghent and long for a forward move.

I cannot, however, bid adieu to Ghent without recording a few notes, which my confined means of observation enabled me to preserve; and be it remembered that, at that period, the continent of Europe was almost a *terra incognita* to Englishmen, to whom everything, therefore, even trifles, bore a degree of interest, which our present intimate acquaintance may cause to appear puerile at the present day.

I need not say that Ghent is a large and populous city, standing upon ground generally flat, intersected and divided into numerous islands by three or four rivers, besides canals, which hold their course through it, nor that it is the birthplace of the Emperor Charles V.; but I may add that Ghent, independent of its historical recollections, is, and ever must be, a most interesting place, particularly to the artist; for where can we see such picturesque street-scenes as are exhibited here ? The streets, bordered by lofty houses generally of a quaint style of architecture, wind their devious way—now narrow, now spreading out to an ample breadth—with an irregularity that certainly leaves no room to complain of sameness. This irregularity attaches as much to the houses as to the streets. These are of every variety—high stepped gables towards the street, little turrets with pointed roofs, others with large French windows, and, again, others all window, as at Bruges. These, intermingled with, and partially seen through, the foliage of the trees, which in many places border the canals, &c., offer most picturesque morsels, precisely such as one sees in the pictures of the old Flemish painters, so that they appeared quite familiar. This effect is considerably heightened by the deep embrasures of the windows, lofty grotesquely ornamented portals, and, above all, the rich deep tone of colouring that pervaded the whole. Chapels and churches, too—some in the Gothic, others Italian, or still more modern styles—intervened continually, the whole forming rich perspectives, animated by the varied and bustling crowds of citizens, peasants, soldiers, &c. One peculiarity struck me as savouring much of indolence and curiosity combined: almost every house, at one or more windows of the first floor, had small square mirrors, sometimes single, sometimes double, so arranged that persons seated within the room could see the passengers on the *trottoir* below without stirring from their seats. In English towns one constantly sees heads peeping over the blinds; here, no one is seen at the windows.

Near the centre of the city is the Place d'Armes, a large square, having the area ornamented by rows of well-grown linden trees, and its houses of a superior character to those in the adjoining quarters. This is the focus of business, and in this neighbourhood one sees all the best shops, some of which astonished us by the profuse display of Indian goods, particularly silk pocket-handkerchiefs, which we found of the very finest quality, and at about half the price they sold at in England. The Place d'Armes is, however, spoiled in a great measure by the shabby wooden railing enclosing the promenade.

In this square was a magnificent hotel, at least as far as outward appearance went. The Duc de Berri had his quarters in it; and one day, as I returned from the barrack, I saw him set off for Alost. This was the first travelling equipage I had seen in the country; and consequently I was much amused with the coxcombry and costume of the postilions—their glazed hats stuck on one side; queues, each with the side-hair neatly plaited in; short, very short jackets; and, above all, the enormous jack-boots. But if the costume amused, the dexterity with which they handled their whips astonished me—" klang-klang-klang," —between them they almost made music. The rapid and dexterous manner in which, flourishing their whips over their heads, they crack them—before, behind, right, and left—is of a piece with that manual dexterity with which our laboratory-boys make ball-cartridges, and our drummers, by quickly-repeated but distinct taps, produce a rolling sound in which the most delicate ear cannot detect a break. But to return from this digression.

The very little time I had to myself did not admit of seeing half the place, and my wanderings were pretty much confined to the neighbourhood of the line between Bruges Straet and the barrack. Sometimes, however, I did extend a little to the right and left, and in one of these excursions got a glimpse, but no more, of some pleasant gardens—public, I suppose —in which numerous walks, overarched with verdure, intersected each other, and presented, as the weather was hot, most inviting retreats. At another time I wandered as far as the Citadel, —I suppose the one built by William III. of England, not that of Charles V., of which not a vestige remains. It must have been but an insignificant work;—the plan, I think, a parallelogram. The mounds of the ramparts remain entire, and the wet ditch. At present it is completely overlooked by the neighbouring houses. From this work, which is situated just without the *barrière* of the road to Thermonde, one commands a prospect, perhaps, of its kind unrivalled. Here are no picturesque or romantic features, but the eye wanders unimpeded over a region as flat as the ocean, and, like it, only terminating in the distant horizon. This region is amongst the richest in the world, and, spite of its flatness, offers to our view a scene at once pleasing and astonishing. Verdant meadows, enameled with myriads of yellow and white flowers, amidst which graze innumerable herds of the finest cattle, extend for miles from the city, and then, intermingled with corn-fields, groves, and thickets, amidst which are seen everywhere villages, farms, and scattered houses, melt gradually away into the blue distance. In the immediate foreground, a singular hillock, crowned by a little chapel and environed by trees, rears its form and enhances

THE CORN-MARKET. 61

the picture by variety of feature and the interesting peeps admitted between the openings of the foliage. The road from Thermonde passes through this grove, and, covered as it generally is (or was, when I saw it) with groups of market-people, carts, and cattle, &c., throws a charming animation into the scene. The lengthened perspective, too, of this road running away in a straight line bordered by trees, and gradually diminishing until lost in the distance, breaks the unvaried flatness of the meadows, and prevents one feeling them monotonous. Returning from the Citadel, I joined the rustic crowd pouring in through the *barrière*, and, following the stream, was brought by it into an extensive square surrounded by lofty and antique-looking houses, apparently the exclusive abode of the humbler classes of merchants or artisans. The crowd here was immense; and it was not without difficulty that I made my way through it. I think this is the Marché aux Grains. Not far from thence I stumbled on the great gun, called the Basilisc,* said to have been

* La Folle Marguerite (?), 18 feet long and 3 feet in diameter, near the Marché de Vendredi; it is called the Mannekens Aert. It is named after a Countess of Flanders celebrated for the violence of her temper. It is also designated the Wonder of Ghent, is made of malleable iron, and, according to another account, was used by Philip Van Arteveldt at the siege of Oudenarde in 1382.—Quin's 'Moselle,' &c., vol. i. p. 160.

cast by order of Charles V., to overawe the Ghentois. As far as I could see, this enormous piece, which reposes on a mass of brickwork in an open space at the turn of the street, is a plain unornamented cylinder of iron (wrought). It was too high for minute inspection. The pedestal upon which it rests serves also as a public fountain, about which are usually groups of gossiping women with their pitchers under their arms, or noisy boys.

Amongst the buildings of Ghent, interesting from their style, the ancient Gothic Hôtel de Ville stands pre-eminent, with its rich and elaborately-ornamented façades. This venerable pile is said to have been built, at least the older part of it, in the beginning of the seventh century. Another remnant of antiquity, perhaps still more old, I discovered in my own neighbourhood— this was the ancient castle, Castrum Ganda (?), a small open space, in the corner of which are the remains of thick walls and one tower still nearly entire—its different storeys affording lodgment to several poor families, from whom, however, I sought in vain for any information respecting these ruins. From the direction of the patches of wall, I conjectured that the open space was once the inner court of the castle.

MEAT AND VEGETABLE MARKETS.

In the same quarter was one of the markets, through which I passed every day in going to and coming from the barrack; it was for meat and vegetables, &c. The latter were exposed for sale in the open air in baskets, as with us; and here, as everywhere else, one could not but be struck with the great abundance and fine quality of every produce of this rich country. One vegetable seemingly in great request was the tender root of the hop plant. This, when peeled and stewed in milk, is really delicious. We had it every day on our table, and it was a general favourite. A principal occupation of the market-women was peeling these roots, which were then thrown into a basin of cold water to keep them fresh, and thus exposed for sale. The meat-market adjoining was under cover and closed in, like the central avenue of Covent Garden, forming a long street of stalls, each full of the finest meat imaginable, cut up into joints, &c., whilst over-head, suspended under the roof, were innumerable whole carcasses of bullocks, sheep, and pigs. Nothing could exceed the cleanliness of this place, or the neatness and propriety of dress of the butchers, their wives, and daughters. Unlike our markets, there was no loud talking, no confused gabbling of tongues; everything seemed conducted with the utmost quiet, order, and decency. The middle of the passage was thronged with well-dressed people of all classes and both sexes. On entering I was struck with a singular dull murmuring sound that pervaded the building, somewhat resembling the sound of a distant mill, which I soon perceived to be produced by the active industry of the women, who, instead of sitting idly waiting for custom, were all busily employed pounding sausage-meat. If ever I could relish a sausage it would be a Ghent one, for nothing can exceed the cleanliness of the operators and their operations, or the goodness of the materials of which they are made. One may form some idea of the abundance of this fine country from the fact that, having been all last year the seat of war, and now everywhere occupied by numerous foreign troops, still there appeared no diminution in the supplies, and the markets of every town exhibit as great a profusion as ever.

With the exception of a slight sandy eminence at Eccloo, the first undulations of the country we had yet seen were at Ghent. On the southern side of the town I ascended with pleasure a hill, which apparently was the commencement of a sort of rolling country extending towards Deynse. From its summit is an excellent view of the city and the fine country around it. Meadows of the liveliest green, intersected by numerous streams, exhibited everywhere immense quantities of linen exposed for bleaching—such was the scene immediately below. In the distance, as the plain became foreshortened, it seemed to be bounded by woods. The city itself was rendered a more pleasing object by having its sombre masses broken and relieved by large plots of garden-ground and the frequent intervention of foliage. On this hill stood a large square building, once a monastery, but suppressed during the Revolution, like many others. To what use it is now turned I could not guess, as not a living soul was to be seen in or about it of whom to make inquiry. The massive pile, with its numerous windows, high roof, and yawning portal, was not an unpicturesque object. I sauntered into its solitary court; grass had almost overgrown the pavement, and desolation was stamped on every feature. I could not look on all this without indulging in a dream, and in my mind's eye embodying fat and lazy monks strolling about the court, or lounging in idle converse on the stone benches against the sunny wall; again, some more venerable figure passing the corridors in silent meditation. On the road from the town, too, I conjured up groups of ascending and descending brothers, and though not approving of their vocation, could not but regret the absence of their picturesque costume. The only convent I saw besides this in Ghent was an inhabited one, and it is to be hoped always will be. This is the Beguinage, to which I hardly know whether the term "convent" should be applied, for it rather resembles a small town. Each of the sisters has a separate dwelling, with a little flower-garden in front of it, much in the style of some of our better kind of alms-houses in England. It appears an old building, and is surrounded by a moat.

The Cathedral of St Bavon being in our neighbourhood, and not much out of the way of my daily walks, I frequently went in to see what was going on; for one goes to these Catholic ceremonies as to any other show. This church makes no great appearance from without, but the interior is imposing and beautiful, as all Gothic interiors are. The panels of the choir over the stalls are a series of paintings exceedingly well executed, representing the acts of St Paul, I believe. The curiosities of the church are the crypt, the tombs, and the pulpit. The former of these probably originated in the unsoundness of the ground rendering such a foundation necessary. Its arches are semicircular, and spring from low but very massive pillars. Mass is sometimes performed here, but only often enough, I should imagine, to prevent its desecration. Of the tombs, there are two of very admirable sculpture — the one in white, the other in black marble—both, I think, of bishops. The pulpit is like that of Bruges— an elaborate piece of carving in wood—notable monument of patience and perseverance. One evening, attracted by the chanting, I walked in, just as a procession wound slowly from behind the choir, and advanced with banners and lighted tapers down the side aisle. The approaching twilight had thrown every part of the church into a mysterious obscurity, harmonising well with such a scene. Two boys in scarlet surplices, with shaven heads, but beautiful faces, came first, swinging about large handsome censers of silver. The atmosphere was soon impregnated with the smoking frankincense, whose odour was well calculated to aid the imposing effect. Two banners, in form resembling the labarum, followed. To these succeeded a train of priests, in variously-coloured, rich, and picturesque dresses, some bearing other banners of different shapes and devices; and a number of boys, all habited like those already mentioned, and equally fair, flanked the procession, and enveloped it in a light haze by the fumes of their incessantly swinging censers. The chant had just died away as I entered the nave, and the procession, with solemn, silent tread, moved slowly down the aisle — the only sound that broke upon the ear being the grating rattle of the censer-lids as they were drawn rapidly up and down the chains. Then again the full impressive harmony of the chant filled the vaulted roof with its sweet and solemn notes, died away, and after another pause was again and again resumed; and thus, having made the circuit of the nave, the procession became gradually lost in the obscurity of the aisle as it slowly retired behind the choir, whence at intervals, softened by distance, the chant still rose over the dividing screen behind the high altar.

Puerile as these exhibitions may be, the effect on me was exciting; and as the last notes were faintly re-echoed through the building, I left it in a frame of mind far different from that in which I had entered.

On the Sunday we passed in Ghent a mass was celebrated expressly for Monsieur (le Comte d'Artois). Expecting something grand, I repaired to the cathedral in company with several other officers. We were received with great civility by the functionaries of the establishment, and provided with seats in the stalls and organ-loft. Our party formed the whole congregation, for there were none of the inhabitants. We had not been long seated ere a slight movement and the shuffling of feet in the direction of the grand entrance announced the approach of the illustrious communicant; and Monsieur entered the choir, followed 'at a little distance by the gentlemen of his suite : a small man of good figure, but of no very distinguished appearance. He was dressed in a blue uniform coat with silver embroidery, white breeches, and silk stockings. He advanced with a quick pace to the steps of the high altar, where a single chair had been placed for him, bowed very low, crossed himself most devoutly, bowed again, and, kneeling on the chair with his arms resting on the back, buried his face in his hands, and in this attitude remained throughout the ceremony. His suite, military and civil, ranged themselves across the choir behind him. A few found chairs, and knelt on them, but the greater part remained standing, and seemed little interested in the service. At length, to my great joy, the last taper was extinguished, and, tired to death, I made my escape, resolved never again to attend a royal mass.

With the interior of the houses in Ghent I had little acquaintance, having seen no more of them than the rooms inhabited by our own officers. In our Quartier de Bruges were many very large and even magnificent ones—some of them in the modern style, with French windows, of three or four stories, or occasionally only one, with a basement entirely blank; others, again, in the heavy antique Flemish style, with large windows in deep embrasures (perhaps with little panes of glass set in lead, and divided by heavy stone mullions)—those on the ground-floor defended by an iron cage, as in Spain; lofty folding-doors, full of iron studs, surmounted by a cumbrous, tasteless pediment, or an equally cumbrous escutcheon, looking gloomily magnificent. In all cases, however, the most scrupulous cleanliness and neatness were general characteristics; and as the street-doors usually stood wide open throughout the day, the eye of the passenger, as it glanced through the darkened perspective of the entrance-hall, was sure to be refreshed by the vivid verdure of vines and acacias decorating the interior court—a never-failing accompaniment, particularly to the older houses.

One of my officers, with whom I had established a breakfast mess, was billeted in a house (or rather palace) of the latter description in the Rue de Poivre (Pepper Straet). The rooms in this were of magnificent dimensions, wainscoted with some dark wood, the doorways and ceilings ornamented with arabesques. They were scrupulously clean, but very bare of furniture, the little there was (merely chairs and tables) clumsy and antique — folding-doors with their ornamented encasements reaching to the ceiling—neither door nor window frames painted. The whole house was as deserted and silent as I have described my own to be—gloomily obscure ; but this, as the weather was hot, formed a recommendation, for it was deliciously cool. The only inhabitants ever seen either by my companion or myself were the lord of the mansion—a most precise, polite, frigid little sexagenarian, and an old domestic in cotton jacket and *bonnet de nuit*, who sometimes assisted Q.'s servant. The old gentleman was, however, most civil in going through the ceremony of offering everything his house afforded, but what that might be there were no means of ascertaining, for we never either saw or smelt his kitchen. The garden, an irregular area of no great dimensions, presented a grove of trees with thickets of underwood, threaded in all directions by narrow serpentine walks; and to prevent a sense of confinement, I suppose, the high boundary-wall was painted from top to bottom in distemper, with the representation of a distant country sky and all. The effect of this, in my opinion, was vastly inferior to that which would have been produced by covering it with vines or flowering creepers. Another of our people dwelt in a house of quite a different description—it was one of those already mentioned as having a blank basement, and giving but a single row of large French windows to the street. My friend's apartments were truly luxurious. The walls were covered with French paper representing the scenery of some tropical region, the furniture (of which there was even a superfluity) all elegant; the large windows, adorned by ample draperies, looked out upon a lovely and luxuriant garden, and the light that entered through them was broken and tempered by festoons of vine leaves that hung across them, whilst the air came redolent of delicious odours from the ocean of flowers below, and the ear was entertained with the sweet warbling of birds suspended in pretty cages of brass wire in all parts of the house. The family consisted of several females—handsome, elegant, and simple in their dress; women-servants, scrupulously neat and clean, but not a man. These ladies must have been people of some consequence, if we may judge from the number and respectability of their visitors. The general aspect of the population of Ghent, as seen in the streets, &c., did not strike me as having anything very peculiar in it to attract the attention of a foreigner; the numbers, however, and to him novel appearance, of the secular clergy form a feature not to be omitted. An Englishman is totally unused to having the Church and its accessories so constantly in his presence as he here finds it. Both eyes and ears remind him perpetually of one and the other. The *carillons*, and the irregular unmeaning jingle-jangle of the bells from the numerous churches, continuing more or less throughout the day — the monotonous nasal chant issuing from every church one passes (and they constantly recur)—the occasional rencontre of some procession, and the number of priests to be seen everywhere in black cassocks and bands, with very small three-cornered cocked-hats stuck formally on their well-powdered heads —never allow one to forget Holy Mother Church as a leading member of the commonwealth. These priests all look sleek and in good case— they are evidently well fed; and it is amusing to see some of them (very young men) gliding along with downcast eyes (*vultus dejectu*) and demure steps, whilst ever and anon a stealthy sidelong glance announces that their thoughts are not entirely abstracted in devotional meditation—that they are not insensible to the excitement of the busy scene around them. To these may be added the dowdy, homely figures of the Beguines in their inelegant black dresses, as inelegant and truly *bizarre* caps of snow-white linen floating like enormous wings on either side of their heads. The remainder of the population, as I have said, offered nothing very striking in the way of costume, at least as far as regarded the higher classes. People everywhere now have adopted, it may be said, a common uniform. All the male world wear round hats, tail or frock coats of sober colours, and trousers. The rich old *bourgmestres*, for instance, are precisely what one would figure to himself a *bourgmestre* to be—fat, portly, aldermanly men, often in cocked-hats and powdered wigs, a sober or sad-coloured suit of good broad-cloth, amply cut, breeches ditto, silver knee-buckles, white or striped silk-stockings, clumsy, square-toed, but well-polished, high-quartered shoes, with enormous silver buckles—quite antiques; the finish, a handsome cane with golden knob, sometimes ruffles, figured silk waistcoats, &c. &c. The peasantry frequenting the markets differed from our people of the same class in the prevalence of short striped cotton jackets, caps, and *sabots*. Many of them, like our rustics, wore smock-frocks, much ornamented about the back, breast, and shoulders by embroidery in coloured worsteds; these frocks, however, are generally dark-blue. The street groups of the middle and lower classes were principally characterised by the frequency of short jackets, generally nankin or striped cotton, breeches of velveteen, with silver knee-buckles and striped stockings; cloth, nankin, or a sort of grey linen, foraging-caps of all shapes — some trimmed with wool or fur, generally having long pendant tassels from the top, and almost all having immense broad shades either of leather, or of the same material as the cap.

Of the manners of a people it would be presumption to speak on so short an acquaintance. The little intercourse we had with them, however, made a favourable impression on us. We found those of the upper classes obliging and polite; the tradesmen civil and attentive; the labouring classes quiet, orderly, and extremely respectful.

In point of religion, the men of the upper classes appeared indifferent or lukewarm, the women very assiduous in the performance of ceremonies, in which it was obvious the heart frequently had little concern. The lower orders were superstitious, priest-ridden, and extremely punctual in the performance of their duties. The peasantry alone seemed quite in earnest. I may characterise the whole population, high and low, as priest-ridden; for, however indifferent the men of the former may be, they are not a whit the less subservient to these their spiritual, and generally temporal, masters.

It would be unjust to condemn as immoral a whole people for the vices found in their cities. We ought not, therefore, to pass unqualified censure on the Flemings because this was exhibited to us openly in the streets of their great cities. I allude to the barefaced manner in which we were tormented incessantly by a number of boys making the most impudent and depraved propositions, and that with a pertinacity not readily repulsed. An instance of moral and religious degradation, I am happy to say, we rarely met with afterwards until our arrival at that hotbed of vice—Paris.

Our last transaction in Ghent was the taking over a number of baggage-mules from Captain Clive's Brigade of the German Legion Artillery. These beautiful animals they had brought with them from Spain, and I shall never forget the grief and indignation with which they parted with them. Affection for, and care of, his horse, is the trait, *par excellence*, which distinguishes the German dragoon from the English. The former would sell everything to feed his horse; the latter would sell his horse itself for spirits, or the means of obtaining them. The one never thinks of himself until his horse is provided for; the other looks upon the animal as a curse and a source of perpetual drudgery to himself, and gives himself no concern about it when once away from under his officer's eye. The German accustoms his horse to partake of his own fare. I remember a beautiful mare, belonging to a sergeant of the 3d Hussars, K.G.L., which would even eat onions. She was one of the very few that escaped after the disastrous retreat of Corunna, and had been saved and smuggled on board ship by the sergeant himself. In the Peninsula the only means of enforcing some attention to their horses amongst our English regiments was to make every man walk and carry his saddle-bags whose horse died or was ill.

CHAPTER V.

April 24.—Orders to march to-morrow morning to Thermonde. At a loss to know where this can be, but find it is Dendermonde. Whether this be in consequence of any movement of the French army, or only for the purpose of concentration, we are in the dark. The other troops of horse-artillery in Ghent have also received orders to march, but we move independently of each other. To-day passed in preparation, visiting, and leave-taking. Called on my host, whom I found in a handsome well-furnished drawing-room at the back of the house, looking over a very nice garden. Had no idea of so much cheerfulness and comfort existing under our roof, nor of the two good-looking women I found with him. After much complimenting we parted.

25*th*.—Fine morning. Marched early; leaving Ghent by the road already mentioned as passing under the Citadel, and crossing that flat but splendid country which I understand extends without interruption to Antwerp, or rather to the Tête de Flandre. This is the Pays de Waes, perhaps the highest cultivated land in Europe. It is said to have been once little better than moving sand, but that the great quantities of manure laid on it for so many successive centuries have completely changed its nature, and produced the fine rich black mould which is now everywhere of considerable depth. If this be true, it will in some measure account for the hillock already spoken of, which is entirely of sand. Passing close under this, I could not but be struck by the circumstance of this sandy mound standing in the midst of an otherwise unbroken level, and conjectured it must be artificial—one of those enormous tumuli erected as the tomb of departed warriors, or as a look-out, which was a common Roman custom, particularly in so flat a region. It is about the height of Silbury, perhaps less, but by no means of so regular a form; its slope, which is covered with trees and bushes, being excavated and broken in numerous places, probably for the sand. Standing as it does amidst a grove of trees, through the boles of which one catches pretty peeps of the blue distance, and crowned by the little chapel, independent of its historical or geological existence, it is really a very interesting object, and forms an admirable foreground to a picture of the Pays de Waes. Every one does not understand the beauty of a landscape the principal feature of which is a dead level. Yet these, like others, have their beauties, which consist principally in the effect under which they are seen, and the delicious tones of the aerial perspective gradually melting into the purply tints of extreme distance. I have often found very exquisite beauty in these flat Flemish scenes, especially when relieved and animated by groups of men and cattle, such as one sees in Cuyp and all the Dutch and Flemish masters. Whether from the richness of the soil, or some peculiar quality of the atmosphere, I know not, but I always fancied the colouring here much more vivid than in England, and the distances much more purply—quite Italian. But I am halting under the hill; so to proceed. Our road led us through the midst of this magnificent Pays de Waes, everywhere exhibiting such crops and such pastures as it is difficult to form an idea of—the latter covered with fine beasts, which I understand are brought hither from Holland to fatten. We passed through several populous villages, particularly Locristy and Seven Eeke, and about fifteen miles from Ghent reached Lokeren, a large manufacturing town, having all the dirty, smoky, dismal appearance of our northern manufacturing places, to which the blackish-coloured stone—somewhat, in colour at least, resembling the slag used about Bristol as a building material—contributes not a little. The houses, of three and four storeys, appeared tenanted each by many families; and the population had all the squalid, filthy character of our own manufacturing population, always excepting those of Stroudwater and the bottoms in Gloucestershire. Cloth is the article fabricated here, but of what quality I know not.

A strong column of Hanoverian infantry, composed of several battalions of militia, crossing our route, detained us at the entrance of the town more than half an hour, to the great amusement of a crowd of gazing weavers and dyers, with upturned sleeves and blue hands and arms, who surrounded us. The Hanoverians were fine-looking troops, generally very young, and completely English in dress and appointments, except that the officers wore particoloured sashes. Each battalion had a very good band, though rather noisy, from the number of jingling instruments entering into its composition — as cymbals, triangles, ottomans, &c. &c.—all which are much more patronised by foreigners than by us. The Chaussée terminating at Lockeren, when we continued our march it was on a bad cross-road, which soon brought us to Zêle—a large populous manufacturing village, having a wide, clean street. Houses in the cottage style, and generally only of one floor. The whole population turned out to see us pass, with the *curé* at their head—a tall, respectable-looking old man, who, judging from the good-humoured countenance with which he scrutinised our column as it passed, and the air *empressé* with which he came forward to offer his advice respecting the road to Dendermonde, I set down either as a very amiable person, or very zealous in the cause of legitimacy: we were feeling our way without a guide, and therefore had to ask. The respectful, quiet, and contented air of his flock spoke also in his favour, and, together with the bright eyes of numerous pretty women among the crowd, left a favourable impression of Zêle.

Henceforward the scenery took a very different aspect, and we exchanged the smiling, populous, well-wooded country we had been hitherto traversing for a lugubrious, marshy tract, devoid of anything that could break its monotony—neither trees nor houses, and but few cattle, were to be seen, whilst the abominable road became so slippery that it was with difficulty our horses could keep their feet.

About half a league from Dendermonde we struck the Scheldt, but could see nothing of it or the opposite country for the high dyke by which the river is here confined, and along the foot of which, for some little distance, our road lay, until it brought us to a wooden bridge elevated nearly thirty feet above the water, and so tottering that it was necessary to pass by single divisions, and even then its vibrations were not pleasant. Our quartermaster, who had been sent in advance, met us here, with orders not to halt in Dendermonde, but to proceed on to St Gille, situated beyond it on the Brussels road. The appearance of things improved here, from the number of trees about Dendermonde, which we soon after entered by a long, straight, narrow, gloomy, mean-looking street of low houses, built of the same dark stone we had seen at Lokeren. This led us to a spacious quay, encompassing what I supposed to be the harbour, for the water was very low, and the mud bare, like Bristol. Passing round the head of this, we soon left the town again, and almost immediately found ourselves at St Gille, which consists of a few mean houses scattered along the Chaussée, the only decent one being that of a *juge de paix*, on which I found myself billeted.

In a country so carefully cultivated as this is, a piece of waste land is a rarity, and therefore we had some difficulty in forming our park, which at last was done in a small enclosed cemetery, not without disturbing the ashes of the dead, and running some risk of breaking our horses' legs and our own necks, for the graves had all been so loosely filled in that the horses sank to their shoulders in the light soil. Our men and horses were dispersed amongst the neighbouring farms of the commune, and though rather widely scattered, yet most comfortably put up everywhere.

Whilst employed at the park my servant had taken my baggage to my billet, so that on repairing thither I found Madame la Juge, *en habit de Dimanches*, already waiting at the door to receive me. A fine and handsome woman, perhaps turned of thirty, and possessing a degree of *embonpoint* which, whilst it added dignity to her air, detracted nothing from the grace of her person. She received me with more than common politeness, with kindness and cordiality, which, as an intruder, I felt I had no right to expect, and, conducting me into the house, assured me that it should be her study to render my stay at St Gille as agreeable as possible, ushering me into an apartment destined for my use, and offering the assistance of her servants—in short, the whole house was at my disposal. All this was not mere compliment, for in good truth she kept her word to the very letter. I never experienced greater kindness, or more sincere hospitality, and under such circumstances soon felt myself perfectly at home in my neat lodgings.

What a contrast was this to the gloomy billet I left in the morning in the silent, solitary Rue de Bruges! Here everything was light, airy, and cheerful. But I must describe my new home. The *apartment* consisted of a saloon of about eighteen feet square, with a little cabinet or sleeping-room adjoining and opening from it. Both were as clean as it was possible to conceive anything could be, and the white walls perfectly immaculate. Furniture of the simplest kind— chairs of oak or walnut ranged along the walls, two tables covered with oil-cloth, neat but scanty window - curtains, with draperies and fringe, and a most brilliant stove, *en faïence*, ornamented with brass - work, standing out nearly in the middle of the floor ; that floor of red tiles, or brick highly varnished, the coolness of which, in the present hot weather, was highly grateful. I have designated this room as light and airy, and truly it was so, for it was illuminated by no less than six windows. Three of these in the front commanded a pleasant view over the well-wooded and beautifully-cultivated country beyond the great Brussels road, which ran beneath them— the fields more resembling extensive gardens than anything else. As this part of the house, projected beyond the *porte cochère,* a window in the side afforded a peep up the road, terminated by the town of Dendermonde, which hence appeared embosomed in trees. Two fine acacias in front of the gateway overshadowed this with their delicate pensile foliage, and screened it from the hot rays of the afternoon sun. The remaining two windows in the back looked into a delicious and carefully-kept garden, divided as usual by those verdant hornbeam walls into different departments. Such was my saloon. My bedroom, if so it may be called, was equally neat and simple in its equipment: a low bedstead without curtains, bedding of humble materials, but so clean that the most fastidious could have found no fault with it, a chair or two, and a small dressing-table in the single window, constituted its whole furniture. Having made arrangements for establishing our mess here, I set off to visit my people, who, as before mentioned, were scattered by threes and fours all over the commune amongst the farmers; and with these good and simple people I found them already quite at home. In most houses I found them seated at dinner with the family—at all they had been invited so to do; and everywhere the greatest good-humour and best possible understanding prevailed between the host and guests. When I asked, "Ist der meister content mit den soldaten?"—gibberish coined for the occasion, as they understood no French, and I no Flemish—the answer was always a hearty "Yaw, mynheer—yaw! ist brav—ist goot"—at the same time goodnaturedly slapping one of them on the back, and leering archly round at the others. Boys, women, and children would all swarm round me, exclaiming "Goot, goot, goot!" Then, anticipating my wish to see the horses, one of them would invite me to the stables, which, though dark, were all warm and comfortable. Here I found our cattle stowed away, perhaps, amongst half-a-dozen of their elephants of horses, literally living in clover, for their racks and mangers were full of it (the finest I ever saw), and their stalls of clean straw up to their bellies. These good people seemed quite proud of having made the lucky brutes so comfortable. I found afterwards from our Juge de Paix that this bounty was in some measure repaid by the dung, which is here so valuable that the production of one horse in four-and-twenty hours is worth at least three or four pounds of hay, and perhaps four times the quantity of clover.

These farming establishments were very much alike, generally speaking; embosomed in orchards, which in their turn are surrounded by lofty elms. The dwelling-house is usually of brick, only one floor, a high roof, under which are the dormitories with garret-windows, sometimes two tiers of them. On the ground-floor the windows are large and open in the French style, outside shutters almost invariably *green*. Commonly there are only two rooms on this floor, one on each side of the passage, the door of which opens on the yards, as do the windows. One of these rooms is the kitchen, or ordinary residence of the family, the other is a *salle de cérémonie*. In the first is the usual display of brass pans, kettles, crockery, &c., which, with some common benches and a large table or two, constitute its furniture. As everywhere throughout this country, the most perfect cleanliness prevails, and the metallic lustre of the brass is brought out as much as scrubbing can effect. The *salle* exhibits a collection of stiff old-fashioned chairs with rush bottoms and high upright carved backs, ponderous oaken tables, snow-white window-curtains, and a series of very common prints, in as common frames, suspended from the walls. These usually represent saints, &c. On the chimney-piece waxen or earthenware figures of animals, fruits, &c.; and frequently affixed to the wall over the centre one sees a kind of deep frame or box with glass front, in which, amongst cut paper, moss, or shell-work, is either a crucifix or a portrait of the Virgin and child. The barns, stables, cow-houses, and other out offices, form the other three sides of a square of which the front of the dwelling is the fourth. A rough pavement of about ten or twelve feet wide runs all round in front of the building; the remainder of the area is one vast dunghill, having a reservoir in the centre to receive its drainings, whilst it receives those of the cow-houses, stables, and dwelling by means of gutters constructed for the purpose. This precious fluid is the great dependence of the Flemish agriculturist, as the principal fertiliser of his fields. When the land is to be manured, it is carted out upon the grounds in a large tub (like a brewing-tub). A boy leads the cart very slowly all over the field, whilst a man, armed with a scoop, keeps scattering it in all dirctions. It must be confessed that the fields after this aspersion do not exhale the most savoury odours, but then nothing can exceed their fertility. The country about Dendermonde was, generally speaking, laid out in long narrow patches, separated from each other sometimes by a belt of turf, sometimes by a footpath, at others by ditches, along the edge of which might be a growth of alders, but no regular hedges anywhere. Towards the Dender, ditches of water were the common division, and these fields were fertilised by irrigation, not by the scoop, and a more beautiful verdure could not be seen, all being pastures; of the other fields or patches, each bore a different crop, some flax, some wheat, some *trèfle* or clover, some buckwheat, some hops—the whole district having the appearance of one vast garden. The soil in general was a light rich mould, but degenerating into sand as it approached the Scheldt, on the north side of St Gille. The absence of hedges was fully compensated by the numerous copses that enriched the scenery in all directions, together with the rows of trees with which almost every road was bordered, so that, although a dead level, nothing could be more pleasing than the pictures it presented, except the tract towards the Scheldt, which was bleak enough.

My rounds finished, I returned to my billet, where I found our people all assembled, and we soon sat down to a most excellent dinner. The wine, which we had procured from the town, was thin, pale, almost white, but of a very piquant flavour, and over it we were enjoying ourselves, when a servant came in, and announced that M. le Juge, having that moment returned from the town, begged permission to pay his respects to M. le Commandant. Permission granted. Enter a little vulgar-looking man, about sixty years of age, whose coarse and by no means prepossessing physiognomy was not improved by the loss of an eye; nor was his person set off to the best advantage by his costume, consisting of a shabby blue frock, dark waistcoat sprigged over with golden flowers, and very long drab pantaloons, hanging about his legs in large folds, evidently unrestrained by any suspensatory process. His head was surmounted by a sort of forage-cap of dark-green velvet, with a band of silver lace, and a silver tassel falling over the crown. Doffing this, with a profusion of bows he casts his sharp single eye inquiringly round our party, exclaiming, " M. le Commandant?" I bow. " M.

le Commandant, se trouve-t-il bien ici?" I assent, and express my gratitude to his better half for her attentions. "De tout, M. le Commandant, de tout! Elle n'a rien fait que son devoir aupres de vous, M. le Commandant! Et de plus, je vous engagé de considerer la maison and les domestiques tous à vôtre service, M. le Commandant—tous, tous, tous!" (pronouncing strongly the final *s* of the last word) "et si, par hazard, M. le Commandant aimerait la solitude, voilà la joli promenade là bas," pointing to the garden. All this passed with us as mere words; but we had formed a wrong estimate of our Juge, who fulfilled to the utmost his professions, and turned out a very worthy fellow. Whilst this colloquy was in progress, our friend had established himself at the table with less ceremony than might have been expected from so complimentary a gentleman, and the bottle, circulating briskly, had the usual effect of loosening tongues and tightening friendship. M. le Juge begged to know where we had obtained our wine, which he did not approve of; it was not such as we ought to drink; begged permission to send for some of a very superior quality from his own cellar. The wine is brought accordingly, a bottle drawn by Monsieur himself with great solemnity and some grim-

ace, relating at the same time its whole history.
Clean glasses are called for, Monsieur fills a bumper, and after contemplating it for a moment against the light, hands it to me with a profound inclination. In colour it exactly resembles what is on the table. I taste it: there is not a shade of difference in the flavour. M. le Juge fills a glass for each of my companions, and hands it to them with the same ceremonious bow. It was easy to see that their opinions coincided with mine; but we did not wish to hurt the good man, and so we one and all smacked our lips, and pronounced it excellent. He immediately ordered a further supply, and insisted on our drinking nothing else. However, the bottles becoming mingled on the table, none of us could distinguish the difference, and our friend himself, I observed, filled his own glass indiscriminately from the one and the other. He meant to treat us, and took this way of accomplishing it, no doubt. We found him an intelligent, facetious companion, although, as we got farther into the night, he did get a little prosy with his anecdotes of the good people of Dendermonde. *En revanche*, he amused us much with a description of the process of enrolling the militia then going on; and droll pictures he drew of the peasantry who were brought

to him for that purpose every day by the *gens-d'armés*. It would seem that these people were forced into the service sorely against their will, being much attached to Buonaparte, and quite averse to the new order of things. This seemed to be the general feeling amongst the bourgeois of Dendermonde, as far as we could learn; and it appeared very doubtful whether our worthy host himself, although a public functionary under the new Government, did not participate in this rage for Napoleon and Impérialisme. Be that, however, as it may, he was so well pleased with our society, that the first cocks crew ere he retired, his hiccoughing adieus and twinkling eye fully demonstrating that, for him at least, the wine was not quite such watery stuff as we had at first imagined. To us *port-drinkers* it was innocuous. The next day we had leisure to look about us, and visit Dendermonde—a place, in my mind, inseparably connected with Corporal Trim and Uncle Toby; and no little amusement was it to my good Juge and his spouse when I related to them the story. They thought it all true for a time.

Whilst my comrades sought the town, I turned to the country, which for me has infinitely more charms. The steeple of a village church peering above the trees about a mile from us, on the Brussels road, attracted me in that direction. The opulent village of Lebbeke, embowered in orchards, appeared peculiarly animated as I approached it. White tents, horses at picket in long lines, groups of artillerymen, peasants and their waggons bringing loads of hay, intermingled amongst the apple-trees, enlivened the scene. Three batteries of 9-pounders were parked in the orchards, and their people partly billeted in the farms, partly encamped near their guns. It was a curious medley of peace and war. Here a large barn by the road-side, its doors thrown wide open, and peasants within busily occupied in threshing, spoke of the former; the guns and their accompaniments in the opposite orchard, of the latter —the horses, looking cool and comfortable under the shade of a fine row of elms, quietly eating their hay, or playfully biting each other. Gunners and drivers, half undressed, were lounging about the tents, or sitting on the wall by the roadside, contentedly smoking their pipes; others busy cleaning their appointments, or raking up the hay in front of the horses.

Large, substantial-looking farm-houses principally formed the village street, and by their comfortable appearance aroused the taste for rural life; but this would be overset by the sight of an officer, his coat unbuttoned, forage-cap on head, and cigar in mouth, lolling listlessly out of a casement, as if perfectly at home—a sight directly antagonistic to the tranquillity of rural retirement. The Flemish waggons, with their teams and drivers, bringing loads of hay, amused me much — long-bodied, and on low wheels, drawn by four, and sometimes five, immense animals, overloaded with fat. The waggoner, walking beside the fore-wheels, guides his team with some dexterity by means of long reins of cord running through holes in the haims. The horses are harnessed two and two, if the team be of four—otherwise two in the wheel and three leaders abreast, always separated from the wheelers by exceedingly long traces; the pole invariably used. The richer farmers, as with us, affect great show in their teams, the harness being gay with fringes and tassels of coloured worsted, and the haims are always particularly fine. These are of wood, flat, about four or five inches broad, the edges frequently studded with brass nails, the front decorated with painted flowers, and often with the Imperial eagle. The overgrown horses are pampered like pet lapdogs, and never required to do

CATTLE AND SHEEP.

one quarter of the work they are capable of. They are noble brutes.

However rich the scenery of this country may be from its cultivation, still, in an Englishman's eye, there is something wanting. Except on the pastures along the Dender, no cattle are ever seen animating the fields. The absence of hedges or other fences obliges the farmer to keep these shut up, except for a short period after the harvest, when they are turned out to pick up what they can along the borders and on the *trèf* layers.

The quantity of manure accumulated by keeping them up is considerable, and no doubt enters into the farmer's calculation. Sheep in small flocks (for I do not see that any large ones are kept) are taken out to pasture by a shepherd and two or three dogs—not at all resembling our sheep-dogs, except in sagacity, but small black curs with long tails. I have seen one of these shepherds dozing on a bank by the roadside, whilst his little flock, grazing in an adjoining slip of grass-land, was quite as efficiently watched as if the fellow had been wide awake. This slip was bounded on three sides by young wheat, and on each of the dividing borders was posted one of these curs. As the flock moved forward or backward so did the dogs; and whilst they fed, these intelligent animals kept incessantly running backwards and forwards on their post like sentinels, instantly darting at any sheep that attempted to break bounds, and driving it back into the grass-plot. The day was exceedingly warm, and their lolling tongues proclaimed that the little animals had no very light task of it, whatever their master's might be.

The town of Dendermonde (of which I saw but little) is situated on the right bank of the Scheldt, at the point where the little river Dender flows into it, as the name imports—Dender mond or mund—*Dender mouth*. This river flows through it, and, being backed up by sluices, forms the basin I noticed on the day of our arrival. It is not large, and its population might be about 5000 or 6000—manufacturers of linens, fustians, &c. &c. The fortifications have nearly disappeared, the only remnant that I saw being something like a ravelin on the Alost side. It is, however, so surrounded by water, and the country is so flat, that an extensive inundation could soon be formed to supply their place if necessary. The general aspect of the town is mean and gloomy, but on the side next to St Gille were several good-looking houses, though all built of the same dark stone. We saw here more pretty women, however, than we had yet met with, always excepting in Zêle.

CHAPTER VI.

Finding all quiet, and that our move hither from Ghent had only been for the purpose of bringing us nearer to the cavalry, whose headquarters were at Ninove, and into a more abundant country for forage, we now gave ourselves up to the amusements our situation afforded, as much as the requisite attention to military duties would allow. Some made excursions to Brussels and Antwerp; some passed their mornings knocking about the balls at a miserable billiard-table upon the rickety floor of an up-stairs room in a neighbouring cabaret; whilst others made a sort of flirting acquaintance with some of the fair damsels of Dendermonde. The time flew quickly, because we were happy.

I was anxious to see Antwerp, and proposed going thither; but day after day something occurred to prevent me, and at last I had the mortifying reflection of having passed six idle days within eighteen miles of it, and yet never been there. My only excursion was to Alost, or Aulst, as they call it. On the 28th Leathes and I set off on this expedition. Until within a mile of Alost, the character of the country we traversed was much the same as that about Dendermonde, but the villages and farm-houses were less neat and more poor in their appearance—ragged thatch instead of slates and tiles, &c.—and the streets of the villages or hamlets narrower and dirtier. During the whole ride we saw but one house that appeared the residence of a gentleman, and that was a large heavy-looking brick building, standing in the midst of an old-fashioned garden, ornamented (if so it may be called) with painted statues of men and monsters quite in the Cockney style. *En effet*, this was the *lusthause* of a wealthy *bourgmestre* of the Ville de Gand. Approaching Alost, we found the character of the country changing, and having seen nothing but a dead-level ever since landing at Ostend, were agreeably surprised at finding ourselves ascending a gentle slope, and surrounded by a gently undulating country, yet so slightly so that we were not aware of it until on it. Passing a sort of advanced barrier, we soon reached the town, and rode into a respectable sort of square, where we dismounted at the Maison d'Autriche. No accommodation for horses here, so we were obliged to resort to a carrier's in an adjoining street, where we with difficulty got stable-room, all being crowded with horses of Louis XVIII.'s cavalry. Being tired when I returned to Dendermonde, I made no note of my visit to Aulst, and therefore can say little about it. All I remember is a fine broad street of handsome houses running up an ascent; a pretty public walk (*en berceau*) called L'Allée d'Amour (as we should say, *Love Lane;* and what town or village is there in England which has not its Allée d'Amour ?); a fine church, in which was a series of paintings (good, I believe) representing the life and adventures of some saint ; the canal harbour, full of boats laden with corn and hay for our cavalry, the contractors having established here their grand depôt, &c. &c.; great crowding and bustling in the streets, occasioned partly by this circumstance, partly by the presence of the Duc de Berri and his troops, and partly by an unusual influx of travellers. Moreover, I remember that we got a most delicious omelet and bottle of very fine Sauterne at the Maison d'Autriche, for which (*garçon* included) we paid only five francs; whilst, *en revanche*, as it were, we had to pay eight to the villain of a carrier for the feed of bad oats which our horses would not eat; that we saddled them ourselves, and sallied from Alost, expecting, in due time and without *contre-temps*, to reach St Gille; that we actually arrived within a mile of Lebbeke, the spire of whose church was closely seen by us above the trees, and towards which we attempted a short cut, which attempt ended in losing ourselves, and wandering about for an hour within 800 yards of St Gille, and always with the spire of Lebbeke in view, without being able to reach one place or the other; and that there we might have wandered till doomsday, had we not fortunately fallen in with a patrol (foot) of *gensd'armés*, who put us into the right way—such is the intricacy of this country, intersected as it is by lanes and ditches, like network, and the view confined to the neighbouring field by the multitudinous little woods. We got home! *Chez moi*, things went on so comfortably that I was quite happy, my worthy host and his spouse treating me and mine quite as part of the family. Of Monsieur, however, I did not see very much, for every morning, immediately after breakfast, he went to his office in Dendermonde, where he remained all day, and he never ventured another soirée with our party. The last year (1814) my position in their *ménage* had been occupied by a French colonel, of whom they spoke in the highest terms, always winding up with, "Ah! il était brave garçon, celui là." When taking leave of them, which the approach of English troops rendered necessary, he added to his adieux, "Mais pour l'année prochaine;" and both these good people confidently expected to see him again, setting it down as certain that the moment the Emperor advanced the English would hasten to their ships, never dreaming that we could resist *him*. So slipped time away, and my present comfort approached its end.

May 1*st*.—I still slept, when, at five o'clock in the morning, our sergeant-major aroused me to read a note brought by an orderly hussar. It was most laconic—*la voici:* "Captain Mercer's troop of horse-artillery will march to Strytem without delay. Signed," &c. &c.

Where is Strytem? and for what this sudden move? These were questions to which I could get no answer. The hussar knew nothing, and the people about me less. One thing was positive, and that was, that we must be under weigh instanter, and pick out Strytem as best we might.

The sergeant-major, therefore, was despatched to give the alert; and having given the hussar a receipt in full for his important despatch, I proceeded to clothe my person for the journey, having hitherto been *en chemise*. As the trumpeter was lodged in a house close by with my own grooms, the "boot and saddle" quickly reverberated through the village, and set its whole population in movement. A gentle tap at my door announced a visitor. What was my surprise on opening it!—there was Madame la Juge *tout en déshabillé*, evidently just tumbled out of bed, and apparently much agitated. Such a scene I did not expect. .

"Ah, Monsieur, vous allez partir!" and she actually began to sob and cry like a child. Was she serious, or was this acting? If the latter, she certainly played her part so well that I could not but give her credit for being in earnest. It is so delightful to believe one's self interesting to a fine woman. Advancing my toilette, I tried at the same time to moderate this outbreak of feeling. She only wept the more. Meantime M. le Juge arrived on the stage, his old blue frock carelessly thrown on, and his nether garment occupying both his hands, one holding it up, and the other arranging it, the eternal green cap stuck on his head, hardly yet quite awake—unwashed, uncombed: the good man did not present the most amiable figure by the side of his neat consort.

Our people were not accustomed to delay, and the road in front of the house was already a scene of bustle from the assembling of the detachments lying nearer home. Although still lachrymose, Madame did not stand idle; but, seeing my servant sufficiently employed packing my portmanteau, set about preparing breakfast, to which I soon sat down, whilst the worthy couple waited on me, recommending this and that, and pressing me to eat, much in the manner of two fond parents hanging over the early meal of their darling boy, about to return to school by the expected coach. I could not but feel grateful for so much kindness, and consequently sorrow at so soon leaving them; and so this breakfast was rather a melancholy one, although the morning sun did shine so bright. The good people were unceasing in their regrets, and repeatedly made me promise that, if I remained in the country, I would pay them another visit—a promise I was never able to fulfil, however.

To my questions respecting Strytem, Monsieur could give no satisfactory answers. "It lay in a very fine country, somewhere in the neighbourhood of Brussels ; and we had better take the road to that city in the first instance, and trust for further information to the peasantry as we went along."

These people are singularly ignorant in this respect, having no knowledge, generally speaking, of any place more than two or three miles from home. Monsieur, however, invited me to follow him to his study—a small room all in a litter—over the gateway, and there, after some hunting amongst books, old clothes, &c. &c., he rummaged out the mutilated fragment of an old but very excellent map, which he insisted on my putting into my *sabretache*, which I did, and still keep for his sake.

At length the moment of departure arrived, the parade was formed, my horse at the door. The tears of Madame flowed afresh as she embraced me. Monsieur led me by the hand to the gateway. Here the great coarse Flemish cook, the corner of her apron applied to her eyes, for she also wept (at the departure of my groom, I suspect), came running out, her clumsy *sabots* with their trimmings of rabbit skin clattering along the stone passage like the hoofs of a cart-horse. My servant had made her a present for her assistance, in her eyes so magnificent that she could hardly express her gratitude, and so poured on me a shower of thanks and blessings, and recommendations to the protection of saints and saintesses, with a volubility which her usual taciturn, phlegmatic manner had not led me to expect. "*Prepare to mount!*" "*Mount!*" The trumpets sound a march, and waiving a last adieu to the group at the gate of my late home, I turn my back on it for ever, perhaps. The men were in high spirits, and horses fat as pigs and sleek as moles—thanks to rest, good stabling, and abundance of *trèf*. Most of the peasants on whom many of our men had been billeted accompanied them to the parade, and it was interesting to witness the kindness with which they shook hands at parting, and the complacency with which, patting the horses on the neck, they scanned them all over, as if proud of their good condition. And yet these were Napoleonists, according to our Juge. For my part, I believe they were utterly indifferent as to whether they lived under the rule of Napoleon or the house of Orange, so long as their agricultural labours were not interrupted: and this alone, I suspect, was the cause of their aversion to being militiamen.

Passing through Lebbeke, we found the three brigades of 9-pounders also getting on march, and the whole village astir. The officers told us their orders were to march direct to Brussels, and they were fully persuaded the French army had advanced.

For about seven miles the road lay through a country differing little from what we had hitherto seen; but then it became suddenly hilly. Ascending the first long but not very steep ascent, we were assailed by a host of beggars, who had stationed themselves here to take advantage of the slow pace at which carriages were obliged to ascend the hill. These were the first I recollect having seen in the country. The ragged boys accompanied the column to the top of the hill, endeavouring to excite, if not compassion, at least admiration of the agility with which they rolled themselves along alternately on hands and feet, like so many wheels—a feat that procured them some coppers.

The country had now totally changed its character; still fertile, highly cultivated, and abundantly populous, yet presenting scenery of a much more interesting nature. Fine swells enabled one to obtain, from time to time, most charming views of the rich distance, instead of, as hitherto, being confined to a few hundred yards of meadow, shut up, as the flat country was, by trees and small copses.

Villages and large farms appeared in all directions, intermingled with extensive woods; the fields exhibited the richest exuberance of crops —wheat, rye, hops, buckwheat, &c., with their lighter tints relieving the more sombre tones of the woodlands. Here the spire of a village church, there the conical roofs and quaint architecture of a chateau, peered above the foliage of the woods, and increased the interest of the scene. To me this change was delightful. I thought I had never seen anything half so rich as the fine landscape spread before me when I turned to look back on gaining the first summit. The height, however, was not sufficient to allow me, at this distance, in a country so thickly wooded, to see Dendermonde again, though my eye eagerly sought it. The large village of Assche (town, I should call it, being marked bourg in the map) crowned this hill, and here we found a battery of Belgian Horse Artillery in quarters. The men lounging about in undress, or without their jackets, without any appearance of a move, induced us to believe our own was, after all, only another change of quarters—and we were right. The people here knew Strytem, which they said was only a few miles distant, to the southward of the road we were on. Accordingly I despatched an officer to precede us, and make the necessary arrangements for our reception; at the same time quitting the chaussée, we plunged into a villanous cross-road, all up and down, and every bottom occupied by a stream crossed by bridges of loose planks, which to us were rather annoying from their apparent insecurity, as well as from the boggy state of the ground for some yards at either end of them. However, if the road was bad, the beauty of the country through which it led made ample amends. Descending from the hill on which Assche is situated, we travelled for two or three miles through a bottom, between two nearly parallel ridges, whose slopes exhibited all the luxuriance of vegetation in splendid crops of grain, &c., and magnificent trees, so peculiar to this country, whilst an almost continued wood occupied their summits. This part of our route reminded me strongly of the valley in which High-Wycombe lies, though there nothing like this exuberance is seen. About a mile, as it proved, from Strytem, for we had not as yet seen anything like a village, we ascended the hill again, and were continuing along the summit when a peasant, in blue smock-frock and white nightcap, came running after us with a scrap of paper in his hand, which he presented to me with a most profound bow, doffing at the same time his dirty cap. A few lines in pencil from Dr Bell informed me that the bearer would lead us to Strytem; and he by signs—for he spoke no French—gave us to understand that we must turn back, having passed the road leading thither. Accordingly a countermarch, by unlimbering, took place, and, following our guide, we descended into a most secluded little valley, green and lovely, the bottom being principally meadow, everywhere surrounded by stately elms. The road, however, became worse than ever—deep tenacious mud, sadly broken up. After marching a short distance we passed a wheel-wright's shop; then came to a broader space, where stood a small mean-looking church, a miserable cabaret, a forge, two very large farm establishments, with a few wretched-looking cottages;—this, our guide gave us to understand, was Strytem. Bell's note spoke of a chateau at the point we were to make for, but here was nothing of the sort. All seemed disappointment, for the miserable place itself was so different from the fine spacious streets and substantial houses of all the villages we had hitherto seen, that one could scarcely imagine it to be the same country. Our guide, however, led on, and after passing this poor collection of dwellings, a high stone wall bounding the road to the left, with a wide gateway in the centre, announced the chateau, which was so completely shut in by the woods, &c., that the first glimpse we got of it was on entering these gates. A spacious green court sloped down to the building, a dreary-looking old pile of brick, forming three sides of a square, and surrounded by a broad moat—nearly as green as the court, from the aquatic weeds floating on its stagnant water. Arched doors; high but narrow windows, composed of small panes set in lead, and encased in heavy stone frames; lofty stepped gables, and a tower occupying one angle of the court, with a conical roof surmounted by an iron cross and weathercock, gave it a most venerable and somewhat imposing aspect. The sombre effect, however, was in some measure relieved by the lively tints of roses and rich verdure of the broad leaves of a vine trained over a trellis along the edge of the moat, as well as the fine fruit-trees everywhere covering the walls of the front court. A broad gravel-drive descended to the moat, which was crossed by a stone bridge, substantial, but not ornamental. On our right were stables, &c., for about half-way down the court; on the left the enormous roofs of barns and farm-buildings appeared over the wall, and beyond them, again, the rather inelegant spire of the village church. An arched doorway communicated on this side with the farmyard. Behind the chateau the view was bounded by the tufted and feathery masses of a superb avenue of beeches and a hill covered with wood seen through the few openings between them, relieving well the reddish sombre tone and formal outlines of the building. Every feature of this place is strongly impressed on my memory as I then beheld it for the first time, not without emotions of disgust; for though rather a picturesque object to look at, I could not suppress a shudder at the idea of its becoming my habitation for an indefinite time. Nothing do I regret more than not having made a sketch of it from this side, although I did several from other points.

The road was so narrow, and the turn so sharp, that it required all the dexterity of our drivers to get decently into the court with their six-horse teams. They did, however, effect it without carrying away the gate-posts, to the no small amazement of some half-dozen boors, whom the novelty of arrival had drawn together, and we finally formed a very compact little park, three pieces and their ammunition-waggons on each side of the central path. The *corps de garde* was established in the loft over the stables in which were lodged the officers' horses; and the rest of the troop were billeted on the neighbouring farms, which, in general, were so large that they took a subdivision, or thirty-two horses, each, and, if I mistake not, that adjoining the chateau a whole division of sixty-four horses. Having despatched this business, we proceeded to examine our own quarters. The old gardener, a tall meagre figure, with a venerable grey head and good-humoured physiognomy, but somewhat bent by age, accompanied by his daughter, a pale melancholy-looking young woman, met us on the bridge, the keys of his fortalice in one hand and his dirty *bonnet de nuit* in the other. (Be it here remarked that although neatness and cleanliness characterise the dwellings of the Flemish peasantry, yet are they not over and above particular in this respect as regards their own persons.) As he could speak nothing but Flemish, Mademoiselle came to officiate as his interpreter, but the *patois* in which she expressed herself was so unintelligible that, after listening for some time to her long-winded story, and comprehending nothing more of it than the constantly-recurring "Mon père dit," &c.,

our politeness gave way, and we begged that the doors might be forthwith thrown open. The burden of her song or chant, for such it was, seemed to be an endeavour to dissuade us from our purpose of lodging there, though I could not well comprehend why. Leaving, then, the good man to replace his bonnet, and Mademoiselle to explain to him something or another, we proceeded to examine the interior, in order to select our rooms. The chateau had been uninhabited for many years, and, though not ruinous, was in a very dilapidated state. Nothing could be more chillingly repulsive than the vast flagged hall into which we first entered. Several doors led from this, right and left, into suites of apartments, and one, low and arched, opposite the entrance, opened on a long bridge leading over the moat to the garden and pleasure-grounds, &c. This hall was totally devoid of furniture. We found the rooms on the ground-floor large, lofty, and of good proportions, but only feebly illuminated by high windows sunk deep in the wall, and of which the heavy stone mullions intercepted nearly as much light as entered between them. The walls were hung with tapestry so ancient and so much decayed that the figures, landscapes, &c., by which it had once been ornamented, were nearly obliterated.

In some rooms old family portraits occupied the places of the wainscot panels, particularly over the doors. The only furniture in any of them was a few ponderous tables, and some high-backed equally ponderous chairs, having both seats and backs stuffed and covered with tapestry. On the floor above, a large corridor or hall—for it was directly over and corresponded in size with the one below—was hung round with full-length portraits of the Van Volden family (to whom the domain belonged), male and female. Some of these were common enough; but there were others evidently the production of no ordinary pencil—one in particular, a lady habited in a costume such as prevailed about our Charles II.'s time—a splendidly beautiful creature of some two or three and twenty years of age, painted in a most masterly style; and, from being in a much more magnificent frame than any of the others, apparently a person of higher consideration. "*Mon-père-dit*" (as we had christened the gardener's pallid daughter), who accompanied us through the rooms, could give no information respecting this fair dame—all she knew was that she had been a person of very high rank, and, she believed, an ancestress of Madame la Baronne, the present proprietress. By the way, Madame Van Volden,

Baronne Von Lombeke et Strytem (such were her titles), was at this time residing in Brussels, where she had a grand mansion—Rue de Dominicans. She possessed also another estate at or near Vilvorde, between which and her town residence she divided her time, so that her Strytem tenants saw her very rarely. Her son, being *maire* of the commune, paid an occasional visit to the village, but then always put up at the farmhouse, so that the chateau had long been locked up and quite neglected. To return from this digression. Having visited the upper apartments, all which were as dismal as those below, we proceeded to choose our quarters, much to the chagrin of Mademoiselle *Mon-père-dit*, who had, no doubt, entertained hopes that the repulsive appearance of things would have deterred us from taking up our residence there. I selected a large salon, immediately off the hall, on the ground-floor. It might have been about 30 feet by 26 or 28, very lofty, with an immense gaping fireplace, but without grate. Two great stone-cased windows looked into the front court, a third across the moat and towards the woods behind the chateau. There were three visible doors—the one leading into the great hall, a second into a sort of vestibule or small hall, whence a staircase ascended to the apartments of the right wing, and the third into a long, narrow, but lofty room, in one corner of which I placed my mattress on an old settee. There was also a door from this room into the vestibule, and beyond that another suite of apartments, in which our surgeon established himself. The walls of my salon, like most of the others, were covered with tapestry, and in the compartments between the windows, over the doors, &c., were grim-looking portraits of *ci-devant* Van Voldens, each having the name and date inscribed at the bottom of it, from which I learned that most of them were of considerable antiquity; some, I think, dating 1537.

I have said that there were three *visible* doors to this room. I had been in it some time ere, by accident, I discovered a fourth, concealed under the tapestry, leading into a very small chapel fitted up with great neatness (except the altar, which was rather gaudy), and evidently the only part of the mansion of which any care had been taken. Such was my new domicile, in which I was soon at home, although it contrasted as strongly with my late cheerful apartment at Dendermonde as that did with the gloomy hole at Ghent. Some of our people found a similar contrast, and could not refrain from grumbling. "By the Lord, gentlemen," said old Lieutenant

Ingleby, "you ought to think yourselves very fortunate in getting such a quarter. In the Peninsula the Duke himself would have thought so, and was often glad to get so good a roof over his head." The grumblers were ashamed, and we heard no more of it. A large salon in the left wing we chose for our mess-room, and the other officers established themselves up-stairs. Fires were soon lighted above and below; servants running up and down;—all was life and movement, and the old place had not been so gay for years before. Indeed, on returning to my room after visiting the billets, there was an appearance of home and comfort about it which I did not expect. A large wood-fire blazed and crackled in the great chimney. My servant had collected chairs enough to make a show, ranged round the walls; on one of the great antique tables in the centre he had placed my writing apparatus and one or two books, together with a map of the Pays bas I had brought from Ghent, in the anticipation of country quarters. Clean linen was airing over the back of one of the tapestry chairs, with other preparations for dressing for dinner; whilst coiled up near the blazing hearth lay my old faithful dog and constant companion for the last ten years.

Our mess-room was as much changed, and the preparations for dinner had given it quite another air to what it had when first seen. Like most of the others, it was spacious, but, unlike them, inasmuch as the windows down to the floor were in the modern French style. Of these there were only two—one looking over the garden and woods, the other over a small field or lawn, bounded on two of its sides by double rows of noble beeches, and on the other two (round which ran the road or lane leading to Brussels) by orchards, hop-grounds, &c. &c. Each had an old iron balcony, so rust-eaten that they seemed ready to drop into the water of the moat which lay below them. Over the elaborately carved antique-looking chimney-piece was a large painting of a castle, with a number of men apparently employed clearing the ditch. The floor had been swept, chairs and tables collected from different parts of the house, and one of the latter covered by a clean table-cloth, and our canteen apparatus laid out for dinner—the whole looking so much more comfortable than we expected, that even our grumblers voted the old chateau not so bad after all, as they sat themselves down to the well-covered board. For the feast, not a despicable one, as well as the arrangement of the salon, we were indebted to the indefatigable activity and unrivalled skill of our friend Karl—a worthy whom I have not yet introduced; so, by way of episode, whilst we are enjoying the good viands of his preparation, let me do so.

On the memorable night of our landing at Ostend, whilst standing on the sands, I was accosted by a very handsome youth of about eighteen or twenty, who asked if I wanted a servant. His costume indicated that he meant himself, for he wore a green livery-coat with red cuffs and collar, and a glazed hat with a cockade in it. His history was, that he had lived some time with General Vandamme, and had accompanied him to Moscow; but on returning into Saxony, although he had been a great favourite with the General, this noble personage one day deserted him most unexpectedly, leaving him, not only without money, but also without a prospect of recovering the long arrears of wages due to him—[there was a mystery in this part of the story]—and after vainly waiting in hopes still that the General might return or send for him, he had set out and found his way thus far towards France, when the chance of getting employment amongst *les officiers Anglais* (and no doubt some of their *guinées*) had occurred to him, and I was the first he had addressed. His figure was rather under the middle size, extremely well made; face beautiful, and address perfect. Moreover, according to his own account, he was a pearl without price. He could speak five or six languages, and cook, cut and dress hair, and a thousand other things I have forgotten; but the great recommendation was a talent he had acquired, when with the French army, of *discovering* and *appropriating* the resources of a country—Anglicé, *plundering*. If Monsieur would but try him, he would find him so attentive, so faithful. For his part, he was sure he should soon love Monsieur —his countenance was so amiable. All would not do—I rejected him; but Leathes took a liking to and engaged him. So thenceforth he became one of us, and soon a general favourite; for although he had sounded his own trumpet, he had in no wise exaggerated his qualifications, nor even told us all, for in addition he was the merriest and most kind-hearted creature I ever met with. He had an inexhaustible fund of stories and songs, and sang beautifully, and in a most sweet and melodious voice; was an admirable mimic, and amongst other things mimicked so well two flutes, that one day, at Strytem, sitting smoking my cigar on the parapet of the bridge, I actually made sure two people were playing a duet in the kitchen; but upon going thither, found only Karl, who, seated on a table, was warbling out a favourite waltz, like a robin on the house-top.

Our language he had soon added to his stock, and being now a tolerable proficient, and evidently so well suited for the office, we had at once nominated him major-domo (spite of his youth) this morning on arriving, and placed all the other servants under his directions. But although understanding and speaking English sufficiently for all common purposes, and to communicate with the other servants, he never would address any of us but in French. To return again to the course of our narrative. Our cheerful meal had been discussed with many an encomium on the provider, and the circulation of the bottle had already produced a genial exhilaration amongst our party, when the door was abruptly thrown open, and in rushed our friend Karl, holding his sides, and unable to speak for laughter. "Why, Karl, what the devil's the matter now?" "C'est l'adjoint, monsieur, qui demande à vous parler." "Well, what of that? Is there anything very comical in this visit?"— " Excusez, monsieur, il est si drôl—est ce que je lui ferai entrer, monsieur," and the merry young dog tried to compose his features. I was about to go out to meet this functionary and learn his business, but the whole mess cried out with one voice to bring him in—curiosity being excited by Karl's obstreperous laughter; so I desired him to be admitted. Karl soon returned, ushering in with most ludicrous gravity the worthy *maire* and his cortège (for it appeared he had not come alone), who, each as he crossed the threshold, making a profound salaam, followed his leader until they were all drawn up in line across the end of the room. The appearance of the party was certainly comic, and for a few moments we contemplated each other in silent amazement. The principal figure of this group—he on the right of the line, Mynheer Jan Evenpoel, *adjoint-maire*—was a short, fat, square-built man, with a head like a pumpkin deeply set (*zabullida*, the Spaniards would say) between his broad high shoulders; countenance stolidity itself; little pig eyes, half hid in the swell of his fat cheeks and the thick overhanging brow; nose pudsy, resembling a lump of brown clay thrown against his face more than a nose; a monstrous wide (now half open) mouth, showing within a row of fangs standing apart like palisades; a great fat dew-lap; the whole phiz finished by two enormous projecting ears. Such was the object that had excited so powerfully the risible faculties of young Karl. Our silent gaze seemed to paralyse him. There he stood, evidently endeavouring to assume some sort of an air of office, but trembling visibly, and as visibly perspiring from his extreme nervousness, twirling his hat in his hand, looking timidly, first at me, then at the formidable party round the table, then inquiringly glancing at his own party. The poor man's evident anxiety must have excited pity, had it not more forcibly excited our risibility, as well as that of Karl.

Three peasants, heavy-looking men, with somewhat more intelligence in their countenances, yet decidedly equally alarmed, arranged themselves next to Mynheer Evenpoel. These, as well as their chief, were all arrayed in their roast-beef suits—jackets of cotton, unmentionables of black or bottle-green velveteen, blue-and-white-striped cotton stockings, clumsy silver knee and shoe buckles,—such was their costume. The eternal *bonnet de nuit* for this time had given place to rather smart round hats, with a profusion of plush on them. Drawn up on their left stood the old gardener, his two sons—stout peasants, clad something like, though more humbly than, the rest—and Mademoiselle "*Mon-père-dit,*" also in her best bib and tucker, trying to look amiable, but evidently most particularly anxious. Lastly, with a brisk, self-satisfied air, stepped in one of the most extraordinary-looking personages of the whole party—a diminutive spare figure with a complexion like mahogany, but upright, and of a most martial bearing. He was clad in a short green uniform coat, with large copper buttons decorated with the imperial eagle of France, green pantaloons, and an enormous leathern cocked-hat, which he touched by way of salute on entering, but, soldier-like, retained on his head. In his hand he carried a sort of javelin, or short hunting-spear. This dignitary, a person of most decided importance, passing the others, stepped briskly up and placed himself at the elbow of the trembling magistrate, who drew a long breath, and gave unequivocal testimony of satisfaction at seeing his tutelary genius by his side.

The important personage just described was the *garde-champêtre*—or *garde-village*, as he was more frequently called—a sort of police officer placed by Napoleon in every village of his empire. I never could ascertain precisely the position and duties of these people; they seemed to be chief police officers, and the *maires* paid them great deference, seldom acting in extraordinary cases without their advice and concurrence. They acted as gamekeepers and constables, billeted troops, and exercised a general surveillance in the commune. No doubt they noted and made reports of all they saw and heard, so that H. I. Majesty had an authorised spy in every village. They were well paid, and the situation appeared to be a comfortable retreat for old soldiers, for such we always found them to be. Our present friend (called familiarly by the peasantry Petit Jean) had served in a regiment of the line under Marshal Suchet in Catalonia, and although still only a middle-aged man, had been pensioned on account of having lost two fingers of his left hand, and placed here for life as *garde-village*. Well, the whole cortège has entered the room, and ranged themselves in line across the lower end of it, close to the wall; the shuffling of feet has ceased, and a profound silence prevails. We sit staring at them, and wondering what the deuce they interrupt us for. Bowing and scraping renewed spontaneously; again silence, but various glances are shot at and signs made to Mynheer Evenpoel, which in his fright he utterly disregards, and stands like an owl, without a movement except the evident shaking of his limbs. After a while old Ingleby, who had been leaning over the back of his chair eyeing the poor devil, utters in his usual gruff Yorkshire way, " *Well, sir?* " without reflecting on the fact of his English not being understood. The tone is enough, however, and it determines the party to bolder measures—the quaking magnate is actually shoved forward to the table. Petit Jean also advances, and again places himself at the poor man's elbow; his right arm, outstretched, bears upon the upright javelin, the butt of which he plants firmly, and with an air, on the floor; in his mutilated left hand he holds up to us an unfolded sheet of foolscap, which we soon ascertain to be inscribed by certain characters calculated to extract hay and corn, &c., from the lofts and granaries of our clients—in short, the requisition for forage and provisions, &c., of our quartermaster-general addressed to the commune of Strytem. The brown little warrior looks complacently round the company as though he would say, "And I also am a soldier; *Moi!*" After repeated applications of a very scanty blue cotton handkerchief to his front—*pour essuyer la sueur*—the worthy magistrate at length, in a trembling, hesitating voice, opens his oration, gains courage as he goes on, warms, and even becomes rather energetic towards the conclusion of nearly a quarter of an hour's talk, to which we have listened, but understood not a word. Mynheer salaams, wipes his front, and stands, mouth half-open, attending the applause due to his exertions, and our reply to his statements, whatever they may be. Petit Jean comprehends the dilemma, steps forward with a military salute, places himself again in an attitude, and, whilst Mynheer stares and seems to envy his self-possession, requests permission of messieurs les officiers to explain what M. l'Adjoint would wish to say, and goes off at score—"M. Evenpoel only expresses the sentiments of the whole commune when he assures messieurs les officiers that the arrival of the brave English has diffused throughout its population the most lively joy. Les Anglais are a people as generous as they are brave, and M. l'Adjoint rests satisfied that under the protection of M. le Commandant the peaceful tranquillity of the commune will remain undisturbed." Here, at a glance from Petit Jean, M. Evenpoel and the whole cortège salaam together, repeating with one consent, " Mais c'est vrai—c'est vrai ! Oui, M. le Commandant, c'est vrai çà !" Petit Jean resumes. "*But*, M. le Commandant, we sensibly regret the poverty of our commune, and are *au désespoir* that Milor Wellington should have sent his brave soldiers to so miserable a place—a place so incapable of affording them the good cheer (bon traitement) that they so richly merit, whilst the surrounding country abounds in rich and populous villages, fully adequate to lodge them comfortably (convenablement) and to supply all their wants. It was only *l'année passée* that this poor commune was oppressed and impoverished by being obliged to provide for a corps of Prussians during several months. These people, undisciplined and *bien méchants*, plundered us all without restraint, and wantonly consumed our whole substance—hardly leaving wherewithal to support our miserable existence. Thus, ruined and impoverished, M. le Commandant, we feel assured, will see that, in spite of our good wishes, we are in an impossibility of supplying the immense rations of forage, &c., here demanded;" and here, taking off his chapeau and making a most profound salaam, he again flourishes before us the obnoxious sheet of foolscap, whilst M. l'Adjoint, beginning to fidget, indicates an inclination to renew his harangue amidst a general buzz of approbation, and a reiteration of "C'est vrai, mon commandant, c'est bien vrai." M. le Commandant silences them by observing, "That a soldier must obey orders—that it is for his general to think and investigate—that Milor Wellington, or those acting for him, had no doubt sufficiently informed themselves as to the resources of the country before they ordered troops thither—that, having done so, right or wrong, these troops must live—that it is evident from the good case of all present, particularly of M. le Maire, that the commune did produce something to eat and drink;—consequently, the gentlemen are invited to allow our partaking with them, or we must help ourselves, which would be bien facheux." A general grunt—" Ah, mon Dieu!"— accompanied by deep sighs on the part of Mademoiselle "*Mon-père-dit.*" I should have stated that M. le Maire and a farmer named Walsdragen were the only two ignorant of French. The former of these had profited by an offered chair, and seated himself during the oration of Petit Jean and my answer. Hearing the concert of sighs and groans, he opens his little pig-eyes to the utmost, and casting them about on the surrounding group, seems to demand an explanation. Petit Jean communicates the awful purport of my answer. Agitation recommences, and I am conjured, for pity's sake, at least to delay until an express be sent to Brussels to acquaint Milor

Vellington of the utter impossibility of so large a body of men and horses being supported by so poor a place. Poor simple people! I should like to have witnessed the reception of the delegate. M. le Commandant observes that M. le Maire may do as to him seemeth best, but cannot be so unreasonable as to expect that we and our horses should wait for supper until his messenger return—ergo, as it is already late, M. le Maire is again invited to lose no more time in talking, but to proceed forthwith in collecting the articles demanded. But, to make a long story short, after a deal of action and whispering in a corner of the room, they made a proposition to furnish one-half the quantity. And here it flashed across me, that these people must be dealt with like the Turkish rayah, who, after protesting his incapability to produce a single egg for a whole hour, at last, upon the application of the Mikmander's whip, brings out a whole store of good things. So I cut the matter short by sending Karl for the quartermaster, who was without awaiting the result of the Maire's visit. The old veteran enters, head erect, shoulders thrown back, and steel scabbard jangling on the floor as he advanced to the table, and silently made his salute. The assembled rustics gape and stare at him in evident alarm, Mynheer trembles, Petit Jean draws himself up, as if imitating old Hall's military bearing, whilst I, pointing him out to the assembled multitude, inform them that in five minutes he will proceed at the head of a foraging party to rummage their barns, granaries, and larders, and help himself. The quartermaster, having received his orders, makes his salute, without deigning even a glance at the Maire and party, amongst whom a precious scene of confusion now takes place, amidst which out they all trundle after old Hall, without even the ceremony of a parting salaam; and we, replenishing our glasses, drank success to our foray, rejoicing in having got rid of the noise. Our quiet, however, was of very short duration, for in the court Hall was already assembling his party, and neither understood their remonstrances nor attended to their grimaces; so with one accord back they came upon us, bursting into the room as unceremoniously as they had just left it, bellowing like so many bulls. A new negotiation opened, and terminated with a promise that everything should be brought in if I would give them *two hours,* after they had vainly struggled for daybreak— and away they went. The two hours had nearly elapsed, and we were still at table, when Petit

Jean, foaming with rage, burst into the room unaccompanied : " Ah, mais ces faquins là bas— ils ne font que se moquer de vous et de vôtre bonté, Monsieur le Commandant. Mais excusez, monsieur, je suis militaire, moi ! et je me suis indigne de voir des militaires se laisser tromper par des vilains paysans ; qui qu'ils sont, connaissent très bien l'accueil q'ils auraient reçus à la main d'un officier Prussien, ou même Français. Avec permission, monsieur, je m'en vais amener avec moi vos fourrageurs faire un fourrage militairement ; " and, without waiting for an answer, the little hero bolted, and following to the hall-door, there we saw him sure enough march out of the gate perched upon one of our immense gun-horses, looking for all the world like a monkey on a dromedary. In two hours bread, forage, and all—nay, more than we had demanded—were brought in.

Meantime our sergeant of the guard comes in for orders as to what he shall do with the mayor. " The mayor ?—what have you to do with the mayor ? " " Why, we have him safe in the guard-room, sir." " The devil you have ! and by whose order ? " " Why, sir, we thought it best to keep him until the foraging-party with *Pitty Jan* returned, least he might try to hinder 'em." Here was a dilemma, should the old man complain to headquarters. However, on sending an officer to release him, and explain the mistake, Mynheer was too frightened to think of anything but rejoicing at gaining his liberty. Perhaps conscience told him that he deserved punishment for the imposition he had attempted to practise on us.

Petit Jean from that moment became our great friend and ally. On almost all occasions he sided with the soldiers in any little difference between them and the boors. On one occasion a complaint had been made to me, by a man who lived near the gate, that one of our gunners had not only plundered his potato-garden, but had also otherwise ill-treated him. On my going to investigate the business on the spot, it turned out that he had struck the gunner. Petit Jean, who had accompanied me officially, on hearing this, turned suddenly on the fellow, " You sacré cochon! frapper un militaire; sacré vilain homme! Quoi!—un vil paysan frapper un militaire? Ah, que cela me révolte!"—and seizing a stake from the hedge, foaming with unfeigned anger, he fell on the poor devil, and fairly chased him out of sight, belabouring him all the way. What English soldier would ever take up the cudgels against his own countryman because the French soldier was his brother-in-arms? Whenever his patrol duty did not call him out, he was sure to be found in the guard-room, or somewhere amongst the men. He might certainly have been a spy in the camp, for Buonaparte had most accurate information respecting the state, positions, and numbers of our army, part of which no doubt was communicated by these *gardes-champêtres*, who, as before mentioned, were all old French soldiers, and did not conceal their attachment to the Emperor. Spy or no spy, Petit Jean was always extremely obliging, and frequently of most essential service to us. Our equipment was in every way too perfect to leave any care as to what might be reported of our state; and as to future movements, we were as ignorant of them as Napoleon himself. But to return to our story. The row was all over, our mess party broken up, and I retired to my room; but, alas! on getting into bed I found sleep impossible—the moat under my window was peopled with millions of frogs, and such was the horrid croaking of these little wretches, that sleep was out of the question, and the Van Voldens were avenged.

CHAPTER VII.

The next morning a most superb breakfast was on my table when I returned from a stroll in the woods—the finest milk, eggs, and butter I ever saw in my life, and in profusion. My servant had procured them at the adjoining farm, and so cheap, that he had brought a large soup-plate full of eggs and an antique jug holding more than two quarts of milk. During our whole stay at Strytem there was never any difference in this respect—always abundance. After breakfast, the usual watering order parade took place in the grand avenue, under the shade of stately beeches. The contented countenances of the men, the sleek coats and frolicksome spirit of the horses, testified sufficiently that neither had fared indifferently. I found, however, that the chateau farm was rather crowded, and therefore detached the 1st division, officer and all, to a small village, with a pretty

OCCUPATIONS AT STRYTEM.

chateau on the hill, about a mile from us—Yseringen. This move made all hands completely comfortable, and so we went on. Nothing could exceed the delicious tranquillity I enjoyed in Strytem. For those who preferred more bustle and more society Brussels was at hand, and thither they frequently repaired; on the other side Ninove, the headquarters of Lord Uxbridge, who commanded the cavalry, was only three or four miles distant, and all the surrounding villages were full of cavalry or horse-artillery. Every one breakfasted in his own apartment. At ten A.M. watering order parade and inspection of horses, &c. Then, after visiting the billets and getting through any casual business, I was at liberty, and, mounting my horse, employed the remainder of the morning in exploring the country. In the evening we all assembled to our social meal. Those who had been to Brussels (or, as we used to say, "Up to town") usually brought some news, or at least some gossip, which added zest to the excellent cheer almost always on our board. How our table was furnished I do not exactly recollect, my notes on the subject being silent,* but believe the meat was ration brought from Ninove every day

---

* The moat supplied us daily a dish of very fine carp, and the gardener's sons occasionally shot us a hare or two.

by our commissary (Mr Coates), so was the bread. Poultry, vegetables, &c. &c., we procured in abunance amongst our neighbours; our wine came from Brussels; candles, wood, &c., from Ninove. After dinner some took a short ride previous to seeing their horses done up for the night. For my part, I preferred enjoying the calm beauties of evening with my cigar under the splendid avenue of beech in rear of the chateau, and when night closed in, retired to my antique saloon, which a blazing fire of fagots and a couple of candles made tolerably comfortable. Here I busied myself in Madame de Genlis's 'Life of Henri IV.,' sometimes until midnight, tranquil and happy. At times, as I occasionally looked up from my book and cast my eyes round, no sound interrupting the solemn stillness save the ticking of my watch as it lay on the table before me, the croaking of the frogs, or the moaning of the wind as it eddied round the old hall, I could almost fancy the deep-toned portraits of *ci-devant* Van Voldens, in their sombre velvet suits and stiff ruffs, actually embued with life, and frowning on my intrusion; or fixing them on the door of the chapel, I would conjure up figures of warriors, *bourgmestres*, or damsels clad all in white, raising the tapestry, and—— but then old Bal, getting up from his place before the fire to scratch himself, or the voice of the sentry in the outer court solemnly proclaiming "All's well," would suddenly recall me from my reverie to a consciousness that it was bed-time; and so to bed I hied me, to sleep as well as the eternal frog concert would allow. Such was the general tenor of our life at Strytem, varied a little at times by circumstances to be related as they occurred, and sometimes disturbed for a moment by reports of hostile movements, or the low murmurs of a distant cannonade. This last, however, was heard so frequently, without being followed by any consequences, that we got accustomed to, and finally disregarded, it. Subsequently we found that it proceeded from the practice and exercising of the Belgic artillery at Mons, or somewhere in that direction. My rides, after a time, brought me somewhat acquainted with the neighbouring country, but only by slow degrees, for surely never was reconnaissance of any country more difficult, —it was a perfect labyrinth.

In the immediate neighbourhood of Strytem the ground arose in a succession of round-topped hills, of no very great height, and all very much alike. Of these, the summits, and frequently the slopes, were clothed with woods of oak, ash, beech, &c. &c., intermixed with coppice of the finest hazel I ever saw, thus forming a number of little valleys running into each other, but all, from the profusion of wood and the overlapping (if I may use the term) of the flanks of the hills, presenting an appearance of the most perfect seclusion. Amongst these woods were scattered large tracts of cultivated ground, laid out in fields of wheat, rye, barley, buckwheat, hops, clover, &c. &c., frequently here enclosed by thick and lofty hedges; quite in the bottoms, and lying along a small stream of water, which ran through almost every one of these little valleys, were meadows of the liveliest verdure, whilst rows of magnificent elms fringed the banks and overshadowed the rippling waters of the rivulets. Villages and detached farms were of constant recurrence, and in all directions one saw the modest spires of the village churches rising above the massed and verdant foliage. Although these woods were, generally speaking, of no great extent —perhaps only a few acres—yet were there some of such extent as to entitle this to the appellation of a woody, or even forest, country. The Bois de Liederkerke, for instance, commenced near the village of Paemêle, and extended no less than four miles in the direction of Assche; everywhere two or three miles wide, including a great variety

RICH CULTIVATION. 143

of ground, and in different directions were several others nearly of the same extent. At first, one is surprised at finding such vast tracts of woodland in a country so populous and so assiduously cultivated; but the thing is easily explained. In addition to the ordinary demands for small wood in husbandry, there are large and numerous hop-grounds requiring a continual supply of poles; but, above all, the enormous quantity of fuel required, not only by the peasantry, but also by the inhabitants of the towns, —wood being almost exclusively used for that purpose.

The kind of country I have been describing extended northward from us as far as Assche— perhaps much further, but of that I know not— and eastward to Brussels. Towards the south the round hills gradually gave place to longer slopes and plateaux, and the woods became less frequent, but the villages were numerous, with the same careful cultivation everywhere. Toward the west, and only a few miles distant, we were bounded by the Dender, holding its course through extensive flat meadows covered with luxuriant crops of hay, or affording pasturage to herds of fine cattle. Beyond the river-valley the country assumed a different aspect: long and less abrupt slopes;

woods fewer and thinner; a total absence of hedges; altogether presenting an aspect in many places bare and cheerless, strongly contrasting with the lovely scenery about Strytem—if I may call scenery lovely where we find neither rock, nor mountain, nor precipice, nor torrent; but it is home scenery, and its character simplicity, luxuriance, abundance, tranquillity, and repose. There one saw the rustic dwellings of the peasantry situated in secluded nooks, and embosomed in orchards and hop grounds; the rural village with its modest church low down in the rich bottom, surrounded by smiling fields of grain or clover; a gentle rivulet slowly winding its devious way amidst the rank luxuriance of vegetation clothing its overhanging banks; the whole encased, as it were, by wavy heights, crowned with thick and verdant woods. One thing, however, was wanting to complete this picture of rural wealth and happiness—it wanted the animating presence of domestic animals, of herds and flocks dotting the fair surface of its fields. The farms in this country are not large as with us; the farmer does not live in a splendid mansion, still more splendidly furnished, nor does he idle away his time in shooting or fox-hunting. The Flemish farmer is a plain honest rustic, clad in homespun grey, a cotton nightcap on his head, wooden shoes on his feet, and the everlasting short pipe in his mouth; he himself holds the plough, guides his team, or assists in thrashing out his grain. Ignorance of their language prevented my acquiring more information concerning them and their affairs than what could be done by observation of outward appearance; therefore I could neither learn the extent of their farms, their ideas on agriculture, the amount of rents, length of leases, nor the value of land, &c. Coarsely fed and coarsely clad, still they are an industrious, hard-working, and contented race; not very intelligent, I allow, but perhaps they are the happier for it;—they are kind to their inferiors, affable and communicative with their equals, and respectful, almost to servility, to their superiors, or those they fancy such.*

Although many of the farming establishments in our neighbourhood resembled in plan and construction those already described about Den-

* Such crops I never before saw, particularly those vividly-green crops of *trèf*, which really appeared so thick that one might walk on them without sinking to the ground. But to me the height attained by the rye was most astonishing. In one field which I rode through nearly every day, it was as high as my head, when mounted on my little horse Cossack, about 14¾ hands high, so that it could not have been less than 7 or 8 feet, the ears remarkably full and looking well.

dermonde, yet were they not universally of this description. That adjoining the chateau was really a very fine one—substantial brick house, barns, out-houses of every kind, all on a great scale, and, as usual, surrounded by a spacious court. But others were very different from this; many were very humble abodes, constructed of wood or clay, with thatched roofs and small casement windows, standing along the edges of the fields, with their barn adjoining but not united, nor any courtyard for manure, &c., the outbuildings all on a small scale, as also, I suppose, were their farms. Others, standing likewise open in the fields, were again of a different character. These had high thatched roofs projecting several feet beyond the walls, and supported by rough posts, forming a sort of verandah; this is filled up to the eaves with firewood—some in logs, some in fagots—which gives to the exterior a very rude appearance, and must make the interior very dark, from the great depth of embrasure thus formed both to door and window; but to balance this, it keeps the house cool in summer and warm in winter. Although the actual village of Strytem consisted of no more than the chateau, the farm, and the few mean houses clustered round the church, yet the commune was extensive, comprising not only many fine farms, but also other and more important villages. The real *maire* was M. le Baron Von Volden, son of the proprietress of our chateau. He, however, seldom came nearer the place than Brussels, leaving to his worthy *adjoint*, Jan Evanpoel, the care of administering the government, and at the time of our arrival either was in Paris, or had but just returned from it. Where the *maire* is thus vested in the person of the *châtelain*, the post seems to be one of much importance—not confined to the police of the village alone, but extending to a general superintendence over the welfare of the commune, the state of the roads, &c. &c. Whether owing to the baron being so much an absentee I know not, but the roads all about Strytem were hardly passable after heavy rain (of which we had a pretty good share), not only from their badness, having no foundations, and receiving little or no repair, but also from the unctuous and slippery soil, which makes riding absolutely dangerous immediately after rain. Some of the worst sloughs, which otherwise would be quite impassable, are repaired, as in Russia, Poland, and America, by laying logs transversely, and covering them with brushwood, and then earth; but these, after a little weathering and wear and tear, become absolutely dangerous from horses slipping in between the logs, sometimes up to the shoulder.

This was one of the drawbacks upon our enjoyment in this otherwise pleasant country; and, having confessed as much, I may as well admit that there were a few others which prevented us from living in a state of absolute and unalloyed happiness. One grievance was the cheapness of gin—a villanous kind of spirit manufactured in the country, and on which a man could get "royal" for twopence; for though our men were really fine fellows and generally very steady soldiers, yet, like other Englishmen, they could not resist a social glass nor avoid its consequences; and, indeed, if excuse it be, they were in a measure driven to the use of this pernicious spirit by the execrable quality of all the beer in the country, which more resembled a mixture of cow-dung and water than anything else. The sale of this poison took place in a small cabaret near the church, which was usually thronged with our people every evening after stable-hour; and, strange to say, where they mixed most sociably with the boors, to my no small astonishment. It is a curious fact, that upon inquiry at the sergeant-major how they could understand each other, he replied that the Yorkshire, Lancashire, and Lincolnshire men, who spoke very broad, could make themselves understood pretty well, and in like manner could comprehend the Flemish of their boon companions. Quarrels would sometimes arise in this *tabagie*, which occasioned a temporary derangement of our tranquil life. But that was a trifle to another grievance which stuck to us incessantly, and was the most serious drawback we endured during our sojourn in the valley of Strytem. I allude to the infernal and eternal frog-concert that nightly disturbed our rest more or less, and kept us in a constant state of irritability. For a few days we bore this curse very philosophically, then began to war against the wretches by pelting them with stones, firing at them with small-shot, beating the water with poles, &c. &c., but all to no purpose, for though we killed them by scores, yet did their numbers never appear to thin nor their detestable "quoah, quoah" to lessen in intensity. Then we made the wheeler construct a raft, and with this some one was always cruising and slaying, yet still no alleviation to the evil. A council was held, and it was determined that nothing short of draining the moat would avail, and therefore drained it should be. Curiosity had some hand in this decision, for we had heard that the moat contained the largest carp ever seen—a fish several feet in length, and weighing I know not what. The old gardener, when acquainted with our resolve and ordered to make the necessary preparations, was perfectly astounded, and (as did Mademoiselle and the sons) used every sort of argument to turn us from it; amongst others, he assured us that *l'année passée* the Prussians had attempted to drain the moat merely to kill all the fish—"les sacré vilains hommes!" but the stench arising from it when low, quickly obliged them to desist. It would not do—we were peremptory; and at length the old man opened the voider, closed the feeder, and to our delight the work of destruction began. Day after day the water gradually receded from the foot of the old walls and from the opposite bank—already in many places the oozy slime of the bottom began to appear—already we rejoiced at the innumerable corpses of our enemies lying on it everywhere; the upper part of the moat was already, not dry, but waterless; and we were on the point of seeing the giant leviathan, when lo! the weather, hitherto cool and showery, became superb, and the heat almost insufferable. Decomposition, animal and vegetable, commenced with alarming rapidity, and the mephitic vapours thus produced pervading every creek and corner of the chateau, obliged us, *bongré malgrè*, to reclose the voider and reopen the feeder,—and thus terminated *la guerre aux grenouilles*. But, alas! our punishment for having resisted the entreaties and warnings of the old gardener was not to close with the sluices. The same hot sun had dried up nearly all the sources whence the moat had been fed, and many a long day of disgust and repentance had we to endure ere the waters again covered the odious slime sufficiently to relieve us from its nauseous stink, and to enable the frogs to renew their song, which, when they did, was to us a song of joy; and we had the further mortification of finding that, with a little patience, we might have saved ourselves all the trouble and suffering, for we had become so accustomed to it that it fell on our ear innocuous.

But the charms of a country life have so occupied my brain as to chase from it all recollection of being a soldier. To be sure, professional occupations did not consume a very great portion of our time, yet still there remain a few little items worthy of being recorded—*imprimis*, drills. So completely is the whole of this country (not occupied by wood) under tillage, that it was long after our arrival at Strytem ere we discovered a spot on which we could even draw out the troop, much less exercise it. At length, and I cannot recollect how, we found a piece of scrubby common of some acres in extent near the village of Denderhout, some miles off on the other side of the Dender, and not far from Alost. Thither, then, we repaired occasionally to practise ourselves, and prevent our people forgetting entirely their drills. Thither also came occasionally His Highness of Berri with his newly-formed corps of cavalry to learn theirs. We frequently met, and as the ground was too confined to admit of both corps working at the same time, the last comers were obliged to dismount and wait until the others had done, for we continued our operations when first on the ground, regardless of the impatience of the royal drill-master, who, though he never said anything to us, did not fail to betray, by a thousand little pettish actions, the annoyance he felt at our want of due respect. One day that they had got in possession and we were obliged to wait, I had a good opportunity of seeing this curious corps and its savage leader. The former presented a most grotesque appearance—cuirassiers, hussars, grenadiers à cheval, and chasseurs, dragoons and lancers, officers and privates, with a few of the new garde de corps, were indiscriminately mingled in the ranks. One file were colonels, the next privates, and so on, and all wearing their proper uniforms and mounted on their proper horses, so that these were of all sizes and colours. There might have been about two hundred men, divided into two or three squadrons, the commanders of which were generals. The Prince, as I have said, was drill-master. A more intemperate, brutal, and (in his situation) impolitic one, can scarcely be conceived. The slightest fault (frequently occasioned by his own blunders) was visited by showers of low-life abuse—using on all occasions the most odious language. One unfortunate squadron officer (*a general!*) offended him, and was immediately charged with such violence that I expected a catastrophe. Reining up his horse, however, close to the unhappy man, his vociferation and villanous abuse were those of a perfect madman; shaking his sabre at him, and even at one time thrusting the pommel of it into his face, and, as far as I could see, pushing it against his nose! Such a scene! Yet all the others sat mute as mice, and witnessed all this humiliation of their comrade, and the degradation of him for whom they had forsaken Napoleon. Just at this moment one of our troop-dogs ran barking at the heels of the Prince's horse. Boiling with rage before, he now boiled over in earnest, and, stooping, made a furious cut at the dog, which, eluding the weapon, continued his annoyance. The Duke, quitting the unfortunate *chêf d'escadron*, now turned seriously at the dog, but he, accustomed to horses, kept circling about, yapping and snapping, and always out of reach; and it was not until he had tired himself with the fruitless pursuit that, foaming with rage, he returned to his doomed squadrons, who had sat quietly looking on at this exhibition. While all this took place, I had made acquaintance with another general officer who appeared to be there in the capacity of aide-de-camp—a gentlemanly sort of man, who, having been many years in England with Louis XVIII., spoke English fluently. This man pleased me much at the time; he was then in adversity. I met him afterwards in prosperity—*nous verrons!*

Now that I have got on military affairs, it may be as well to record the manner in which this country was occupied—at least as far as my knowledge on the subject goes. First, then, headquarters of the cavalry and horse-artillery at Ninove, where was also the principal depôt of forage and provisions. The reason for assembling the cavalry thus at some distance from the expected scene of operations was the great fertility of this part of Brabant, and the facility of communication with Alost, to which place, the Dender being navigable, advantage could be taken of the rich Pays de Waes. The villages, farms, &c., all round Ninove were full of troops.

Okegem.—Major M'Donald's troop horse-artillery.
Paemêle.—Sir Robert Gardiner's do.
Strytem and Yseringen.—Captain Mercer's do.
Lombeke, Nôtre Dame.—Captain Sinclair's brigade of 9-pounders.
Lennik, St Martin.— Headquarters of Lieutenant-Colonel Hawker, Royal Artillery, commanding two batteries somewhere in his neighbourhood.
Beyond Ninove, westward, were the troops, horse-artillery, of Majors Bull, Ramsay, and Webber Smyth—forget names of villages.
Liederkerke, Denderlue, and vicinage.—Life Guards and Blues.
Schandelbeke and Vicinage.—The three huzzar regiments, 10th, 15th, 18th.
Lerbeke, &c.—23d Light Dragoons.
Castre, &c.—16th do.
Meerbeke.—Headquarters Sir O. Vandeleur with 12th and 13th Light Dragoons.
Grammont.—Foot Guards.

Enghien.—Foot Guards.

Schaepdale, &c.—Brunswick Infantry; all boys.

Brussels.—*The* headquarters—92d Highlanders, Rifles, Hanoverian infantry, and some Belgian dragoons and huzzars; grand depôt of forage and provisions, and of artillery stores, &c. &c.

Mons.—English artillery and Dutch troops of different arms.

Assche.—Troop of Belgian horse-artillery.

Courtray, Atto, Tournay.—Believe huzzars of the K.G. Legion.

Visitors from England were at this time flocking over in great numbers, and travelling about amongst the cantonments; but ours was so secluded, being distant from every great road, that none of them found us out, until Sir G. A. Wood (our Colonel commanding), coming over to review the horse-artillery, brought with him the Knight of Kerry and another Irish gentleman (name forgotten), who passed a day with us in the old chateau, and were mightily pleased with our snuggery. The inspection took place on the little common at Denderhout. Six troops[*] were drawn out, and made a splendid show—for finer, as to equipment, men, horses, &c. &c., could not possibly be seen. Mine was generally allowed to

[*] The *captains were*—viz., Lieutenant-Colonel Sir Hew D. Ross, Major Bull, —— Ramsay, Lieutenant-Colonel W. Smyth, Major M'Donald, Captain Mercer.

be the finest (old G), though there was some hesitation in deciding between it and Webber Smyth's.

The line was scarcely formed when his Royal Highness of Berri arrived, and as usual got into a pet at finding himself forestalled. Sir Augustus Frazer, however, with his excellent manners and as excellent French, soothed him by expressions of regret, &c. &c., and stating that some of our people had come a long distance, and unless soon despatched, would hardly be able to get home before night. Roads bad, &c., otherwise, &c. &c. &c. The Duke cooled down, and condescended to accompany Sir G. Wood through the ranks. We then marched past, and off home.*

The French officers were all admiration and astonishment: they had never seen anything so complete, nor any troop so mounted.

At Waterloo, on the 18th June, there were present eight troops of British and two of Hano-

---

* The Duke of Wellington was so indifferent to the manner in which officers dressed, that they indulged in all sorts of fancies. I remember, at this inspection, Ramsay wore the light-cavalry belt instead of a sash; Bull wore beard and mustache; so did Newland; I wore the mustache. The usual dress of hussars was frock-coat open, with a red waistcoat richly laced with gold. At that time our regimental pantaloons were *pepper-and-salt*, with straps of brown leather inside the legs and round the bottom, and a red stripe down outside seam.

verian horse-artillery. The British, as far as I can recollect, were:—1. Lieutenant-Colonel Sir Hew D. Ross's; 2. Major Bull's; 3. Major M'Donald's; 4. Major Ramsay's; 5. Lieutenant-Colonel Webber Smyth's; 6. Lieutenant-Colonel Sir Robert Gardiner's; 7. Major Beane's; 8. Lieutenant-Colonel Sir A. Dickson, *alias* Captain Mercer's; also Captain Whinyate's rocket troop. These were armed as follows:—Major Bull's, six heavy $5\frac{1}{2}$-inch howitzers; Lieutenant-Colonel Gardiner's and W. Smith's, five light 6-pounders, and one light $5\frac{1}{2}$-inch howitzer—these two being attached to the hussar brigades; Captain Whinyate's rockets and light 6-pounders; each of the others had five 9-pounders and one heavy $5\frac{1}{2}$-inch howitzer; and these "heavy drags" (as we called them) were destined, by Sir Augustus Frazer, who commanded the horse-artillery, together with Bull's howitzers, to form a grand battery in reserve, to be applied as he might find occasion—a formidable reserve it would have been. However, it never came into play in that manner; for in the general orders of the army organising it, we were all posted to different brigades of cavalry, consequently Frazer's *grande batterie* vanished in smoke. In this allotment I fell to the first division, Lord Edward Somerset, composed of the three Household regiments—the Scots Greys, 1st Dragoon Guards, and 6th or Inniskillings. We continued, however, at Strytem, neither reporting to, nor receiving orders from, Lord Edward; nor did we ever join the division until 21st June, near Mons, whence we marched with them to Paris, and then again separated.

Of the field-artillery I know very little, but remember that, about the beginning of June, Sir Augustus Frazer, who was Sir G. Wood's *right-hand man*, told me that, including the horse-artillery, there were then twenty brigades of British artillery, or 120 pieces, ready to take the field. More arrived, I believe, after this; I know Beane's troop of horse-artillery did. What number of Hanoverian, Dutch, Belgic, &c., there might be, I never knew.

Whence it originated, I cannot conjecture, but, certes, much indecision did exist about this time as to our armament. Shortly after our arrival at Strytem, we were ordered to send our light 6-pounders to Ghent, there to be exchanged for *heavies*. These, after a few days, were to be sent back and replaced by the 9-pounders, which eventually we kept.

These changes, whilst in progress, cost me considerable anxiety, from the dread of a move taking place whilst my guns were absent—an event the more to be dreaded, since the Duke never attended to any justification if anything went wrong; nor would he have looked to my superiors, but myself alone, and thus I should have borne the whole weight of his anger.

At length, about the beginning of June we were complete, when my troop establishment was as follows, viz. :—

5 guns, 9-pounders, and 1 heavy 5½-inch howitzer—8 horses each,	48
9 ammunition-waggons — viz., 1 to each piece, and a spare one per division—6 horses each,	54
1 spare-wheel carriage—6 horses,	6
1 forge, 1 curricle-cart, 1 baggage-waggon—4 horses each,	12
Total in draught,	120
6 mounted detachments—8 horses each,	48
2 staff-sergeants, 2 farriers, 1 collar-maker,	5
6 officers' horses, lent them by the Board of Ordnance,	6
6 officers' mules, for carrying their baggage,	6
Total,	185
Additional horses unaccounted for above, spare, &c.,	30
General total of animals,	214
Besides which, each officer had his own two horses, and the surgeon one, making 11 more—so that, including these, we had	226

The *personnel* consisted of—Second Captain, Mercer, commanding; Captain Pakenham (subsequently Newland) as Second Captain; Lieutenants Bell, Hincks, Ingleby, and Leathes—the former acting as adjutant to Sir A. Frazer, the latter as supernumerary; and before we left Strytem, Ingleby exchanged with Lieutenant Breton, and joined Sir Robert Gardiner's troop; so that, finally, it stood: Breton, Hincks, Leathes—surgeon, Hitchins; 2 staff-sergeants, 3 sergeants, 3 corporals, 6 bombardiers, 1 farrier, 3 shoeing smiths, 2 collar-makers, 1 wheeler, 1 trumpeter, and 1 acting do., 80 gunners, 84 drivers — the 1 acting trumpeter not included. The organisation was in three divisions, of two subdivisions each—a subdivision being one piece of ordnance, with its ammunition-waggon and detachment. Each division had one spare ammunition-waggon and a proportion of the other carriages, &c. The division was commanded by a lieutenant, and the subdivisions, the right of the division by a sergeant, the left by a corporal—a bombardier to each subdivision. On parade, the $5\frac{1}{2}$-inch howitzer was the right of the centre division. Perhaps at this time a troop of horse-artillery was the completest thing in the army; and whether broken up into half-brigades under the first and second captains, or into divisions under their lieutenants, or subdivisions under their sergeants and corporals, still each body was a perfect whole.

CHAPTER VIII.

I HAVE confessed a little farther back that the happiness of our sojourn in this lovely country was not without some alloy; and having done so, I may add one or two more items to this balance, *per contra*.

Soon after our arrival at Strytem, an officer of the commissariat was attached to the troop, for the purpose of feeding us and our animals. His first care was to secure a sufficient number of country waggons, with their drivers and horses, intending to keep them together ready for a move. The farmers, finding this a grievance, besieged me, personally and through Mynheer Evenpoel, to allow them to remain at home until wanted. This Mr Coates (who, by the way, was an experienced and excellent commissary) strongly opposed, foretelling the consequences but too truly; however, I yielded, upon a solemn promise of M.

l'Adjoint that they should be held ready to move at a moment's notice. Having committed this folly, I was well punished for it by the anxiety I experienced at every report of a move; and at last when the hour did come, they were called and found wanting, and poor Mr Coates had to mount and hunt them up, when they ought to have been loaded and on the road. This was a lesson to me.

Another misery I endured was the constant apprehension of falling under the Duke's displeasure for systematic plundering of the farmers by our people, which I could not well check without risk of incurring the same on another score—*i.e.*, for not doing it! This is enigmatical; let me explain. Our allowance of forage, though sufficient to keep our horses in pretty good condition when idle, was not sufficient when they were hard worked; nor was it sufficient at any time to put on them that load of flesh, and give them that rotundity of form which Peninsular practice had established as the *beau ideal* of a horse entering on a campaign, the maxim being — "The more flesh a horse carries, the more he has to lose, and the longer he will be able to bear privation." To keep up this, therefore, it was necessary to borrow from the farmers; and at this time of the year the superb crops of the *trèfe* offered themselves most opportunely. The practice was general amongst cavalry and artillery, so that all the horses were equally in good case; and it would have been a most dangerous proceeding, by abstaining from it, to let your horses appear thinner than those of your neighbour. The quick eye of the Duke would have seen the difference, asked no questions, attended to no justification, but condemned the unfortunate victim of samples as unworthy of the command he held, and perhaps sent him from the army. We therefore, like others, plundered the farmers' fields; with this difference, however, that we did it in a regular manner, and without waste—whereas many of the cavalry regiments destroyed nearly as much as they carried away, by trampling about the fields. The dread of this being reported kept me continually in hot water, for my farmers (who, under the reign of the Prussians, would never have dared utter a complaint), hearing how strictly plundering was forbidden by the Duke, soon became exceedingly troublesome with their threats of reporting me.* How we escaped it is difficult to say, but

* A report *was* sent to Brussels, but it never reached the Duke, for the simple people went in the first instance to Sir G. Wood, and there it was strangled.

certainly we continued helping ourselves; and latterly St Cyr, and some other farmers, getting more docile, would themselves mark out where we were to cut. Our neighbour at the chateau farm (Walsdragen) was the most troublesome. The Duke was not partial to our corps, which made it still more fortunate for me that these people never put their threats in execution. It is difficult to say why, but his Grace certainly treated us harshly, and on many occasions unjustly. Of his harshness *voici un exemple.* Captain Whinyates having joined the army with the rocket troop, the Duke, who looked upon rockets as nonsense, ordered that they should be put into store, and the troop supplied with guns instead. Colonel Sir G. Wood, instigated by Whinyates, called on the Duke to ask permission to leave him his rockets as well as guns. A refusal. Sir George, however, seeing the Duke was in a particular good humour, ventured to say, " It will break poor Whinyate's heart to lose his rockets." "D—n his heart, sir; let my order be obeyed," was the answer thundered in his ear by the Duke, as he turned on the worthy Sir George. Let me return to the country and its charms.

With me one of the most delightful occupations is the exploring a new country; so that, whilst others could not exist except in Brussels, I found abundant occupation for my leisure riding about the neighbourhood of Strytem. One of my first rides was, as in duty bound, to Ninove. Instead of taking the main road from Brussels thither, which runs through Meerbeke, I took a by one to Liederkerke, and, turning to the left a short distance from this place, crossed the gently-flowing Dender, opposite the little village of Okegem, by a rustic bridge supported on posts, so narrow and fragile that it was not without demur, and at last leading my horse, that I ventured over. I found the officers of the troop here very humbly lodged—in mere cottages, and that of a poor description. Nothing here comparable to our lordly tapestried saloons at Strytem—to the which, by the way, we were becoming attached, more particularly since the fine weather had set in, and taught us to appreciate their coolness and refreshing *demi-jour*.

The country, after passing the river, was not interesting, as I have mentioned elsewhere, but the scenery improved somewhat on drawing near Ninove, which place, with the immense monastery of white stone built on the higher part of the ground, had a somewhat imposing appearance: drawing still nearer, some fragments of old walls begin to make their appearance amongst the trees, which now became more numerous, and we enter the place under a dark-browed picturesque arch, flanked by two circular towers, partly in ruins and overgrown with ivy, the whole half concealed, until one turns short upon it, by the clustering foliage of some handsome elms and the thick shrubbery of bushes growing out of the old walls. As my horse's feet resounded under the archway, a flash of romance came across me, and I thought of the counts of Burgundy and their romantic court, and pictured in my mind's eye some lordly pageant streaming from out the archway in all its glittering array. Sober reality soon banished romance. A short street brought me from the gate to the head of the principal one—long, broad, clean; houses low, and of rather a humble description; on the whole, looking more like the street of an English country town than anything I had seen in the Pays Bas here; and standing across it was the monastery which had formed so conspicuous a feature in the aspect of the town from without. This, instead of representing the sort of ecclesiastical building one would expect a monastery to be, was a magnificent modern-built house of three storeys, pierced with numerous large sashed windows, looking airy and cheerful—anything rather than the house of sorrow, repentance, and abstinence. It is, I suspect, a modern restoration of the monastery of Premonstrantine monks mentioned by Blau, and the only one he does mention. It was suppressed in 1792. Wandering into the court, which was overrun with grass and weeds, I met the only remaining brother of the order, the dress of which he wore. His appearance was venerable, but whether it was that he was naturally morose, or because I was a heretic, he would answer none of my questions, only making a waive of the hand in answer to my inquiry whether I might walk over the premises. That this reserve did not arise from ignorance of French, his immediately turning and giving directions to a labourer in that language testified. Lord Uxbridge and his staff having taken up their abode here restricted my observations to the exterior of the building. I saw enough, however, to learn that the Premonstrantine monks had once been lodged like princes, and so passed on to look at the town.

Ninove is prettily situated on the left bank of the Dender, from which its spacious street ascends by a gentle acclivity; and at this time it presented a very gay and bustling appearance, from the presence of the cavalry staff and the active operations of the commissariat. It may contain about 3000 inhabitants, and was once surrounded by a wall, with flanking towers, of which some vestiges still remain. I believe much weaving is done here, and I saw several mills and tanneries. Blau says the ancient name was "Nienevem, Ninoviam, Ninovam, *vulgus* Kandrorum; *nunc* Ninovam—Gallo belgæ Ninof appellant; Belgia regalis," &c. So much for Ninove. For that time I bid it adieu, and passing the bridge at the bottom of the street, took my road homewards through the pretty and interesting country to the southward of it. Old Blau says there was some joke against the people of Ninove connected with its ancient name Ninevem, which he compares with the Nineveh of Assyria. In my way home, passing through Meerbeke, I saw a handsome chateau, where Sir Ormsby Vandeleur had his divisional headquarters. It was a picturesque object, and truly Flemish in style, though in situation, &c., it resembled an English country-house—two storeys, with numerous large windows, and the usual double tier of dormitory windows in the high roof. It was flanked at either end by a round tower, with the characteristic conical roof. The grounds were quite English. A level lawn of smooth and verdant turf extended from the front to the road. Shrubberies of laburnums, &c., surrounded it on three sides, concealing the offices, and these were backed by a thick wood of lofty forest trees. To judge from externals, an agreeable quarter.

The great Bois de Liederkerke afforded me a fine field for exploration, and many a delightful ride I took amongst its grateful shades. In one of these I discovered, in the very heart of it, a cleared spot of a few acres, part of which was occupied by the blackened ruins of some building, and part exhibited the very melancholy appearance of a once handsome garden, run wild and gone to decay—even the very ruins were nearly overrun by brushwood and weeds. A peasant, whom I met with after leaving the wood, told me that although he had never seen these ruins, he supposed they must be the remains of a convent of nuns which once existed somewhere in the wood, but had been burned many years ago. Ignorance of his language prevented my understanding a long story he told me—partly in Flemish, partly in French—but I picked out that the nuns of this convent had all been ladies of considerable, some of very high, rank.

The main road to Alost, by Liederkerke and

Denderlue, runs through this wood, and, emerging from it on that side, one exchanges the gloomy obscurity of the forest and confined view amongst the trees for the broad light of day and a wide expanse of fine meadows, covered with herds of cattle, through which the Dender runs brawling and bubbling along over its pebbly bed, crossed at this point by a long wooden bridge, immediately beyond which is the village of Liederkerke, at the time of my visit full of our Household troops.

It was a curious sensation that of seeing Lifeguardsmen lounging about the street and before the houses—these people are so intimately associated in one's mind with London, the Park, Horse Guards, &c. Nor was the contrast between their tall full figures and rosy complexions and the gaunt awkward figures and sallow complexions of the Flemish peasantry—the smart tight-fitting scarlet or blue jackets of the one, with the coarse homely garbs and dingy-coloured smock-frocks of the other—less curious.

Both banks of the river, which here approach each other and are rather steep, are well clothed with trees, and form a picturesque scene. Immediately above and below the bridge, these banks, retiring from each other, leave between their bases and the river a wide level of meadow-land, which, being everywhere bounded by low thickly-wooded hills, and, as before mentioned, thickly sprinkled with herds of fine cattle or luxuriant crops of hay, now almost ready for mowing, afford scenes of a different but not less pleasing character. On the right the hills, projecting like a promontory, and blending themselves with those on the left, enclose these fine meadows in an amphitheatre of beautifully variegated and tufted foliage, unbroken by buildings or any indication of the haunts of man; whilst the left bank, less thickly wooded, presents here and there intervening fields, the high thatched roofs of farms and cottages, and, pre-eminent amongst the whole, the spire of Denderlue peeping through the foliage. Amongst other excursions, one was of a more than commonly interesting nature, since it brought me acquainted, not only with a very lovely spot, but also with a singularly eccentric character—one whose history is of so romantic a nature, that I ever regret not having made myself master of it in all its details; I mean Paul Visconti, Marquis d'Acornati and Lord of Gaesbeke, the chateau of which he inhabits. The first notice we had of this singular man was from some officers of the 23d Light Dragoons, who had been cantoned in his village. On their first arrival the old gentleman was quite furious at the insult offered him in sending troops thither at all, but especially without his having been consulted. The officers, having quartered their men, proceeded to take up their own abode in the chateau, and the Marquis, being aware of this, closed his gates, and made preparations to resist. His garrison consisted of two or three ancient domestics and six or eight young boys. On approaching the gates, the officers were somewhat surprised at seeing guns pointed at them from several embrasures, and at the same time a venerable turbaned head, projecting from one of them, demanded, in good English, how they dared trespass on the property of the Marquis d'Acornati, peremptorily bidding them to depart, or take the consequences. The captain, a true English gentleman, having heard something of the Marquis's peculiarities from the villagers, instead of resenting the opposition, humoured the old man's whim, and commenced a parley in the true language and all the forms of chivalry. This was touching the Marquis in a tender point. The gates were thrown open, as were his arms, to these courteous strangers, whom he received and entertained with the hospitality of the olden times during their stay, mourned their departure, and never mentioned them afterwards but in the highest terms of praise. Some of my officers had already visited Gaesbeke, and their accounts excited my curiosity to see this extraordinary man. Accordingly one day mounting Nelly I set out. The road lay through the large village of Lennik St Martin, remarkable in the distance for its handsome spire, towering above the more humble ones of the surrounding villages. Here I found Lieutenant-Colonel Hawker and his adjutant, Lieutenant Anderson. The colonel commanded a division composed of two batteries, 9-pounders, which were cantoned in his immediate neighbourhood, but not in Lennik. Hence the country was exquisite—the scenery acquiring a greater degree of interest from the increasing height of the hills, though in luxuriance and verdure, both of arborific and cereal vegetation, it could not exceed that which I had left behind me.

At length, after a pleasant ride of about twelve miles, on attaining the summit of a hill, the noble Chateau de Gaesbeke appeared in front, on the edge of a deep ravine, which separated me from it, surrounded by thick woods, the sombre verdure of which harmonised well with the mellowed tone of its antique brick walls and towers, whilst their round tufted tops were finely contrasted with its sharp angles and pointed conical roofs.

Crossing the ravine, I arrived on a plateau of rich velvety turf, ornamented by a few clumps of the most superb beech-trees I ever saw in my life, some of their boles rising almost straight forty or fifty feet, without a twig to break the smooth rounded surface of their glossy grey bark. Fine as those composing the great avenue at Strytem were, still they were far exceeded in size, luxuriance, and beauty of form by these. Artificial means are employed to produce these magnificent ornaments of the park or pleasure-ground. Whilst the tree is young it is constantly watched, and every bud carefully eradicated the moment it pierces the bark, until, having attained a certain height, nature is permitted to take her course and push out lateral branches, leaving between them and the soil a stupendous column of timber. A broad carriage-road, winding amongst these clumps, led to the great gate of the chateau, now unsuspicious of another military invasion, standing wide open. It was approached by a stone bridge thrown over a ditch, which, running along the front of the chateau, imperceptibly lost itself in the steep declivity to the right and left. The lofty arched portal was flanked by round towers, having semicircular embrasures on the first floor, and above them a row of arched win-

THE CHATEAU DE GAESBEKE. 177

dows with rusty iron balconies, extending across the gateway also. Toward the right, the two tiers of large French windows gave a more modern air to the curtain (if I may so call it), which was terminated in that direction by an immense elliptical tower, the steep roof of which finished in a short ridge with ornamental iron-work, and a weather-cock at either end. To the left, the blank wall ended in a round tower of smaller dimensions, and without the usual conical roof, its picturesque antique form only partially seen through the foliage of the trees, which formed a screen before that front.

I entered the castle court without seeing a soul, or any indication of the place being inhabited. True, there was little of ruin. The old walls appeared generally in good repair; the glass in the windows was sound, not a pane broken—yet a forlorn deserted aspect reigned over all; and the bent iron ornaments of the roofs, the grass-grown court, and the shattered remains of two or three low-wheeled carriages, lying half buried in the rank vegetation of weeds which had sprung up around them, added not a little to the cheerless desolate aspect of the whole. To the right on entering was a long range of two storeys (which, from the lofty windows, appeared to be the state apartments), terminating at either end with a tower. From the gateway into the angle on the same side similar features indicated other suites of apartments. To the left of the gateway, extending to the tower on that side, were stables and coach-houses. From this tower a parapet-wall followed the outline of the ground along the edge of the declivity, running out in semicircular bastions at intervals of about fifty yards, until, joining the tower at the extremity of the right wing, it completed the enclosure of the court, forming an area of an irregular figure, the low parapet allowing to the windows of the main building a most striking and extensive view over the rich country to the westward. The defence of this front was further increased by a range of casemated apartments, with narrow loop-holes, probably intended for arrows; but whether they extended the whole length of the front, or only under the bastions, I forget. They are entered by a narrow staircase from the court above. In the centre of this court, upon a rude pedestal, was the fragment of a man in a sitting posture, of which the Marquis afterwards gave me a printed explanation, drawn up by himself, tending to show that this must be a remnant of the celebrated Torse de Belvedere, and that the whole constituted a figure of Ulysses, seated, and in the act of discharging an arrow from his bow. But to return. After taking a cursory glance at the general arrangement of the buildings, and finding that the sound of my horse's feet had no effect in extracting their inhabitants, I rode up to and thundered at a low-arched door which stood half open in the great tower. The appeal was answered by a sallow-faced dirty boy of fifteen, with long uncombed flaxen locks hanging about his ears, and giving him a peculiarly wild and savage appearance as he stood staring at me with widely-distended eyes. To my inquiry if the Marquis were at home, he only answered by a nod, and then disappeared in the gloom of the dark vaulted passage whence he had emerged. Returning almost immediately, he had found his tongue, and begged me to go to the principal entrance to the right wing (what had once been handsome panelled folding-doors), which he unbolted within, and, taking my horse as I dismounted, ushered me into a large and lofty vestibule of handsome proportions, but quite unfurnished, and in a miserable state of decay. On the opposite side of this, at the desire of my guide, I entered a fine lofty room, with a coved roof, painted in blue and white stripes in imitation of the interior of a Turkish tent, and at the corners, where the drapery was supposed to be gathered up, ornamented with an imitation of golden cords and tassels. Round the walls were suspended trophies formed of swords, daggers, pistols, &c., all richly mounted, and almost all Oriental. The furniture consisted of large ottomans, covered with a striped stuff to match the pattern of the tent. These were ranged round the walls, and there was neither chair nor table in the room, which was lighted by an arched window opening upon a clumsy wooden balcony, and commanding a beautiful view over the distant country and of the deep wooded ravine below. After waiting here about ten minutes, the object of my curiosity made his appearance, followed by a rather vulgar-looking fattish man, with whom he had been engaged, and whom I discovered to be a lawyer of Brussels, and his man of business. This gentleman soon took his leave, and left me *tête-à-tête* with his client. Let me draw his portrait, while still fresh in my memory: Below the middle size, and a little bent by age; thin, light, and active; a countenance embrowned by southern suns, if not natural; regular features, and a face that had evidently once been handsome; quick, sparkling, intelligent eyes giving to his physiognomy a vivacious expression, rather at variance with the wrinkled cheek of the *octogénaire*. His costume was completely Turkish. A white muslin turban, somewhat soiled, but plentifully beset with precious stones, covered his head; an ample caftan of blue cloth, vest and trousers of the same—the former tied across the chest with strings, the latter large and full-gathered, and at bottom stuffed into a pair of extremely short boots, strangers apparently to Day and Martin or their kindred of the Pays Bas. A crimson silk sash girded his waist, in which was stuck an Oriental poignard, having its handle entirely covered with precious stones, and scabbard tastefully enchased in silver filigree. In his right hand he carried a short hunting-spear, and in his left a small *cor de chasse*. His address, easy and affable, was evidently that of one accustomed to the best society. The reception he gave me was most flattering, and even affectionate; and he incessantly repeated his admiration of England and her sons. For my part, I told only half the truth in stating that the celebrity of his chateau and gardens had procured him the honour of this visit, never hinting how great a lion he was himself. After a short conversation, he proposed showing me his chateau, &c., and conducting me through several apartments on the ground-floor, we arrived at his own bed-room in the extremity of the building. Nothing can be conceived more desolate and cheerless. Superb as to dimensions and form, these apartments were completely unfurnished, and in a most melancholy state of dilapidation. The painting soiled and faded, the elaborately-moulded ceilings and cornices coming down piecemeal and covering the floors with their fragments; these floors themselves rotten, and sinking in many places into holes. The shutters of the high and numerous windows, some closed entirely, others only half; others, again, with one leaf, perhaps, on the floor, and one hanging by a single hinge. Such was the appearance of these once lordly rooms. I shuddered as I traversed this scene of former splendour—of present degradation. The mind, always busy on these occasions, called up the beruffed slashed-sleeve cavalier of other days; the courtly dame, the stomacher resplendent with costly jewels, ebon locks falling in ringlets over her bare, well-turned shoulders and swelling bosom. How changed the scene! The lordly *châtelain* has given place to the little curved Turkish figure before me; the brilliant assemblage of knights and dames to desolation and solitude.

The dormitory of mine host, where at least

some comfort might have been expected, was only of a piece with the rest. Coarse, scanty, and not very clean-looking bedding, lying in a confused heap upon a low bedstead of common deal, without curtains—in short, such a bed as one sometimes sees in an ostler's room over the stables—a rickety deal table, and a couple of old chairs. None of the appurtenances of the toilet, nor any apparent means of stowing his wardrobe; bare walls, and nought else. One might have imagined it the abode of some poor devil whom charity had admitted to occupy a nook in the deserted mansion. The Marquis showed all with perfect *sang-froid*, unconscious that there was anything strange in a man of his princely fortune living like a pauper, and continued leading me from room to room, until we arrived at one smaller than the rest, and a little less dilapidated, which he announced as his study—a title to which a huge table, occupying the greater part of it, and covered with a heap of papers, pictures, and writing material, all intermingled in most glorious confusion, seemed to give some colour; and here were also two or three common chairs. From amongst the litter on the table, after a little hunting, he rummaged out a small miniature of a female, which he thrust into my hand with an air of exultation, as much as to say, "There!—what think you of that?" and evidently supposing me as intimate with its features as himself, and as evidently mortified at my asking who the original might be, whilst, with rather a haughty air, he informed me that it was the portrait of his dear mistress (kissing it respectfully), the Empress Maria Theresa, whom he had had the honour to serve as an officer of Hungarian hussars many years. Whilst laying the miniature again on the table, he hurried out of the room, motioning me to follow him. The old man was quite chivalric when speaking on this subject, and apparently quite in earnest.

Our next visit was to the kitchen, whither he took me to see the thickness of the walls, which were no less than 10 feet. Such a den as this never before sullied the respected name of kitchen. From the smallness of the windows, or port-holes, and the enormous thickness of the walls, it was, even at this time of day, almost dark enough to require candles; spacious and vaulted, with a floor all decayed—and no wonder, for it was in great part covered by an immense heap of potatoes, and quite devoid of furniture. Its occupants were a second Dame Leonarda, and three or four dirty boys, lounging indolently about. A wood-fire blazed on the ash-encumbered hearth, over which was suspended an iron pot filled with potatoes. He then led me through the casemates or subterraneous defences on the western side, before mentioned; and having thus completed our survey of the castle, we sallied from the portal to visit the gardens and *pleasaunce*, the Marquis stepping out with all the briskness of youth. We had got about half-way over the lawn, under one of the magnificent clumps of beeches, when suddenly my conductor, stopping, put his horn to his mouth and blew such a peal as made the woods ring again. No result followed, and as he had not explained himself, I was at a loss to conjecture the meaning of this, unless it were to let me hear the echo. After waiting impatiently a few minutes, the sound was repeated, and an instant afterwards out came all the boys scampering through the portal and over the turf towards us, with an activity strongly contrasted with their former listlessness. This, however, did not satisfy their master, who, rating them soundly for their inattention to his first summons, ordered them to bring out the *carriole*. In a few minutes one of the old carriages I had seen in the court was drawn out by a miserable half-starved-looking beast, hardly deserving the name of a horse, and with harness to match—that is, old, rusty, broken, and mended with bits of cord, &c. Into the suspicious-looking vehicle we both got, and having exchanged his hunting-spear for a shabby whip, the Marquis proceeded to do coachman, and conducted me through his lovely domain; for lovely it really was, in spite of the neglect evident in all directions—a circumstance, however, that one scarcely regretted, since it threw such an air of wildness over the scenery as to make it most charming.

The ground on which the castle stood ran out in knolls, with very abrupt slopes, forming deep ravines, at the bottom of which streams of limpid water ran bubbling along, until finding their way to the main trunk, or great ravine, under the western front, they there united there waters and formed a small lake, whose placid surface was animated by swans and whole flocks of wildfowl, which here found an undisturbed retreat. The whole of the ground above described, excepting the level lawn in front of the great gate, was thickly covered with wood—in some parts impervious from the thick shrubbery of undergrowth, in others clear from this encumbrance— affording splendid forest vistas between the boles of the magnificent trees—the ground beneath carpeted with the most beautiful variety imaginable of mosses and wild-flowers—innumerable creepers hanging in festoons from the branches, with here and there a venerable ruin, fallen against and only supported by its neighbours, increasing the wildness and charm of this enchanting scenery. At times, after following a path winding through the thick shrubberies, and overshadowed by the luxuriant branches of the forest trees, so as to be in perfect twilight, we suddenly came upon a small cleared space, carpeted with turf, in the centre of which, perhaps, was a rustic altar, or the fragment of a column, the marble of which, stained by damps or the encroachments of variously-coloured lichens, harmonised well with the tints of the sylvan scene around it. Some of these were simple cylinders; others were angular, with projecting cornices. Offerings of flowers there were on many of them— evidence of the feelings and peculiar sentiments of the noble proprietor, and that, although neglectful as far as repairs went, he still had eyes to see and a heart to feel the beauties of his lovely domain. Again emerging from the *demi-jour* of the cool *berceau*, the road wound round the face of a knoll, affording a charming view of the distant country, with the lordly chateau towering in the foreground; then replunging into obscurity, it opened again on a scene as extensive but of a totally different character—the country towards Hal, with its long and more thinly-wooded slopes and summits. In one place, a clearing of three or four acres, bearing a crop of potatoes, presented precisely such a scene as one meets with in America—the ground still encumbered with roots and branches, the lofty surrounding wall of grey stems, here and there a tree fallen against its neighbours, or hanging forward as if ready to come to the ground at a touch; in short, a scene of such savage wildness as one would hardly expect to meet in this land of culture and improvement.

After a delightful drive, we returned to the chateau, passing under the ramparts of the garden, which, lying on the slope of the hill, are banked up in such a manner as to form a succession of nearly level terraces. These are laid out in parterres, ornamented with statues and fragments, &c. In the centre of these, a circular wooden tower rises to a great height, forming a conspicuous object from all the neighbouring country, over which the gallery on its summit commands a most extensive view. The walls of this tower are of open work, and, as well as the

HISTORY OF THE CHATEAU. 189

winding staircase within, are said to be a *chêf d'œuvre* of carpentry.

As it was growing late, I was obliged to decline my host's invitation to visit his farm in the valley below; and having, with the assistance of one of his young pages, saddled my horse, I took leave, and returned to Strytem highly pleased with my excursion.

A few days afterwards the Marquis sent me a bundle of papers containing the history of Gaesbeke and its counts; but being unable from want of leisure to copy any of it, I can only remember that the chateau was built about the middle of the thirteenth century by one of the Counts of Brabant, of whom it long continued to be the principal residence. Of the present proprietor I could learn little except what was imparted by himself during our ride, in substance as follows:
—Paul Acornati Visconti, an Italian by birth, inherits Gaesbeke in right of his mother, and by the father's side is of the celebrated family of Visconti of Milan. Early in life he entered the Austrian army, and served as lieutenant and captain of Hungarian hussars during the Seven Years' War. At the peace of 1763, finding himself free, and in possession of a princely fortune, he gave himself up to his vagabond propensities, and passed

his time in wandering over Europe, &c. &c. In this way he ran over all Germany, France, and much of Russia and Poland; traversed Denmark, Sweden, and Lapland as far as the North Cape. Either Dr Clarke or Acerbi mentions meeting him at Tornea, or having heard of him there. He then visited the British Islands, where he remained some time (I think he told me he had been twelve times to England), extending his wanderings to the remotest corners of Ireland, the Highlands of Scotland, and the Western Isles. Here (in England) he became acquainted with many of our celebrated characters—civil, military, and literary—of whose intimacy he was not a little proud. He was delighted with England and its inhabitants, but his fondness for both yielded to the unaccountable mania with which he was subsequently seized for Turkey, the Turks, their manners, their institutions, and everything belonging to them; and after a prolonged residence amongst them, only returned to his own country when the management of his extensive estates in Italy and the Pays Bas imperatively required his presence. What his religious sentiments might have been I know not, but in every other respect he had become a complete Turk, and so determined to remain; thus he has always dressed in the Oriental costume, as I found him, and in every other way conforms to their customs. I have already described the person of this curious character. His health and activity are remarkable; and although a little curved, there is nothing of the old man in his step, which is firm, light, and active; his usual pace is a little trot. His manner of living is extremely simple; his diet, I believe, principally vegetable, and his beverage water. He seldom goes to bed before midnight, rising again at three o'clock in the morning; and to this habit of early rising he assured me he was indebted for his good health. Whether he had ever been married I know not, but that he had a daughter I know, since in the note of invitation to a fête he intended giving at Brussels, he particularly mentioned his wish to introduce me to her. Amongst the people of the neighbourhood I found he bore various characters, some ascribing his eccentricities to a deranged intellect, others to philosophy. Others believed him to be a magician, wherefore the peasantry in general stand in great awe of him. All, however, allow that he is a most charitable, good man. It is said that his liberality towards even his most distant relations is so great, that they amongst them enjoy more of his wealth than he does himself.

That he is wealthy is out of the question; his property is immense. Besides the Gaesbeke estate, he possesses others both in the Pays Bas and in Italy. Most of the best houses in Brussels are his, and the Gaesbeke property alone comprises seventeen villages and parishes. His own house in Brussels is said to be a magnificent one; in it he gave the fête to which I was invited, which I afterwards heard was very splendid, the first people of the country and many of our most distinguished officers having been present. He seldom resides in Brussels for any length of time, nor are his visits to that city frequent, as he prefers retirement and the country.

The establishment at Gaesbeke consisted only of a gardener, an old woman as cook, &c., and some five or six boys, from twelve to sixteen years of age, whom he sometimes dressed in the Hungarian hussar uniform, at others as Orientals—so said the people. Be that as it may, they all wore the usual dress of the country when I saw them. After this first visit the lovely domain of Gaesbeke became a favourite lounge, and I passed many a delicious morning wandering about its cool shady walks. Sometimes the Marquis was at home, sometimes not, but it made little difference—he always received me with the same kindness, and seemed not a little flattered at the pleasure I took in his favourite woods; but we neither of us interrupted the pursuits of the other, for if he were employed he continued his employment, otherwise he would sometimes accompany me himself, or send one of his young pages, if there were anything to be done or seen that required assistance or a guide. It was not without regret that, eventually, I was obliged to leave his neighbourhood without having had an opportunity of taking leave of him.

There was another extraordinary character—a man of great wealth, too—residing within a few miles of us, at Ternath, or St Ulris Capelle; but him I only heard of from Leathes, who had visited him, which I never had an opportunity of doing. This man differed from Acornati in having his chateau splendidly furnished and his pleasure-grounds, described as vieing in beauty with those of Gaesbeke, kept in most excellent order. He had, moreover, a choice collection of paintings.

CHAPTER IX.

WHILST our army thus revelled in luxury in this fine country, that of the enemy, we understood, was concentrating on our frontier, preparatory to the grand blow which was to drive us into the sea. To meet the threatened invasion, it was generally understood in the army that the Duke had made choice of two positions in the neighbourhood of Brussels—the one a little beyond the village of Waterloo, the other at Hal, the point where the roads from Ath and Mons unite. In one or the other of these, it was said, he intended to await the attack, according as the enemy might advance. Frequently, attended only by an orderly dragoon, he would visit these positions, studying them deeply, and most probably forming plans for their occupation and defence. In confirmation, too, of the reports that the French army would shortly advance, we about this time received an order to divest ourselves of all superfluous baggage, and were given to understand that, in case of passing the frontier, the army must be prepared to forego all shelter but what would be carried with it, since the operations were to be of the most active nature. Curious to see these positions, I one day rode over to Hal, which was the nearest to us. The country through which I passed for a long way was like that about Strytem; but on approaching Hal it became more open, free from wood, and without any kind of enclosures. This little town is situated on the Senne, here a good deal interrupted in its course by milldams, &c., so that it forms numerous ponds in and about the place, only to be crossed by the stone bridge over which the road from Braine le Leud and Braine le Chateau, &c., passes, and in the town unites with the two great roads from Ath and Mons, which have previously crossed a small rivulet descending from the north-west, and thus ascends the steep street in the direction of Brussels. On this side the ground rises to a considerable height, giving a great command over the valley and roads winding through it, which may be seen at a considerable distance descending from the opposite hills, which recede so much to the southward as to be of no avail against the positions, although considerably higher.

The town, as already stated, lies on a steep slope; the houses are of stone, many of them large and of most respectable appearance; street wide and airy; many mills, &c., in the lower part, and tan-yards.

I was obliged to content myself with a very superficial view of Hal; for, having miscalculated the distance from Strytem, I had no time for more than to ride through it and back again. The only thing I saw on the road worth notice was a very pretty villa, small, but exceedingly neat, standing in the midst of well-kept pleasure-grounds, quite unlike anything else in the country that I had hitherto seen.

I have as yet been so wrapped up in the country that I have passed over Brussels, to which, however, I had already made several visits, and to which I must now devote a page. So—to begin at the beginning—my first visit was about four or five days after our arrival at Strytem. The weather was particularly favourable. It was one of those lovely days of spring, succeeding rain, when all nature seems bursting into new life—when we are ourselves sensible of the renovating effects of the season, and the elasticity of our spirits is such, that everything appears beautiful to our sight—when all is exhilaration and delight, and we are disposed to be in good humour with everything around us. The country through which my route lay, rich in the bounties of nature, and exhibiting a pleasing variety of feature, made this ride peculiarly agreeable. About half-way, at the villages of Itterbeke and Dilbeke, the appearance of several riflemen in grey or black uniforms, round hats having the brim looped up on one side, and decorated with pendant green plumes, scattered about the fields, the roads, and posted behind trees, somewhat surprised me. Near the roadside, too, on the point of a green knoll, stood one of those rude Rembrandt-like mills, so common in this country; and on the wooden stairs leading up to the door sat several men, with their rifles in hand or lying across their knees, whilst their attention seemed steadily fixed on the surrounding country, as if something interesting was transacting there. A dropping shot now and then re-echoing amongst the woods, seemed to confirm the truth of my apprehensions that the French army had advanced, and that I had no time to lose in regaining Strytem. The sergeant of the party on the mill-steps, however, dissipated my apprehensions. These people belonged to the Duke of Brunswick, and, being all young soldiers, he obliged them to live in their cantonments, as if in face of an enemy, with all their videttes and advanced-posts out. The firing, I found, proceeded from a party practising with their rifles at targets cut in the shape of, and painted to resemble, French soldiers. This was my first interview with men (*mere boys!*) with whom subsequently I had to stand shoulder to shoulder in the great struggle. My approach to the city was announced by the occurrence of several pretty country-houses or villas, much in the same style as that I had seen on the road to Hal, but no indication in the distance—no towers, spires, or lofty building towering over the trees— until, passing the summit of a hill, Brussels suddenly burst on my sight, covering the slope of the hills on the opposite side of the valley—a glorious picture, and one not readily to be erased from my memory. From this point, and under such a sky, she showed herself to the utmost advantage, and the atmosphere was so pure that even from this distance every detail was distinctly visible. The cathedral of St Gudule, standing upon a terrace, formed a striking feature. The tufted verdure of the trees on the ramparts enclosing the city enabled one easily to follow their outline along the summit of the heights, whilst on the face of the slope the ramparts themselves, with their venerable grey towers, gave additional interest to the scene; the houses, rising in terraces, as it were, tier above tier, and everywhere intermingled with foliage; innumerable churches and chapels; palaces, too, amongst which, most conspicuous, was that of Prince d'Aremberg and the Cour de Flandres, and in the lower town the beautiful Stadthuys;—all united to form the glorious picture.

In the vale below, the river Senne wound its way slowly along amidst green meadows, the surface of which was broken by long stripes of white linen, spread there to bleach. In the west and south it was closed by a belt of black forest —the ever-memorable Forest of Soigney. The Senne was ravishing—it seemed as if one could never tire of looking on it; and as I lingered to do so, the more prominent features in the history of that fair city came crowding on my mind, and, now that the scene of action lay before me, embodied themselves to my mind's eye. At first the city seems to have been confined to the borders of the marsh, and thence gradually to have crept up the hillside, until at last it was circumscribed by a rampart—the lower part of the town being evidently the older, and of a different style entirely from the upper.

Descending the hill, I entered this lower town by the Barrière de Gand ' and a long winding narrow street, bordered on either side by houses of black stone, three storeys (generally) high, but of a mean appearance, without *trottoirs* for the foot-passengers, and the mud above my horse's fetlocks; a little farther on I passed the fish-market, and a fearful penance it was—for the strongest stomach, I should think, could hardly resist its noisome smell, arising from a fearful accumulation of garbage flung beneath the tables.

Passing along, I found the streets in this part of the town crowded with commissariat waggons, coming for or taking supplies to the neighbouring cantonments, so that between these and the multitude of Hanoverian soldiers it was not without difficulty that I made my way along and reached an expansion of the street where the Marché aux Herbes is held, much as it used to be in the fore street at Exeter ere the present market-place was built. The bustle, gaiety, groups of females, the colour and smell of flowers and herbs, &c., always make a vegetable-market an agreeable scene. This one was enhanced by the various uniforms of the British, Belgic, and Hanoverian soldiery, and the handsome shops surrounding it. These exhibited in their windows every variety of the choicest productions of India and Europe; and pre-eminent amongst them all were the jewellers and pipe-sellers, or tobacconists, with their splendid displays of meerschaums, Turkish pipes with amber mouth-pieces, rich tobacco-pouches, &c. &c. The Montagne de la Cour, though restricted after passing the market, still a broad street, ascended right in front; and at the foot of this a large hotel (d'Angleterre) occurred so opportunely that I rode into its court, and, leaving my orderly in charge of my horse, set off at once, eager to explore this new and interesting ground.

My first impulse was to seek the park, of which I had so often heard, and instinctively I ascended la Montagne de la Cour, which proved the direct road to it. At the top of the ascent I found myself in a pretty little square (Place Royale) surrounded by handsome houses, but having very much the appearance of pasteboard. Turning thence into a broad street, I found myself in a most magnificent square, far exceeding in beauty, if not in size, any of ours in London — pretty lawns and thick shrubberies, with fine trees, &c., enclosed by a handsome iron railing, and surrounded by fine houses, the façades ornamented by Ionic pilasters, and painted in delicate tints of buff, green, &c., or white, and the whole forming a splendid spectacle and delicious spot. The park is laid out in walks winding through shrubberies and dingles, affording varied and pleasing scenery, some part of the ground being broken and uneven. In the centre is a sort of pavilion where refreshments are sold, and near it is a sheet of water, &c. *Park* is a misnomer; consider it a *square*, in our acceptation of the term, and it is one of the most beautiful in Europe. Its beauty is considerably increased by the old ramparts with their fine umbrageous trees overtopping by far those of the park, and completing one side instead of a row of houses. The glimpse I here got of those ramparts naturally attracted me thither, and I was delighted with the lovely, airy, and commanding promenade they afforded. This promenade round the ramparts is the most delightful imaginable, elevated as they are so much above the highest houses of the city (on the east and north-east sides), and overshadowed by stately elms, affording beautiful views over the city and neighbouring country, always having in the foreground some imposing and picturesque mass of ancient masonry, overrun with a rank vegetation of large-leaved weeds, &c.; some grey and venerable tower—a remnant of antiquity. Descending the hill on either hand, the height of these ramparts decreases to that of the ordinary fortifications of the middle ages; but here, in the lower part, the walls and towers in themselves are far more picturesque, and exhibit much greater antiquity. They are here, I suspect, the same that were built when the city was first fortified in 1044, whilst those above are the more modern fortifications of 1379. Above, as I have before mentioned, the ramparts present a stupendous mound, with large square towers, this elevation being there necessary to protect the city—lying as it does on a declivity—from the higher ground beyond; whilst here below they are only of moderate elevation and breadth, with round or octagonal towers, the masonry time-worn and sombre, almost to blackness, and eminently picturesque.

But this, my first visit, was too short, and there was too much to see to admit of lingering long on any one spot; so, reluctantly quitting the ramparts, I hurried with eager curiosity from street to street and square to square, catching a slight, and but a slight, glimpse of anything, yet delighted, and devouring all. There is a charm which I cannot describe in the contemplation of these heavy and old-fashioned yet picturesque structures, with their sculptures, pointed gables, and eccentric variety of windows, such as most of those (either Gothic, Flemish, or Spanish) with which La Grande Place is surrounded. Here, too, is that most beautiful building, the Hôtel de Ville, flanked by hexagonal towers, and surmounted by its celebrated belfry, rising to a height, it is said, of more than 360 feet; its construction is of open work, and it is impossible to imagine anything combining at once such majesty, grace, elegance, and lightness. One would scarcely imagine that a work so delicate could be enduring; and yet this lovely tower, even now in appearance fresh and perfect, has already stood more than three, nay, nearly four, centuries—having been built in 1445. The statue of St Michael which surmounts it would, in my opinion, be better away; yet this is a feature more vaunted than the elegant form of the building or its admirable workmanship. The saint stands upon one foot, and pirouettes with every breeze. The Hôtel de Ville was commenced in 1380. After a lapse of four centuries, and notwithstanding the boasted "march of intellect," where is the man who could now sit down and conceive such a structure? Many there are, perhaps, who by help of books and existing examples, might compile something of the sort, but I doubt whether any modern architect be capable of the *original conception;* and I am sure that, spite of the 'Mechanic's Magazine' and the present philosophical studies of our masons, none of them could produce more perfect or better work. Like painting, architecture has had its day. Sir Christopher Wren himself acknowledged his astonishment at the boldness of the arches of King's College Chapel, Cambridge, and confessed his ignorance as to their construction and mode of placing the key-stones.

After all, the Hôtel de Ville is irregular in its construction, and the placing the tower at one extremity of the façade instead of the centre I have heard censured as a grievous fault; — I like it—there is originality even in that. The general effect is most imposing.

Nor is the varied throng frequenting this fine place on market-days unworthy of it,—their quaint and original costume harmonising well with the character of the architectural setting around. Many were my visits to Brussels, and always was I delighted. If I did not see all that I now speak of at that first one, *n'importe.* The effect of St Gudule's (the cathedral) is in this respect very good, situated upon a terrace to which one ascends by a broad flight of stairs to the fine Gothic portal, flanked by two handsome towers, and looking out over the city on the country beyond. Up this flight of steps I did ascend with solemn pace and slow, and into its beautiful nave : but the celebrated sculptured pulpit obtained from me no more observation or admiration than those of Ghent and Bruges. The emotion I feel on entering a Gothic cathedral is of a nature too solemn to admit of dwelling upon, or even noticing, such things.

How strikingly Spanish are the charming Bruxellaises in their mantillas, gracefully crossed on the bosom ! I have often heard and read that they are so, but had no recollection of the circumstance at the moment the fact struck me. The mantilla itself, so Spanish, has its testimony of their ancestry confirmed by the brilliant black eyes sparkling beneath it; and the prevalence of black dresses amongst the groups frequenting the park, or *allée-verte*, complete the illusion, and for a second we forget that these are not Andalusians. Never having been in company with any of the fair dames of Brussels, it would be presumption to say more than what I saw of them in public ; my say, therefore, amounts to the having seen many lovely faces and graceful figures, though I had once foolishly fancied that all Flemish women must be of the same breed as Anne of Cleves, or the strapping wenches with whom Rubens and others have made us familiar —forgetting that, as the offspring of some of the finest men and handsomest women in Europe, the Austrians, Spaniards, and French, they ought to show well. From outward appearance it would be, perhaps, difficult to decide the origin; but in the ladies the Spanish blood generally seems to predominate.

In wandering about Brussels one is struck with the frequent occurrence of ecclesiastical ruins— these are generally the remains of monasteries suppressed at the Revolution in 1793. The extensive, and apparently once handsome, house of the Capucines exhibits now only a heap of rubbish, with about five or six feet of the massive walls here and there; another, of which the chapel remained pretty entire, was used by our commissariat as a magazine for hay, straw, &c. &c.

A more striking scene, perhaps, cannot be imagined than the *allée-vert*, with its long vista overarched by thickly-clothed branches of the stately elms lining it in double rows on either hand, the broad expanse of calm water covered by crowded and gaily-painted barges, ornamented with flags and streamers, and enlivened with music and singing. The spacious roads on each bank gay with carriages, equestrians, and numerous pedestrians—all apparently happy, consequenty smiling and merry. I took this route one Sunday with the intention of visiting the Palace of Lavickens, but, alas! the luxury of lounging amidst the merry crowd under the shade of the elms, and amongst these joyous groups, detained one in such wise that, on arriving at the first lock, time no longer served, and my project was necessarily abandoned. As I turned homeward, the well-known overture to Lodoiska resounding from a neighbouring cabaret attracted me thither, and what was my surprise at finding the orchestra by which it was performed to consist of two pretty girls, each with a violin, whilst the old mother accompanied them on the violoncello. I afterwards heard these girls at a café near the Park, where, the audience being more refined, their performance was more careful. I thought their music exquisite, as well as their singing, which they sometimes mingled with it. Had their expressive black eyes and coquettish *cornettes* of red-striped cotton anything to do with it? In my subsequent visits to Brussels, instead of continuing to frequent the Hôtel d'Angleterre, I found a brother officer whose horses were billeted on the Hôtel d'Aremberg, and who offered me stalls whenever I came to town—an arrangement so convenient that his Highness was patronised by me during the remainder of my sojourn at Strytem. I am not sure that I ever saw my princely host, but believe that a tall, thin, elderly man, with a powdered head, a most amiable countenance, and most gentlemanly bearing, who one day crossed the stable-yard whilst I was there, must have been the Prince. We looked at, but did not condescend to bow to, each other. His being on the wrong side of politics was the cause of his domain being thus invaded by strangers, and the billetmaster was careful to keep him full.

One of our lounges at Brussels now was the exhibition of paintings just opened—a pleasant thing enough, as all the world assembled, and there was a daily squeeze in the rooms. As for the articles we were supposed to come to look at, they were below mediocrity—mere daubs, mostly portraits, and many of British officers.

The 19th of May 1815 was with us a memorable day; our friend Sir Augustus Frazer gave a grand, and a very good, dinner to all the horse-artillery officers, English and German, on the occasion of his being appointed lieutenant-colonel of that arm. The dinner was at the Hôtel de la Paix, Place Royale; excellent claret, sauterne, and champagne flowed in abundance, and the utmost hilarity prevailed. Many of us then met for the first time, many after a separation of years, and many for the last time. My friend Bolton sat next to me. I had not seen him since we were cadets together, but a few weeks afterwards he was gathered to his fathers on the field of Waterloo. Frazer had promised me a bed at his friend's (Lieutenant-Colonel Maxwell, 21st) lodgings; accordingly, slipping away from the party, I found my way thither somehow or other, and his servant showing me my room I was soon fast asleep. From this I was aroused some time after by persons coming into the room, and, to my infinite horror, found that I had occupied the bed intended for Bob Cairns. A long dialogue of regrets, &c. &c., ensued, but I continued obstinately to sleep, as indignant at having been deceived as they were at my usurpation; so in the morning I arose early, and left the house and explanation to Sir Augustus. A few days afterwards poor Bob also was gathered to his fathers.

With an aching head I repaired to the beautiful promenade on the ramparts, and made the circuit of the city, lingering about in the fresh morning air until I thought people would be stirring, and then adjourned to my friend Bell's, where, being renovated by an excellent breakfast, I mounted my horse and returned to Strytem—to see Brussels no more.

For some time past it had been generally understood that our army would advance into the French territory on or about the 20th June, in anticipation of which event I sometimes amused myself speculating on the probable events of the campaign. I drew out a written plan, in which we were to fight three battles and arrive in sixteen days at Paris, finishing by a grand *embrâsement*. This, as will be seen, was in some measure prophetic, since three battles were fought (Quatre Bras, Waterloo, and St Denis by the Prussians), and we did arrive in sixteen days, and the catastrophe was with difficulty prevented by the Duke.

CHAPTER X.

May 29*th*.—GRAND cavalry review near Grammont, in the fine meadows on the banks of the Dender, for the use of which, it is said, as much as £400 or £500 were paid.

The day was lovely, and we marched from Strytem in the cool of the morning. The roads, although pretty good, were in places so cut up by the passage of other troops before us, that it became necessary at times to halt until our men filled up the holes with brushwood and earth. About noon we arrived on the ground, than which nothing could be more favourable for the purpose.

The Dender, flowing through a broad tract of rich meadow-land perfectly flat, makes a bend from Grammont to the village of Jedeghem, the ground on its left bank rising in a gentle slope, whilst on the right the meadows extend back for about half a mile, and then terminate at the foot of an abrupt wooded height, which forms, as itwere, a chord of the arc described by the river. This was the arena chosen for the review, and a more favourable one could scarcely have been chosen. We were formed in three lines. The first, near the banks of the river, was composed of hussars in squadrons, with wide intervals between them, and a battery of horse-artillery (6-pounders) on either flank. Opposite the centre of this line was a bridge (temporary, I believe) by which the cortège was to arrive on the ground, descending from the village of Schendelbeke. The second line—compact, or with only the usual squadron intervals—was composed entirely of heavy dragoons, having two batteries—the one of 24-pounder howitzers, the other of 9-pounders—in front of the centre, and a battery of 9-pounders on either flank. The third was a compact line like the second, but entirely of light dragoons, supported also on either flank by a battery of 9-pounders.

It was a splendid spectacle. The scattered line of hussars in their fanciful yet picturesqe costume; the more sober, but far more imposing, line of heavy dragoons, like a wall of red brick; and again the serviceable and active appearance of the third line in their blue uniforms, with broad lappels of white, buff, red, yellow, and orange—the whole backed by the dark wood of the declivity already mentioned—formed, indeed, a fine picture. There were, I understood, about 6000 men on the field; and as I looked and admired their fine appearance, complete equipment, and excellent horses, I wondered how any troops could withstand their attacks, and wished Napoleon and his chiefs could but see them as they stood. My wish was in part gratified, for we afterwards learned beyond all question that numbers of French officers had not only been present, but actually were so in full uniform (many of them of high rank), and had mingled in the cortège of the Duke, and so rode through the ranks—the safest plan they could have pursued, it being impossible to say whether they did or did not belong to the corps of the Duc de Berri, who, as I said, still wore the imperial uniforms in which they had come over to the royal party; and this was still more favoured by a ridiculous scene which occasioned the absence of the French party from the review. It was as follows: Arriving on the ground covered with dust, the different corps had no sooner formed in their position, and dismounted, than off went belts, canteens, and havresacks, and a general brushing and scrubbing commenced ; for the Duke, making no allowance for dusty or muddy roads, expected to see all as clean as if just turned out: accordingly, we had not only brought brushes, &c., but even straw to wisp over the horses. The whole line was in the midst of this business, many of the men even with jackets off, when suddenly a forest of plumes and a galaxy of brilliant uniforms came galloping down the slope from Schendelbeke towards the temporary bridge. "The Duke!" "the Duke!" "the Duke's coming!" ran along the lines, and for a moment caused considerable bustle amongst the people ; but almost immediately this was discovered to be a mistake, and the brushing and cleaning recommenced with more devotion than ever ; whilst the cavalcade, after slowly descending to the bridge and debouching on the meadows, started at full gallop toward the saluting point already marked out, the Duc de Berri, whom we now recognised, keeping several yards ahead, no doubt that he might clearly be seen. At this point he reined up and looked haughtily and impatiently about him; and as we were now pretty intimate with his manner, it was easy to see, even from our distant position, that he was in a passion. The brushing, however, suffered no interruption, and no notice was taken of his presence. One of his suite was now called up and despatched to the front. What further took place I know not, but, certes ! the messenger no sooner returned than his Highness was off like a comet, his tail streaming after him all the way up the slope, unable to keep pace with him, for he rode like a madman, whilst a general titter pervaded our lines as the report flew from one to the other that Mounseer was off in a huff because we did not give him a general salute. Many were the coarse jokes at his expense; and I was amused at one of my drivers, who, holding up the collar from his horse's chest with one hand, whilst with the other he brushed away under it, exclaimed, laughing aloud, "I wouldn't be one of them 'ere French fellows at drill upon the common to-morrow for a penny; if they're not properly bullyragged, I'm d——." It turned out afterwards that he had sent his aide-de-camp to claim the reception due to a prince of the blood-royal, but Lord Uxbridge excused himself by saying he had no instructions on that head, &c. &c. About two o'clock the Duke of Wellington and Prince Blucher, followed by an immense cortège, in which were to be seen many of the most distinguished officers and almost every uniform in

Europe, arrived on the ground. Need I say that the foreigners were loud in praise of the martial air, fine persons, and complete equipment of the men and horses, and of the strength and beauty of the latter? and my vanity on that occasion was most fully gratified, for on arriving where we stood, the Duke not only called old Blucher's attention to "the beautful battery," but, instead of proceeding straight through the ranks, as they had done everywhere else, each subdivision—nay, each individual horse—was closely scrutinised, Blucher repeating continually that he had never seen anything so superb in his life, and concluding by exclaiming, "*Mein Gott, dere is not von orse in dies batterie wich is not goot for Veldt Marshal:*" and Wellington agreed with him. It certainly was a splendid collection of horses. However, except asking Sir George Wood whose troop it was, his Grace never even bestowed a regard on me as I followed from subdivision to subdivision. The review over, and corps dismissed, I resigned my command to my second captain, and proceeded direct to Ninove, Lord Uxbridge having invited all commanding officers to meet his illustrious guests at dinner. On repairing to the monastery, I found a numerous company assembled, comprising some of the most distinguished characters in Europe.

The room in which we assembled, as well as the dining-room, was of splendid dimensions, but totally void of ornament: plain white stuccoed walls, and no furniture in the one but a few travelling articles of our noble hosts; and in the other the dinner-table, chairs, and benches of the most ordinary kind, evidently brought in for the occasion. Long corridors running the whole length of the two wings (standing at right angles to each other), with numerous rooms of similar dimensions opening from them, seemed to be the plan of the building. I suppose the dining-room must have been nearly 100 feet long, nearly square, and about 18 or 20 feet high. In this the tables were laid horse-shoe fashion. In the centre of the cross-table sat Lord Uxbridge; on either hand Blucher and Wellington; then the Duke of Brunswick; the hereditary Prince of Orange; his brother Prince Frederick; Gneiseneau; Ziethen; Kleist; Dornberg; a Danish general whose name I forget; Sir Frederick Arentschild, K.G.L. (the Duke of Wellington's favourite old hussar); Sir Sidney Smyth; Lords Hill, Pack, Picton, Elly; and a host of illustrious names, foreign and British, but not one Frenchman that

THE DINNER.

I recollect. (Perhaps the affair of the morning might have caused the absence of the Duc de Berri, &c.) What names!—names familiar to every ear in the history of those exciting times— names we pronounce with respect regarding those who bear them as being removed above everyday life. But to have sat at table with them, to have heard them called out in the familiarity of everyday conversation—how strange! One can hardly imagine himself thoroughly awake on such occasions. But to return.

It was my good fortune to sit between Colonel Sir F. Arentschild and another no less celebrated officer of the German Legion, Lieutenant Strenuwitz, a Pole by birth, who had signalised himself on more than one occasion in the Peninsula by attacking and capturing outposts. We broke up at an early hour (too early, I think, for old Blucher, who seemed to enjoy himself much), and retired to another room, where coffee was served, and after some little conversation we dispersed. In leaving the dining-room the Duke of Wellington stopped for a few minutes to converse with old Arentschild, and, pinned in a corner by them, I had time to contemplate, well and closely, our great leader. At that time he certainly had not a grey hair in his head.

It was getting dusk when I mounted my horse to return home, and the people were beginning to discharge squibs and crackers on the street of Ninove; the houses were decorated with garlands of laurel and green boughs, so that everything wore an air of festivity.

May 30*th.*—How delightful the tranquillity of Strytem appears after the stir and bustle of yesterday! The fields look more gay, the woods and pleasure-grounds more lovely than ever. Yesterday morning was passed amidst the din of arms and pomp of war—amidst crowds of crested warriors and the clang of martial music—the evening in festivity, amidst magnates of the earth.

How differently has this lovely day glided by! The morning I passed in a quiet peaccable ride amidst the charming scenery of the neighbourhood—wandering through corn-fields, orchards, and hop-grounds, and exploring the shady recesses of the Bois de Liederkerke; the evening in voluptuous indolence, sauntering up and down under the magnificent beeches of the great avenue, indulging in fairy dreams, and listening to the rural sound that, from time to time, broke on the stillness of the hour, whilst the smoke of my cigar hung in wreaths around me as I occasionally stopped to contemplate the scene. No living soul interrupted the solitude, except once the gardener's son, in his blue smock-frock, wooden shoes, and dirty night-cap, with a long rusty old gun under his arm and a short pipe in his mouth, crossed the avenue, marched up the central path of the garden, and disappeared amongst the thickets of the *pleasaunce* beyond. He went, I knew (for he always said so), to the Chasse aux Lièvres for the supply of our table ; but as that was badly supplied, we might have fancied our gamekeeper a bad shot, had not our worthy doctor one evening (for what purpose he could best say) also taken a ramble in the said *pleasaunce,* where, to his infinite surprise, he stumbled upon our chasseur making love to his sister's *adjointe* (a great Flanderkin of a Maritornes), which instantly explained the deficiency of supply. There he went then, as I said, for either purpose—his short pipe leaving a long gossamer-like film of smoke behind him. And this digression brings me to the close of this delightful day.

The genial month of May thus terminated amidst the delightful enjoyments of a country life, and June commenced under happy auspices, little dreaming of the far different scenes we were destined to witness ere yet another month had passed.

The only event that marked this period of our

tranquil, even-flowing existence was the remova of our 1st division from the chateau farm, in compliance with the urgent request of the farmer (Walsdragen), to the pretty village of Yseringen, about a mile off, on the hill above us. I regretted this separation of the troop, but could not withstand the poor man's solicitations, who expected every hour his wife's *accouchement*. As for the division, it benefited by the change. The officer (Leathes) got most excellent quarters in a comfortable well-furnished chateau, whilst his men and horses were equally well lodged in the adjoining farm. Poor Walsdragen, however, could not enjoy this relief, for, a few days after, the impending event took place, and he lost his wife. I shall not forget in a hurry this melancholy circumstance, for I charged myself with unkindness towards him in his affliction by having so long withstood his solicitations to be relieved of our people. I was walking in the avenue, as usual, after dinner, enjoying my weed; the evening was calm and serene, the sun just setting; no sound disturbed the stillness save the hum of insects or the croaking of the frogs. Suddenly one of the most terrific shrieks I ever heard burst forth, until the woods rang again. At first, startled as I was, there was no saying whence the sound came, and taking my cigar from my mouth, I had scarcely assumed a listening attitude when, again and again, it was repeated in a manner so appalling as to make my very flesh creep. It evidently proceeded from the farm; but what could occasion such horrid cries? This time they were succeeded by loud lamentations of many voices, male and female. I hurried towards the farm, hardly knowing what to conjecture. The first idea that flashed on me was an irruption of some French party, who were plundering, murdering, &c. &c., and this, in the first instance, seemed in some measure borne out when several men, without hats, came rushing out of the farmyard with lamentable cries, and passing by me without notice, proceeded to the bridge of the chateau, and there, throwing themselves on their knees before an image of the Virgin and child standing in a niche outside the chapel already mentioned, commenced a most dolorous mixture of lamentation and half-chanted supplication—part of a litany, I presume. I stood somewhat puzzled. After a few minutes of this devotional exercise, one of them ran away and brought a spade, with which he cut a large sod, and the whole party hurried back to the house, carrying it with them. At this moment St Cyr (one of our farmers, and the best amongst them) came up, and, making Mynheer Walsdragen's compliments, reported from him, and at his desire, the death of his wife, which had just taken place—a strange piece of etiquette at such a moment. The sod, I learned, was to put under her head, an ancient practice invariably observed.

My first idea of an irruption of the enemy did not seem just now quite so improbable, for we almost daily heard a good deal of firing in the direction of Mons, and the peasantry were continually bringing accounts of movements of the French army, none of which ever proved true; and the firing, we afterwards learned, proceeded from the practice of the Dutch or Belgic artillery at Mons.

Our host, the Baron van Lombeke, paid us a visit about the beginning of this month for the first time. The ostensible motive for this visit was an inspection of the roads, which he said were immediately to be put in a complete state of repair. He stayed three or four days with us, during which his excursions never extended further than the major's or the curé's, so that he saw but little of the roads—which, together with the circumstance of his having arrived only a few days before from Paris, induced a suspicion that his real business was of a very different nature — possibly to ascertain the strength and positions of our cavalry corps, or something of the sort.

It seemed odd enough receiving a man as a guest in his own house; our servants prepared a room for him, and he was waited upon by the old gardener. Of course he dined, or rather supped, with us; for I believe he usually partook of the curé's dinner at one o'clock. Although what we should call rather vulgar-looking, yet we found M. le Baron exceedingly well-informed, perfectly the gentleman in manners, and upon the whole an agreeable acquisition to our little party. His gardens, and everything about the place, he begged us to consider as our own. We had done so already; however, we took the thing as it was meant—a mere compliment; but we felt that there was more sincerity in the contrast he drew between ourselves and the Prussians, and the repeated assertions of his satisfaction in having his chateau occupied by us instead of by them.

Finding me in want of books, he kindly promised to send me some from Brussels; and I was agreeably surprised at his punctuality, when, a day or two after his departure, the old gardener brought me the five volumes of 'The Hermit of the Chaussée d'Antin'—a work new to me, and to which I was indebted for several most agreeable evenings.

The day marked for our advance into France now approached; and although no confirmation of the rumour reached us, yet we began to prepare for it as confidently as if already given out in general orders. Meantime, as will be seen, our friends beyond the border were scrutinising our intentions pretty closely.

It was on the evening of the 15th June, and about sunset or a little later, that an officer of hussars rode into the village of Yseringen, Leathes being at the time at dinner with me at our chateau. He was dressed as our hussars usually were when riding about the country—blue frock, scarlet waistcoat laced with gold, pantaloons, and forage-cap of the 7th Hussars. He was mounted on a smart pony, with plain saddle and bridle; was without sword or sash, and carried a small whip;—in short, his costume and *monture* were correct in every particular. Moreover, he aped to the very life that "devil-may-care" *nonchalant* air so frequently characterising our young men of fashion. Seeing some of our gunners standing at the door of a house, he desired them to go for their officer, as he wished to see him. They called the sergeant, who told him that the officer was not in the village. In an authoritative tone he then demanded how many men and horses were quartered there, whose troop they belonged to, where the remainder of the troop was quartered, and of what it consisted? When all these questions were answered, he told the sergeant that he had been sent by Lord Uxbridge to order accommodation to be provided for two hundred horses, and that ours must consequently be put up as close as possible. The sergeant replied that there was not room in the village for a single additional horse. "Oh, we'll soon see that," said he; pointing to one of the men who stood by, "Do you go and tell the *maire* to come instantly to me." The *maire* came, and confirmed the sergeant's statement, upon which our friend, flying into a passion, commenced in excellent French to abuse the poor functionary like a pickpocket, threatening to send a whole regiment into the village; and then, after a little further conversation with the sergeant, he mounted his pony and rode off just as Leathes returned to the village. Upon reporting the circumstance to the officer, the sergeant stated that he thought this man had appeared anxious to avoid him, having ridden off rather in a hurry when he appeared, which, together with a slight foreign accent, then for the first time excited a suspicion of his being a spy, which had not occurred to the sergeant before, as he knew there were several foreign officers in our hussars, and that the 10th was actually then commanded by one—Colonel Quentin. The suspicion was afterwards confirmed, for upon inquiry I found that no officer had been sent by Lord Uxbridge on any such mission. Our friend deserved to escape, for he was a bold and clever fellow. A brother emissary, however, who visited Lombeke Notre Dame the same evening, was not quite so prudent nor so fortunate, for he was caught by the sentinel in the act of examining the guns of Sinclair's Brigade by aid of a dark-lantern and made prisoner; but in the hubbub of marching the next morning made his escape, and was heard of no more. We afterwards learned that a number of officers had been sent the same evening into our cantonments to ascertain whether we remained quiet, &c. &c.

Spite of my eagerness for more active service, it was not without regret that I saw the time approach when I expected to leave for ever the tranquil abode of Strytem; and some such thoughts occupied me this very evening (15*th*), as I sauntered about the great avenue after Leathes had left me. Most of the other officers had gone to the ball at Brussels, and I remained quite alone. The balmy softness of the air, the beauty and repose of the scenery, were, I thought, more exquisite than ever; and I continued in the avenue until the increasing obscurity of the evening drove me in to enjoy an hour or two with 'The Hermit of the Chaussée D'Antin' ere. I retired for the night.

CHAPTER XI.

June 16*th*.—It would appear that our Quartermaster-General of the cavalry took a peculiar pleasure in disturbing people at very unseasonable hours. He served me so at Dendermonde, and now he has done precisely the same at Strytem. As on that occasion, I was sound asleep when my servant, bustling into the room, awoke me *en sursaut*. He brought a note which an orderly hussar had left, and ridden off immediately. The note had nothing official in its appearance, and might have been an invitation to dinner; but the unceremonious manner in which the hussar had gone off without his receipt looked curious. My despatch was totally deficient in date, so that time and place were left to conjecture; its contents pithy—they were as follows, viz. :—

" Captain Mercer's troop will proceed with the

utmost diligence to Enghien, where he will meet Major M'Donald, who will point out the ground on which it is to bivouac to-night.

Signed,   *   *   *

D.A.Q.M.-Gen."

That we were to move forward, then, was certain. It was rather sudden, to be sure, and all the whys and wherefores were left to conjecture; but the suddenness of it, and the importance of arriving quickly at the appointed place, rather alarmed me, for upon reflection I remembered that I had been guilty of two or three imprudences. First, all my officers were absent; secondly, all my country waggons were absent; thirdly, a whole division (one-third of my troop) was absent at Yseringen. "*Send the sergeant-major here,*" was the first order, as I drew on my stockings. "*Send for Mr Coates*" (my commissariat officer), the second, as I got one leg into my overalls. "*William, make haste and get breakfast,*" the third, as I buttoned them up. The sergeant-major soon came, and received his orders to turn out instanter, with the three days' provisions and forage* in the havresacks and on the horses;

* We had been ordered nearly a fortnight ago to keep this quantity ready, and the hay rolled, &c. &c.

also to send an express for the first division. He withdrew, and immediately the fine martial clang of "boot-and-saddle" resounded through the village and courts of the chateau, making the woods ring again, and even the frogs stop to listen.

The commissary soon made his appearance. "What! are we off, sir?" "Yes, without delay; and you must collect your waggons as quickly as possible." "I fear, Captain Mercer, that will take some time, for St Cyr's are gone to Ninove." My folly here stared me full in the face. Mr Coates said he would do his utmost to collect them; and as he was a most active, intelligent, and indefatigable fellow, I communicated to him my orders and determination not to wait, desiring him to follow us as soon as he possibly could. My first-enumerated care was speedily removed, for I learned that the officers had just arrived and were preparing for the march, having known of it at Brussels ere we did. The two divisions in Strytem were ready to turn out in a few minutes after the "boot-and-saddle" had resounded, but, as I feared, the first kept us waiting until near seven o'clock before it made its appearance. This delay allowed us time to make a hearty breakfast; and, in the uncertainty of when we should get another meal, we each stowed away a double portion of Walsdragen's fine eggs. At length the first division arrived, and the animating and soul-stirring notes of the "turn-out" again awoke the echoes of the hills and woods. Up jumped my old dog Bal, and away to parade and increase the bustle by jumping at the horses' noses and barking, as parade formed. Away went the officers to inspect their divisions, and Milward is leading my impatient charger Cossac up and down the court. I linger to take a last look of my antique apartment, and bid farewell to my mute companions the Van Voldens.

The gardener, his son, and Mdlle. Mon-Père-dit, with her pale face rendered still paler by the agitation of the morning, stand drawn up in the court, precisely in the same order and on the same ground as on the day of our arrival. With a profusion of blessings, &c., they thank me for the great care we have taken of the chateau, and for the very liberal gratuity which our paymaster, the doctor (Hitchins), had bestowed upon them. They wish me all manner of success, but fear we shall have bloody work. The old man mutters something about Buonaparte *capôte*, which I do not understand, but take for granted is something friendly, so return thanks, mount my horse, and, once more, adieu Strytem.

We had cleared the village and marched some miles well enough, being within the range of my daily rides; but, this limit passed, I was immediately sensible of another error—that of having started without a guide, for the roads became so numerous, intricate, and bad, often resembling only woodmen's tracks, that I was sorely puzzled, spite of the map I carried in my *sabretache*, to pick out my way. But a graver error still I had now to reproach myself with, and one that might have been attended with fatal consequences. Eager to get on, and delayed by the badness of the roads, I left all my ammunition waggons behind, under charge of old Hall, my quartermaster-sergeant, to follow us, and then pushed on with the guns alone, thus foolishly enough dividing my troops into three columns—viz., the guns, ammunition waggons, and the column of provision waggons under the commissary. For this piece of folly I paid dearly in the anxiety I suffered throughout this eventful day, which at times was excessive.

Rid of all encumbrances, we trotted merrily on whenever the road permitted, and, arriving at Castre (an old Roman legionary station), found there the 23d Light Dragoons just turning out, having also received orders to march upon Enghien. A Captain Dance, with whom I rode a short distance, told me he had been at the ball at Brussels last night, and that, when he left the room, the report was that Blucher had been attacked in the morning, but that he had repulsed the enemy with great slaughter, was following up the blow, and that our advance was to support him. The road for the last few miles had been upon a more elevated country, not so wooded—a sort of plateau, consequently hard and dry; but immediately on passing Castre, we came to a piece which appeared almost impassable for about a hundred yards—a perfect black bog, across which a corduroy road had been made, but not kept in repair, consequently the logs, having decayed, left immense gaps. The 23d floundered through this with difficulty, and left us behind. How we got through with our 9-pounders, the horses slipping up to the shoulders between the logs every minute, I know not; but through we did get, and without accident, but it took time to do so. About noon, after threading our way through more mud and many watery lanes, doubtful if we were in the right direction, we came out upon a more open and dry country close to a park, which, upon inquiry, proved to be that of Enghien. To the same point various columns of cavalry were converging, and under the park wall we found Sir Ormsby Vandeleur's brigade of light dragoons, dismounted and feeding their horses. Here we also dismounted to await the arrival of Major M'Donald; and as I looked upon the day's march as finished, deferred feeding until our bivouac should be established—another folly, for an officer in campaign should never lose an opportunity of feeding, watering, or resting his horses, &c. Attracted by the novelty of the scene and the fineness of the day, we had numerous gay visitors here—ladies and gentlemen—who had stationed themselves within the park, enhancing by their presence the gaiety of the scene, for we had halted immediately under the park wall, and at the point where the road to Braine le Comte by Steenkerke branched off from the one we were on. All the corps as they arrived, I observed, took this road, and continued onwards, which made me somewhat impatient lest I should have halted short of my destination. Having waited a good half-hour, and no Major M'Donald appearing, I began to look about for some one who could give me information, but no staff-officer was to be seen, and no one else knew anything about the matter. Corps after corps arrived and passed on, generally without even halting, yet all professing ignorance of their destination. Pleasant situation this! Sir Ormsby's dragoons were by this time bridling up their horses and rolling up their nosebags, evidently with the intention of moving off. Seeing this, I sought out the general, whom I found seated against the bank, that, instead of a hedge, bordered the road. Whether naturally a savage, or that he feared committing himself, I know not, but Sir Ormsby cut my queries short with an asperity totally uncalled for. "I know nothing about you, sir! I know nothing at all about you!" "But you will perhaps have the goodness to tell me where you are going yourself?" "I know nothing at all about it, sir! I told you already I know nothing at all about *you!*" and starting abruptly from his seat, my friend mounted his horse, and (I suppose by instinct) took the road towards Steenkerke, followed by his brigade, leaving me and mine alone in the road, more disagreeably situated than ever. I now began to reflect very seriously on the "*to stay*" or "*not to stay*." In the former case I bade fair to have the ground all to myself, for although everybody I spoke to denied having any orders, yet all kept moving in one and the same direction. In the latter case, my orders in writing certainly were to stay; but circumstances might have occurred since to change this, and the new order might not have reached me. Moreover, it was better to get into a scrape for fighting than keeping out of the way, so I made up my mind to move forward too. Accordingly I had already mounted my people when Sir H. Vivian's brigade of hussars, followed by Major Bull's troop of our horse-artillery, passed. Bull I found was, like myself, without orders, but he thought it best to stick close to the cavalry, and advised me to do the same, which I did, following him and them on the road to Steenkerke. The country about this place appeared more bare and forbidding than any I had yet seen in the Pays Bas. Just as we moved off, the column of Household troops made its appearance, advancing from Ninove, and taking the same direction.

It was now that the recollection of my absent waggons began to torment me, and I actually feared never to see them again. However, there was no help for it now, and I continued onward.

A few miles farther we crossed the Senne by an old stone bridge, and about four in the afternoon arrived at Braine le Comte, almost ravenous with hunger, and roasted alive by the burning sun under which we had been marching all day. The country had improved and become more wooded, so that the town looked pretty, surrounded as it is by gardens and trees. We were not allowed (why, I know not) to see more; for on arriving at one end of it we turned into a road on the left, and so, making a circuit round the back of the gardens, came out at the other end on a piece of bare ground, where we found several regiments drawn up in close columns, dismounted and feeding. It was somewhere between Enghien and Braine le Comte that we met an aide-de-camp (I believe one of the Duke's) posting away as fast as his poor tired beast could get along, and dressed in his embroidered suit, white pantaloons, &c. &c., having evidently mounted as he left the ball-room. This, I remember, struck us at the time as rather odd, but we had no idea of the real state of our affairs.

We had formed up, and were feeding also, but the nosebags were scarcely put on the poor horses' heads than the cavalry corps, mounting again, moved off, one after the other, and we were constrained to follow ere the animals had half finished. Here, as before, I could obtain no intelligence respecting our march, the direction and meaning of which all I spoke to professed a profound ignorance. Whilst halting, Hitchins, slipping into the town, brought us out a couple of bottles of wine, the which we passed round from one to the other without any scruple about sucking it all out of one muzzle. This renewal of our march was a sad disappointment, for on finding the cavalry assembled here, we made sure they were only waiting until the different bivouacs could be arranged, when we should settle ourselves for the night.

In marching round the town, many of the houses had a sort of gallery behind them, which were filled with spectators, particularly many priests. The gardens were very pretty, and I could not but contrast the comparative luxury of these people, snug and comfortable, and sure of their bed when night came on, with our own vagabond situation.

The country beyond Braine le Comte was pretty, the usual rich and wooded champaign extending to the foot of an abrupt ridge of hills, covered with forest to the summit, and toward which our road lay.

A little hamlet (Long Tour, I think) lay at the foot of the hills, the straggling street of which we found so crowded with baggage-waggons of some Hanoverian or other foreign corps, that for a long while we were unable to pass. The cavalry, therefore, left us behind, for they broke into the adjoining fields until they had cleared the impediment. Although annoyed at being thus hindered, I could not but admire the lightness, and even elegance, of the little waggons, with their neat white tilts, and as neat and pretty *jungfrauen* who were snugly seated under them. We found the ascent of the hills more difficult than we expected, the road, which went up in a zigzag (indeed, it could not have been otherwise), little better than a woodman's track, much cut up, and exceedingly steep—so much so, that we found it necessary to double-horse all our carriages, by taking only half up at once. This delayed us considerably; but, impatient as I was to get on, I was pleased at not being hurried through this charming forest-scenery. The hills, as I said, rose abruptly, and with a very steep acclivity, their sides being covered with noble forest-trees, amongst the boles of which the eye ranged without impediment—there being little or no underwood — occasionally catching glimpses through the foliage of the rich and varied plain which we had left, and of the grey buildings of Braine le Comte embosomed in verdure. Groups of dragoons and hussars, mingling with our guns, &c.,

all scrambling up the steep ascent, seen amongst the gigantic trunks of the trees and by the softened light of the forest, presented delicious pictures. Nor were these less interesting from the accompanying sounds — the dull tramp of the horses, the rattling of sabres, and the voices of command, all magnified by the echo of the forest, which was such that one might have fancied himself speaking under a vault.

At length the whole of our carriages were on the summit, but we were now quite alone, all the cavalry having gone on; and thus we continued our march on an elevated plateau, still covered with forest,* thicker and more gloomy than ever—here and there passing a farm and small clearing of a few fields, and then again plunging into the cool dark woods. At one of these farms I got a draught of new milk—very grateful after such a hot march and long fast. At length we had crossed the forest, and found ourselves on the verge of a declivity which stretched away less abruptly than the one we had ascended, consequently presenting a more extensive slope, down which our road continued. A most extensive view lay before us; and now for the first time, as emerging from the woods, we became

* I believe this is the Bois de la Houssier.

sensible of a dull, sullen sound that filled the air, somewhat resembling that of a distant water-mill, or still more distant thunder. On clearing the wood, it became more distinct, and its character was no longer questionable—heavy firing of cannon and musketry, which could now be distinguished from each other plainly. We could also hear the musketry in volleys and independent firing. The extensive view below us was bounded towards the horizon by a dark line of wood, above which, in the direction of the cannonade, volumes of grey smoke arose, leaving no doubt of what was going on. The object of our march was now evident, and we commenced descending the long slope with an animation we had not felt before.

It was here that Major M'Donald overtook us, and without adverting to the bivouac at Enghien, of which probably he had never heard, gave me orders to attach myself to the Household brigade, under Lord Edward Somerset, but no instructions where or when. I took care not to tell him they were in the rear, lest he might order us to halt for them, which would have been a sore punishment to people excited as we now were by the increasing roar of the battle evidently going on, and hoped that by marching faster they might soon overtake us. Just at this moment a cabriolet, driving at a smart pace, passed us. In it was seated an officer of the Guards, coat open and snuffbox in hand. I could not but admire the perfect *nonchalance* with which my man was thus hurrying forward to join in a bloody combat—much, perhaps, in the same manner, though certainly not in the same costume, as he might drive to Epsom or Ascot Heath. The descent terminated in a picturesque hollow, with a broad pool, dark and calm, and beyond it an old mill, perfectly in keeping with the scene. The opportunity of watering our poor brutes was too good to be missed, and I accordingly ordered a halt for that purpose. Whilst so employed, an aide-de-camp, descending from a singular knoll above us, on which I had noticed a group of officers looking out with their glasses in the direction of the battle, came to summons me to Sir Hussey Vivian, who was one of them.

On ascending the knoll, Sir Hussey called to me in a hurried manner to make haste. "Who do you belong to?" said he. I told him, as also that the brigade was yet in the rear. "Well," he replied, "never mind; there is something serious going on, to judge from that heavy firing, and artillery must be wanted; therefore bring up your guns as fast as you can, and join my hussars: can you keep up?" "I hope so, sir." "Well, come along without delay; we must move smartly." In a few minutes our people, guns and all, were on the hill. The hussars mounted, set off at a brisk trot, and we followed. Alas! thought I, where are my ammunition waggons? Neither this anxiety, however, nor the excitement of the moment, were sufficient to shut my eyes to the beautiful picture on that knoll. Conceive a point of ground standing forth with precipitous slopes over the hollow already mentioned, with its picturesque mill and calm glassy pool; on this ground, happily grouped, a band of warriors, in dresses not less picturesque, beneath a huge cross of the rudest workmanship; a few Salvator-like trees complete the foreground, the distance presenting a rich and varied scene of corn-fields (now yellow), and pastures of the liveliest green, and sombre wood—the whole extending away till in the distance all the features are massed and mellowed into indistinctness and purply vapour. Such was the scene. The hussars, to lighten their horses, untied the nets containing their hay, and the mouths of their corn-bags, which falling from them as they trotted on, the road was soon covered with hay and oats. We did not follow their example, and, although dragging with us 9-pounders, preserved our forage, and also our place in the column.

By-and-by a large town appeared in front of us, and the increasing intensity of the cannonade, and volumes of smoke about the trees, led us to suppose the battle near at hand, and on the hill just beyond the town. This town was Nivelle.

Another beautiful scene, and one full of excitement, now presented itself. We were descending by a gentle slope toward Nivelle, which lay spread out before us—its towers and masses of building, especially what appeared to be the ruins of an ancient castle, sweetly touched by the golden light of the setting sun, whilst the greater part lay in deep-toned purple obscurity. Fine trees, with dark overhanging foliage, bordering the road, formed a foreground and frame, as it were, to this picture. Beyond the town the ground rose, also in shadowy obscurity, crowned with sombre woods, over which ascended the greyish blue smoke of the battle, now apparently so near that we fancied we could hear the shouts of the combatants—a fancy strengthened by crowds of people on the heights, whom we mistook for troops — inhabitants of Nivelle, as we soon discovered, seeking to get a sight of the fearful tragedy then enacting. Before entering the town we halted for a moment, lighted our slow matches, put shot into our leathern cartouches, loaded the guns with powder, and stuck priming wires into the vents to prevent the cartridges slipping forward, and, thus prepared for immediate action, again moved on.

On entering the town what a scene presented itself! How different from the repose of the country we had been traversing all day! There all was peace and tranquillity, undisturbed—absolutely undisturbed, except by the hurried march of successive columns along the highroad. There the rustic pursued his wonted labours as in profound peace, the mill went its rumbling round, the birds carolled on the spray. True, the sounds of battle came borne on the evening breeze—the brattle of musketry and the boom of cannon shook the air; but it was distant—very distant —and might be heard, and the ascending smoke seen, with that sort of thrilling sensation with which we witness the progress of the storm when we ourselves are secure from its effects. Here, on the contrary, all was confusion, agitation, and movement. The danger was impending; explosion after explosion, startling from their vicinity, and clattering peals of musketry, like those lengthened thunder-claps which announce to us

so awfully the immediate neighbourhood of the
electric cloud. The whole population of Nivelle
was in the streets, doors and windows all wide
open, whilst the inmates of the houses, male and
female, stood huddled together in little groups
like frightened sheep, or were hurrying along with
the distracted air of people uncertain where they
are going, or what they are doing. The scene
was strangely interesting. In a sort of square
which we traversed, a few soldiers, with the air of
citizens (probably a municipal guard), were drawn
up in line, looking anxiously about them at the
numerous bleeding figures which we now began
to meet. Some were staggering along unaided,
the blood falling from them in large drops as they
went. One man we met was wounded in the
head; pale and ghastly, with affrighted looks and
uncertain step, he evidently knew little of where
he was, or what passed about him, though still
he staggered forward, the blood streaming down
his face on to the greatcoat which he wore rolled
over his left shoulder. An anxious crowd was
collecting round him as we passed on. Then
came others supported between two comrades,
their faces deadly pale, and knees yielding at
every step. At every step, in short, we met numbers, more or less wounded, hurrying along in

search of that assistance which many would never live to receive, and others receive too late. Priests were running to and fro, hastening to assist at the last moments of a dying man; all were in haste—all wore that abstracted air so inseparable from those engaged in an absorbing pursuit. There were women, too, mingling in this scene of agitation. Ladies, fair delicate ladies, stood on the steps at the doors of several handsome houses, their hands folded before them, as if in the agony of suspense, and with an air of deprecation, their eyes wandering over the excited crowd, whilst ever and anon they would move their lips as if in prayer. I thought as we passed along they looked at us, and prayed for our safety and success. I gave them credit for it, at least, and the very idea had the effect of inspiration. Strange that the sight —nay, often the recollection—of all that is tender and compassionate, of woman, should have the effect of stimulating us to martial deeds. The little knots of excited citizens assembled on our route would cease their energetic declamations, and turn to look at us as we passed along. Many would run up, and, patting our horses' necks, would call down benedictions on us, and bid us hasten to the fight ere it were yet too late, or utter trembling and not loud shouts of " Vivent les

Anglais!" A few there were who stood apart, with gloomy discontented looks, eyeing their fellow-citizens with evident contempt, and us with scowls, not unmixed with derision, as they marked our dusty and jaded appearance. Through all this crowd we held our way, and soon began to ascend the hill beyond the town, where we entered a fine chaussée bordered by elms, expecting every moment to enter on the field of action, the roar of which appeared quite close to us. It was, however, yet distant.

The road was covered with soldiers, many of them wounded, but also many apparently untouched. The numbers thus leaving the field appeared extraordinary. Many of the wounded had six, eight, ten, and even more, attendants. When questioned about the battle, and why they left it, the answer was invariably, "Monsieur, tout est perdu! les Anglais sont abimés, en déroute, abimés, tous, tous, tous!" and then, nothing abashed, these fellows would resume their hurried route. My countrymen will rejoice to learn that amongst this dastardly crew not one Briton appeared. Whether they were of Nassau or Belgians, I know not; they were one or the other—I think the latter. One red-coat we did meet— not a fugitive though, for he was severely wounded.

A WOUNDED HIGHLANDER.

This man was a private of the 92d (Gordon Highlanders), a short, rough, hardy-looking fellow, with the national high cheek-bones, and a complexion that spoke of many a bivouac. He came limping along, evidently with difficulty and suffering. I stopped him to ask news of the battle, telling him what I had heard from the others. "Na, na, sir, it's aw a damned lee; they war fechtin' yat an I laft 'em; but it's a bludy business, and thar's na saying fat may be the end on't. Oor ragiment was nigh clean swapt off, and oor Colonel kilt jist as I cam awa." Upon inquiring about his own wound, we found that a musket-ball had lodged in his knee, or near it; accordingly Hitchins, dismounting, seated him on the parapet of a little bridge we happened to be on, extracted the ball in a few minutes, and, binding up the wound, sent him hobbling along towards Nivelle, not having extracted a single exclamation from the poor man, who gratefully thanked him as he resumed his way. A little further on, and as it began to grow dusk, we traversed the village of Hautain le Val, where a very different scene presented itself. Here, in a large cabaret by the roadside, we saw through the open windows the rooms filled with soldiers, cavalry and infantry; some standing about in earnest conversation, others seated round tables, smoking, carousing, and thumping the board with clenched fists, as they related with loud voices— what ?—most likely their own gallant exploits. About the door their poor horses, tied to a rail, showed by their drooping heads, shifting legs, and the sweat drying and fuming on their soiled coats, that their exertions at least had been of no trivial nature.

CHAPTER XII.

THE firing began to grow slacker, and even intermitting, as we entered on the field of Quatre Bras —our horses stumbling from time to time over corpses of the slain, which they were too tired to step over. The shot and shells which flew over our line of march from time to time (some of the latter bursting beyond us) were sufficient to enable us to say we had been *in* the battle of Quatre Bras, for such was the name of the place where we now arrived, just too late to be useful. In all directions the busy hum of human voices was heard; the wood along the skirts of which we marched re-echoed clearly and loudly the tones of the bugle, which ever and anon were overpowered by the sullen roar of cannon, or the sharper rattle of musketry; dark crowds of men moved in the increasing obscurity of evening, and the whole scene seemed alive with them. What a moment of excitement and anxiety as we proceeded amongst all this tumult, and amidst the dead and dying, ignorant as yet how the affair had terminated! Arrived at a mass of buildings, where four roads met (*les quatre bras*), Major M'Donald again came up with orders for us to bivouac on an adjoining field, where, accordingly, we established ourselves amongst the remains of a wheat crop.

Our men dismounted, and the horses tied up to the wheels of the carriages, every one was despatched with canteens and water-buckets to a well at the farm, to procure water for themselves and horses. This being the only water in the immediate neighbourhood, the crowd of all arms was so great about it that our people were employed fully two hours after halting ere they had completed watering their horses. They were then fed with corn, whilst eating which, a patch of wheat still standing was discovered near our bivouac. This we immediately cut or pulled up, and thus saved our hay, for there was sufficient to employ the poor brutes all night, if they preferred eating to sleeping.

Our animals cared for, the next consideration was ourselves. The men had provisions ready cooked in their havresacks, and therefore soon made themselves comfortable ; but we had nothing, could procure nothing, and were likely to go supperless to bed. We had assembled in a little circle, discussing the events of the day previous to lying down, when, to our no small joy, the doctor made his appearance, followed by one of the servants bearing the remnant of a large meat-pie that yesterday had formed *part* of our dinner at Strytem, and which he, with laudable zeal and presence of mind, had in the hurry-scurry of the morning thrust into our little cart, thinking, good man, it might prove useful. No one can doubt that it did so in a degree ; but the sixth part of the *remnant* of a pie went little way to satisfy the cravings of our stomachs, which had had so long a holiday. However, it was something, and we were grateful for it, and thankful to our worthy Esculapius for having been so provident. The meal ended and cigars lighted, we sat enveloped in our cloaks, chatting and listening to the Babel-like confusion at the well, where crowds were still struggling for water, until, one by one, we sank on the ground, overcome by sleep, which for my part remained unbroken until the grey dawn began to peep of the

17th June, when a popping fire of musquetry, apparently close at hand, aroused me again to consciousness of my situation. At first I could not imagine where I was. I looked straight up, and the stars were twinkling over me in a clear sky. I put out a hand from beneath my cloak, and felt clods of damp earth and stalks of straw. The brattle of musketry increased, and then the consciousness of my situation came gradually over me. Although somewhat chilly, I was still drowsy, and, regardless of what might be going on, had turned on my side and began to dose again, when one of my neighbours started up with the exclamation, "I wonder what all that firing means!" This in an instant dispelled all desire to sleep; and up I got too, mechanically repeating his words, and rubbing my eyes as I began to peer about. One of the first, and certainly the most gratifying, sights that met my inquiring gaze, was Quartermaster Hall, who had arrived during the night with all his charge safe and sound. He had neither seen nor heard, however, of Mr Coates and his train of country waggons, for whom I began now to entertain serious apprehensions. From whatever the musketry might proceed, we could see nothing—not even the flashes; but the increasing light allowed me to distinguish numberless dark forms on the ground all around me, people slumbering still, regardless of the firing that had aroused me. At a little distance numerous white discs, which were continually in motion, changing place and disappearing, to be succeeded by others, puzzled me exceedingly, and I could not even form a conjecture as to what they might be. Watching them attentively, I was still more surprised when some of these white objects ascended from the ground and suddenly disappeared; but the mystery was soon explained by the increasing light, which gave to my view a corps of Nassau troops lying on the ground, having white tops to their shakos. Daylight now gradually unfolded to us our situation. We were on a plateau which had been covered with corn, now almost everywhere trodden down. Four roads, as already mentioned, met a little to the right of our front, and just at that point stood a farmhouse, which, with its outbuildings, yard, &c., was enclosed by a very high wall. This was the farm of Quatre Bras. Beyond it, looking obliquely to the right, the wood (in which the battle still lingered when we arrived last night) stretched away some distance along the roads to Nivelle and Charleroi, which last we understood lay in front, but far out of sight. Along the continuation of the Charleroi road, and in the direction of Brussels, a little in rear of our right, a few cottages scattered along it had their little gardens enclosed by banks, with here and there an elder or some such bush growing on them; and these were the only enclosures to be seen, all the rest being a wide extent of corn-land without hedge or wall. On the farther side of the road, beyond the cottages, the fields were interspersed with thickets of underwood and a few clumps of trees, which shut in the view in that direction. To the rear the country appeared perfectly naked and open. To the left (I always speak with reference to the enemy whom we fronted) the ground descended very gradually for about two miles, where it appeared bounded by a long wood extending far away towards Brussels. In front it descended more abruptly; and then there was a plain about a mile in breadth extending along our front, from the wood on the left to that on the right. The great road from Nivelle to Namur, crossing that from Brussels to Charleroi at Quatre Bras, ran along this plain, whilst the direction of the latter was nearly perpendicular to our position. Beyond this plain the ground rose again to a height somewhat superior to that on which we stood, and another large wood extended on it from opposite the one on our left, apparently half-way to that on the right, having the declivity towards us laid out in fields enclosed by pretty thick hedges. Between these two woods the opening gave us an extensive view over the country, in the direction of Gembloux and Namur.

On the Charleroi road and in the plain was a small village (Frasnes), with its church, just beyond which the road ascended the heights, on the open part of which, between the road and the wood towards the left, was the bivouac of the French army opposed to us. Its advanced posts were in the valley near Frasnes, and ours opposite to them — our main body occupying the ground between Quatre Bras and the wood on the left. A smart skirmish was going on amongst the hedges, &c., already mentioned, and this was the firing we had heard all the morning. Our infantry were lying about, cleaning their arms, cooking, or amusing themselves, totally regardless of the skirmish. This, however, from our position, was a very interesting sight to me, for the slope of the ground enabled me to see distinctly all the manœuvres of both parties, as on a plan. After much firing from the edge of the wood, opposite which our riflemen occupied all the hedges, I saw the French chasseurs suddenly make a rush forward in all directions, whilst the fire of our people became thicker and faster than ever. Many of the former scampered across the open fields until they reached the nearest hedges, whilst others ran crouching under cover of those perpendicular to their front, and the whole succeeded in establishing themselves—thus forcing back and gaining ground on our men. The fire then again became sharper than ever—sometimes the French were driven back; and this alternation I watched with great interest until summoned to Major M'Donald, who brought us orders for the day. From him I first learned the result of the action of yesterday—the retreat of the Prussians, and that we were to do so too. His directions to me were that I should follow some corps of infantry, or something of the sort; for what followed caused me to forget it all: "*Major Ramsay's troop,*" he said, "*will remain in the rear with the cavalry, to cover the retreat; but I will not conceal from you that it falls to your turn to do this, if you choose it.*" The Major looked rather conscience-stricken as he made this avowal, so, to relieve him, I begged he would give the devil his due and me mine. Accordingly all the others marched off, and as nothing was likely to take place immediately, we amused ourselves by looking on at what was doing.

AN ALARM.

Just at this moment an amazing outcry arose amongst the infantry at the farm, who were running towards us in a confused mass, shouting and bellowing, jostling and pushing each other. I made sure the enemy's cavalry had made a dash amongst them, especially as the fire of the skirmishers became thicker and apparently nearer, when the thing was explained by a large pig, squealing as if already stuck, bursting from the throng by which he was beset in all directions. Some struck at him with axes, others with the butts of their muskets, others stabbed at him with bayonets. The chase would have been amusing had it not been so brutal; and I have seldom experienced greater horror than I did on this occasion when the poor brute, staggering from the repeated blows he received, was at last brought to the ground by at least half-a-dozen bayonets plunged into him at once.

All this time our retreat was going on very quietly. The corps at Quatre Bras had retired early in the morning and been replaced by others from the left, and this continued constantly— every corps halting for a time on the ground near Quatre Bras until another from the left arrived, these moving off on the great road to Brussels, ceding the ground to the new-comers.

At first every one, exulting in the success of yesterday—the having repulsed the enemy with a handful of men, as it were, unsupported by cavalry and with very little artillery — anticipated, now our army was united, nothing less than an immediate attack on the French position. We were sadly knocked down, then, when the certainty of our retreat became known. It was in vain we were told the retreat was only a manœuvre of concentration; the most gloomy anticipations pervaded every breast. About this time Sir Alexander Dickson paid me a visit, having just arrived from New Orleans, where he commanded the artillery, to be our Deputy-Quartermaster-General. He only stayed a few minutes.

As the infantry corps on the plateau became fewer, the fire of the skirmishers amongst the hedges gradually relaxed, and at length ceased—the Rifles, &c., being withdrawn, and following the line of retreat. At last, about noon, I found myself left with my troop, quite alone, on the brow of the position, just by the farm of Quatre Bras—the only troops in sight being a small picket of hussars, near the village of Frasnes, in the plain below; a few more in our rear, but at some little distance, amongst the houses; and a brigade of hussars* far away to the left (about two miles), close to the wood in that quarter. Thus solitary, as it were, I had ample leisure to contemplate the scene of desolation around me, so strangely at variance with the otherwise smiling landscape. Everywhere mementoes of yesterday's bloody struggle met the eye—the corn trampled down, and the ground, particularly in the plain, plentifully besprinkled with bodies of the slain. Just in front of the farm of Quatre Bras there was a fearful scene of slaughter—Highlanders and cuirassiers lying thickly strewn about; the latter appeared to have charged up the Charleroi road, on which, and immediately bordering it, they lay most numerously.

In communicating to me the orders of our retreat, Major M'Donald had reiterated that to join Lord Edward Somerset's brigade without delay, but still he could not tell me where this brigade was to be found. Meantime Sir Ormsby Vandeleur's brigade of light dragoons having formed up in front of the houses, and supposing from this that all the cavalry must be nigh, as one step towards finding Lord Edward I crossed the road to the right of these dragoons, and rode towards

* Sir Hussey Vivian's, I believe.

the part where, as before stated, the light was intercepted by trees and bushes. On passing through these I had an uninterrupted view of the country for miles, but not a soldier or living being was to be seen in that direction. As I pushed on through the thickets my horse, suddenly coming to a stand, began to snort, and showed unequivocal symptoms of fear. I drove him on, however, but started myself when I saw, lying under the bush, the body of a man stripped naked. This victim of war was a youth of fair form, skin delicately white, and face but little darker; an embryo mustache decorated the upper lip, and his countenance, even in death, was beautiful. That he was French I conjectured, but neither on himself nor his horse was there a particle of clothing that could indicate to what nation he belonged. If French, how came he here to die alone so far in the rear of our lines? I know not why, but the rencontre with this solitary corpse had a wonderful effect on my spirits— far different from what I felt when gazing on the heaps that encumbered the field beyond. Seldom have I experienced such despondency—such heart-sinking—as when standing over this handsome form thus despoiled, neglected, and about to become a prey to wolves and carrion crows—

the darling of some fond mother, the adored of some fair maid. His horse, stripped like himself, lay by—they had met their fate at once. Returning to my troop, I found Sir Augustus Frazer, who had come to order my ammunition-waggons to the rear that the retreat might be as little encumbered as possible, and to tell me that what ammunition was used during the day would be supplied by my sending for it to Langeveldt, on the road to Brussels, where that to Wavre branches from it.

Thus divested of our ammunition, it was evident that our retreat must be a rapid one, since with only fifty rounds a-gun (the number in the limbers), it could not be expected that we could occupy any position longer than a few minutes. In the end, this measure had nearly led to very disagreeable results, as will be seen anon.

It was now about one o'clock. My battery stood in position on the brow of the declivity, with its right near the wall of the farm, all alone, the only troops in sight being, as before mentioned, the picket and a few scattered hussars in the direction of Frasnes, Sir O. Vandeleur's light dragoons two or three hundred yards in our rear, and Sir H. Vivian's hussars far away to the left. Still the French army made no demonstration of an advance. This inactivity was unaccountable. Lord Uxbridge and an aide-de-camp came to the front of my battery, and, dismounting, seated himself on the ground; so did I and the aide-de-camp. His lordship with his glass was watching the French position; and we were all three wondering at their want of observation and inactivity, which had not only permitted our infantry to retire unmolested, but also still retained them in their bivouac. "It will not be long now before they are on us," said the aide-de-camp, "for they always dine before they move; and those smokes seem to indicate that they are cooking now." He was right; for not long afterwards another aide-de-camp, scouring along the valley, came to report that a heavy column of cavalry* was advancing through the opening between the woods to the left from the direction of Gembloux. At the same moment we saw them distinctly; and Lord Uxbridge, having reconnoitered them a moment through his glass, started up, exclaiming, in a joyful tone, "By the Lord, they are Prussians!" jumped on his horse, and, followed by the two aides, dashed off like a whirlwind to meet

* These appear to have been the cuirassiers of Milhaud, together with the light cavalry of the corps commanded by Count Lobau, sent to assist Ney in his attack on Quatre Bras.—See O'Meara's 'Translation of Memoir of Napoleon,' lib. ix. cap. v. p. 109.

them. For a moment I stood looking after them as they swept down the slope, and could not help wondering how the Prussians came there. I was, however, not left long in my perplexity, for, turning my eyes towards the French position, I saw their whole army descending from it in three or four dark masses, whilst their advanced cavalry picket was already skirmishing with and driving back our hussars. The truth instantly flashed on my mind, and I became exceedingly uneasy for the safety of Lord Uxbridge and his companions, now far advanced on their way down the valley, and likely to be irretrievably cut off. My situation now appeared somewhat awkward: left without orders and entirely alone on the brow of our position—the hussar pickets galloping in and hurrying past as fast as they could—the whole French army advancing, and already at no great distance. In this dilemma, I determined to retire across the little dip that separated me from Sir O. Vandeleur, and take up a position in front of his squadrons, whence, after giving a round to the French advance as soon as they stood on our present ground, I thought I could retire in sufficient time through his intervals to leave the ground clear for him to charge. This movement was immediately executed; but the guns were scarcely unlimbered ere Sir Ormsby came furiously up, exclaiming, "What are you doing here, sir? You encumber my front, and we shall not be able to charge. Take your guns away, sir; instantly, I say—take them away!" It was in vain that I endeavoured to explain my intentions, and that our fire would allow his charge to be made with more effect. "No, no; take them out of my way, sir!" was all the answer I could get; and, accordingly, I was preparing to obey, when up came Lord Uxbridge, and the scene changed in a twinkling. "Captain Mercer, are you loaded?" "Yes, my lord." "Then give them a round as they rise the hill, and retire as quickly as possible." "Light dragoons, threes right; at a trot, march!" and then some orders to Sir Ormsby, of whom I saw no more that day. "They are just coming up the hill," said Lord Uxbridge. "Let them get well up before you fire. Do you think you can retire quick enough afterwards?" "I am sure of it, my lord." "Very well, then, keep a good look-out, and point your guns well." I had often longed to see Napoleon, that mighty man of war —that astonishing genius who had filled the world with his renown. Now I saw him, and there was a degree of sublimity in the interview rarely equalled. The sky had become overcast since the morning, and at this moment presented a most extraordinary appearance. Large isolated masses of thundercloud, of the deepest, almost inky black, their lower edges hard and strongly defined, lagging down, as if momentarily about to burst, hung suspended over us, involving our position and everything on it in deep and gloomy obscurity; whilst the distant hill lately occupied by the French army still lay bathed in brilliant sunshine. Lord Uxbridge was yet speaking, when a single horseman,* immediately followed by several others, mounted the plateau I had left at a gallop, their dark figures thrown forward in strong relief from the illuminated distance, making them appear much nearer to us than they really were. For an instant they pulled up and regarded us, when several squadrons, coming rapidly on the plateau, Lord Uxbridge cried out, "Fire!—fire!" and, giving them a general discharge, we quickly limbered up to retire, as they dashed forward supported by some horse-artillery guns, which opened upon us ere we could complete the manœuvre, but without much effect, for the only one touched was the servant of Major Whinyates,

* That this was Napoleon we have the authority of General Gourgand, who states that, irritated at the delay of Marshal Ney, he put himself at the head of the chasseurs (I think), and dashed forward in the hope of yet being able to catch our rear-guard.

who was wounded in the leg by the splinter of a howitzer shell.

It was now for the first time that I discovered the Major and his rocket-troop, who, annoyed at my having the rear, had disobeyed the order to retreat, and remained somewhere in the neighbourhood until this moment, hoping to share whatever might be going on. The first gun that was fired seemed to burst the clouds overhead, for its report was instantly followed by an awful clap of thunder, and lightning that almost blinded us, whilst the rain came down as if a water-spout had broken over us. The sublimity of the scene was inconceivable. Flash succeeded flash, and the peals of thunder were long and tremendous; whilst, as if in mockery of the elements, the French guns still sent forth their feebler glare and now scarcely audible reports—their cavalry dashing on at a headlong pace, adding their shouts to the uproar. We galloped for our lives through the storm, striving to gain the enclosures about the houses of the hamlets, Lord Uxbridge urging us on, crying, "Make haste!—make haste! for God's sake, gallop, or you will be taken!" We did make haste, and succeeded in getting amongst the houses and gardens, but with the French advance close on our heels. Here, however, observing the chaussée full of hussars, they pulled up. Had they continued their charge we were gone, for these hussars were scattered about the road in the utmost confusion, some in little squads, others singly, and, moreover, so crowded together that we had no room whatever to act with any effect—either they or us.

Meantime the enemy's detachments began to envelop the gardens, which Lord Uxbridge observing, called to me, " Here follow me with two of your guns," and immediately himself led the way into one of the narrow lanes between the gardens. What he intended doing, God knows, but I obeyed. The lane was very little broader than our carriages—there was not room for a horse to have passed them! The distance from the chaussée to the end of the lane, where it debouched on the open fields, could scarcely have been above one or two hundred yards at most. His lordship and I were in front, the guns and mounted detachments following. What he meant to do I was at a loss to conceive : we could hardly come to action in the lane ; to enter on the open was certain destruction. Thus we had arrived at about fifty yards from its termination when a body of chasseurs or hussars appeared

there as if waiting for us. These we might have
seen from the first, for nothing but a few elder
bushes intercepted the view from the chaussée.
The whole transaction appears to me so wild and
confused that at times I can hardly believe it to
have been more than a confused dream—yet true
it was;—the general-in-chief of the cavalry exposing himself amongst the skirmishers of his
rear-guard, and literally doing the duty of a
cornet! " By God! we are all prisoners" (or
some such words), exclaimed Lord Uxbridge,
dashing his horse at one of the garden-banks,
which he cleared, and away he went, leaving us
to get out of the scrape as best we could. There
was no time for hesitation—one manœuvre alone
could extricate us if allowed time, and it I
ordered. " Reverse by unlimbering" was the
order. To do this the gun was to be unlimbered,
then turned round, and one wheel run up the
bank, which just left space for the limber to
pass it. The gun is then limbered up again and
ready to move to the rear. The execution, however, was not easy, for the very reversing of the
limber itself in so narrow a lane, with a team of
eight horses, was sufficiently difficult, and required
first-rate driving. Nothing could exceed the
coolness and activity of our men; the thing was

done quickly and well, and we returned to the chaussée without let or hindrance. How we were permitted to do so, I am at a loss to imagine; for although I gave the order to reverse, I certainly never expected to have seen it executed. Meantime my own situation was anything but a pleasant one, as I sat with my back to the gentlemen at the end of the lane, whose interference I momentarily expected, casting an eye from time to time over my shoulder to ascertain whether they still kept their position. There they sat motionless, and although thankful for their inactivity, I could not but wonder at their stupidity. It seemed, however, all of a piece that day—all blunder and confusion; and this last I found pretty considerable on regaining the chaussée. His lordship we found collecting the scattered hussars together into a squadron for our rescue, for which purpose it was he had so unceremoniously left us. Heavy as the rain was and thick the weather, yet the French could not but have seen the confusion we were in, as they had closed up to the entrance of the enclosure; and yet they did not at once take advantage of it. Things could not remain long in this state. A heavy column of cavalry approached us by the chaussée, whilst another, skirting the enclosures, appeared pushing forward to cut us off. Retreat now became imperative. The order was given, and away we went, helter-skelter—guns, gun-detachments, and hussars all mixed *pêle-mêle*, going like mad, and covering each other with mud, to be washed off by the rain, which, before sufficiently heavy, now came down again as it had done at first in splashes instead of drops, soaking us anew to the skin, and, what was worse, extinguishing every slow-match in the brigade. The obscurity caused by the splashing of the rain was such, that at one period I could not distinguish objects more than a few yards distant. Of course we lost sight of our pursuers altogether, and the shouts and halloos, and even laughter, they had at first sent forth were either silenced or drowned in the uproar of the elements and the noise of our too rapid retreat; for in addition to everything else the crashing and rattling of the thunder were most awful, and the glare of the lightning blinding. In this state we gained the bridge of Genappe at the moment when the thundercloud, having passed over, left us in comparative fine weather, although still raining heavily.

The town of Genappe stands on the slope of a hill rising immediately from the little verdant valley through which the Lys flows—here little better than a brook. Arrived at the bridge, we slackened our pace, and ascended leisurely the narrow winding street, in which not a living soul was visible. The shutters were all closed, and stream of water pouring from the roofs formed a perfect torrent of the gutter running down the middle of it. This solitude was rather a disappointment, for I had hoped here to have got fire to relight our slow-match.

For the last mile or so we had neither seen nor heard anything of our lively French friends, and now silently wound our way up the deserted street, nothing disturbing its death-like stillness save the iron sound of horses' feet, the rumbling of the carriages, and the splashing of water as it fell from the eaves,—all this was stillness compared with the hurly-burly and din from which we had just emerged.

On gaining the high ground beyond the town, we suddenly came in sight of the main body of our cavalry drawn up across the chaussée in two lines, and extending away far to the right and left of it.

It would have been an imposing spectacle at any time, but just now appeared to me magnificent, and I hailed it with complacency, for here I thought our fox-chase must end. " Those superb Life

Guards and Blues will soon teach our pursuers a little modesty." Such fellows!—surely nothing can withstand them. Scarcely had these thoughts passed through my mind ere an order from his lordship recalled us to the rear. On debouching from the town, seeing nothing in the country right and left of us, and fearful of impeding the retreat, whilst our hussars retired skirmishing through the street (the French having again come up), we had continued onward to gain the position occupied by our heavy cavalry, from which we were still separated by a small dip of the ground. We returned then to the end of the town, where the flight of shot and shells over us (the road was here sunk between two high banks) gave very intelligible information as to the reason of our recall. The enemy's horse-artillery, having taken up a position in the meadows near the bridge, were annoying our dragoons as they debouched from the town. The ground was heavy from the rain, and very steep, so that it was only by great exertion that we succeeded at last in getting our guns into the adjoining field. The moment we appeared the French battery bestowed on us its undivided attention, which we quickly acknowledged by an uncommonly well-directed fire of spherical case. Whilst so employed, Major

M'Donald came up and put me through a regular catechism as to length of fuze, whether out of bag A or B, &c. &c. Although much vexed at such a schooling just now, yet the Major appeared so seriously in earnest that I could not but be amused; however, to convince him we knew what we were about, I directed his attention to our excellent practice, so superior to that of our antagonist, who was sending all his shot far over our heads. The French seemed pretty well convinced of this too, for after standing a few rounds they quitted the field, and left us again without occupation. The Major vanishing at the same time, I sent my guns, &c., to the rear, and set off to join Lord Uxbridge, who was still fighting in the street. Our ammunition was expended, the waggons having been taken away by Sir Augustus Frazer at Quatre Bras.

On regaining my troop, I found Major M'Donald and the rockets with it. They were in position on a gentle elevation, on which likewise were formed the lines of cavalry extending across the chaussée. Immediately on our left, encased in the hollow road, the Blues were formed in close column of half-squadrons, and it was not long ere Lord Uxbridge, with those he had retained at Genappe, came sweeping over the hill and joined us. They were closely followed by the French light cavalry, who, descending into the hollow, commenced a sharp skirmish with our advanced-posts. Soon squadron after squadron appeared on the hill we had passed, and took up their positions, forming a long line parallel to ours, whilst a battery of horse-artillery, forming across the chaussée, just on the brow of the declivity, opened its fire on us, though without much effect. To this we responded, though very slowly, having no more ammunition than what remained in our limbers. In order to amuse the enemy and our own cavalry, as well as to prevent the former noticing the slackness of our fire, I proposed to Major M'Donald making use of the rockets, which had hitherto done nothing. There was a little hesitation about this, and one of the officers (Strangways) whispered me, "No, no—it's too far!" This I immediately told the Major, proposing as a remedy that they should go closer. Still there was demur; but at last my proposition was agreed to, and down they marched into the thick of the skirmishers in the bottom. Of course, having proposed the measure myself, I could do no less than accompany them. Whilst they prepared their machinery, I had time to notice what was going on to the right and left of us. Two double lines of skirmishers extended all along the bottom—the foremost of each line were within a few yards of each other—constantly in motion, riding backwards and forwards, firing their carbines or pistols, and then reloading, still on the move. This fire seemed to me more dangerous for those on the hills above than for us below; for all, both French and English, generally stuck out their carbines or pistols as they continued to move backwards and forwards, and discharged them without taking any particular aim, and mostly in the air. I did not see a man fall on either side; the thing appeared quite ridiculous; and but for hearing the bullets whizzing overhead, one might have fancied it no more than a sham-fight.

Meanwhile the rocketeers had placed a little iron triangle in the road with a rocket lying on it. The order to fire is given—portfire applied— the fidgety missile begins to sputter out sparks and wriggle its tail for a second or so, and then darts forth straight up the chaussée. A gun stands right in its way, between the wheels of which the shell in the head of the rocket bursts, the gunners fall right and left, and, those of the other guns taking to their heels, the battery is deserted in an instant. Strange; but so it was.

I saw them run, and for some minutes afterwards I saw the guns standing mute and unmanned, whilst our rocketeers kept shooting off rockets, none of which ever followed the course of the first; most of them, on arriving about the middle of the ascent, took a vertical direction, whilst some actually turned back upon ourselves—and one of these, following me like a squib until its shell exploded, actually put me in more danger than all the fire of the enemy throughout the day. Meanwhile the French artillerymen, seeing how the land lay, returned to their guns and opened a fire of case-shot on us, but without effect, for we retreated to our ridge without the loss of a man, or even any wounded, though the range could not have been above 200 yards. As we had overtaken the rear of our infantry, it became necessary to make a stand here to enable them to gain ground. Major M'Donald therefore sent me in pursuit of my ammunition-waggons, since all in our limbers was expended. Having before sent for these, we calculated that they could not now be very far off. In going to the rear I passed along the top of the bank, under which, as I have said, the Blues were encased in the hollow road. Shot and shells were flying pretty thickly about just then, and, sometimes striking the top of the bank, would send down a shower of mud and clods upon them.

The ammunition-waggons I found coming up, and was returning with them when I met my whole troop again retiring by the road, whilst the cavalry did so by alternate regiments across the fields. The ground offering no feature for another stand, we continued thus along the road. The infantry had made so little progress that we again overtook the rear of their column, composed of Brunswickers—some of those same boys I used to see practising at Schäpdale in my rides to Brussels. These poor lads were pushing on at a great rate. As soon as their rear divisions heard the sound of our horses' feet, without once looking behind them, they began to crowd and press on those in front, until at last, hearing us close up to them, and finding it impossible to push forward in the road, many of them broke off into the fields; and such was their panic that, in order to run lighter, away went arms and knapsacks in all directions, and a general race ensued, the whole corps being in the most horrid confusion. It was to no purpose that I exerted my little stock of German to make them understand we were their English friends—a frightened glance and away, was all the effect of my interference, which drove many of them off. We, however, still kept on our way, and soon after passed a few houses by the roadside, which I afterwards found was La Belle Alliance. Hence we crossed another valley, and on rising the opposite hill I found a capital position on the top of an old gravel-pit, which I occupied without loss of time. Behind the ground on which my guns were formed was a long hedge * (a *rara avis* in this country), which prevented our seeing anything beyond; and as no troops were in sight except those following us across the valley, we had then no idea that we had arrived in the position where our whole army was assembled, nor that we then stood upon ground which, ere to morrow's sun were set, would for ever be celebrated throughout all generations!

We did not long remain idle, for the guns were scarcely loaded ere the rear of our cavalry came crowding upon the infantry corps we had passed, and which were then only crossing the valley, the French advance skirmishing with these, whilst their squadrons occupied the heights. We waited a little until some of their larger masses were assembled, and then opened our fire with a range across the valley of about 1200 yards. The echo

* This was the spot where Picton fell on the morrow, and in this hedge was the so well-known Wellington Tree.

of our first gun had not ceased, when, to my astonishment, a heavy cannonade, commencing in a most startling manner from behind our hedge, rolled along the rising-ground, on part of which we were posted. The truth now flashed on me; we had rejoined the army, and it is impossible to describe the pleasing sense of security I felt at having now the support of something more stanch than cavalry.

The French now brought up battery after battery, and a tremendous cannonading was kept up by both sides for some time. The effect was grand and exciting. Our position was a happy one, for all their shot which grazed short, came and struck in the perpendicular bank of our gravel-pit—and only one struck amongst us, breaking the traversing handspike at one of the guns, but neither injuring man nor horse. Our fire was principally directed against their masses as we we could see them, which was not always the case from the smoke that, for want of wind, hung over them; then against their smaller parties that had advanced into the valley to skirmish with the rear-guard of our cavalry. Here for the second and last time I saw Napoleon, though infinitely more distant than in the morning. Some of my non-commissioned officers pointed their guns at the numerous cortège accompanying him as they stood near the road by Belle Alliance; and one, pointed by old Quartermaster Hall, fell in the midst of them. At the moment we saw some little confusion amongst the group, but it did not hinder them from continuing the reconnaissance.

Whilst we were thus engaged, a man of no very prepossessing appearance came rambling amongst our guns, and entered into conversation with me on the occurrences of the day. He was dressed in a shabby old drab greatcoat and a rusty round hat. I took him at the time for some amateur from Brussels (of whom we had heard there were several hovering about), and thinking many of his questions rather impertinent, was somewhat short in answering him, and he soon left us. How great was my astonishment on learning soon after that this was Sir Thomas Picton! The enemy, finding us obstinate in maintaining our position, soon slackened, and then ceased firing altogether; and we were immediately ordered to do the same, and establish ourselves in bivouac for the night. This we proceeded to obey as a most welcome order, and retiring from our position down the hill, came to a large farm, where, breaking through a quickset hedge, we formed our park in the adjoining orchard, preferring its green turf to the plashy, muddy fields around, that morning covered with fine crops of wheat, now little better than sloughs. We were not long, however, in discovering that it was only exchanging the frying-pan for the fire, since our smiling turf was nearly ankle-deep in water, the orchard lying low and hollow, somewhat below the level of the road. But it was already growing dark, consequently too late to hunt out another, so we were obliged to put up with it.

Thoroughly wet—cloaks, blankets, and all—comfort was out of the question, so we prepared to make the best of it.

Our first care was of course the horses, and these we had ample means of providing for, since, in addition to what corn we had left, one of our men had picked up and brought forward on an ammunition waggon a large sack full, which he found in the road near Genappe. Thus they, at least, had plenty to eat, and having been so well drenched all day, were not much in need of water. For ourselves we had nothing!—absolutely nothing! and looked forward to rest alone to restore our exhausted strength. Rather a bore going supperless to bed after such a day, yet was there no help for it.

But our poor animals were not all of them destined to repose, and much as they had undergone during the last six-and-thirty hours, some of them were yet obliged to pass the night on the road, and in harness. Completing our limbers with ammunition from two of the ammunition waggons, a non-commissioned officer was despatched with these, as soon as the horses had been fed, to Langeveldt near Brussels, where Sir Augustus Frazer had told me in the morning we should find a depôt from whence to supply what had been expended during the day.

These cared for, came the care of ourselves. Our gunners, &c., soon stowed themselves away beneath the carriages, using the painted covers as additional shelter against the rain, which now set in again as heavy as ever. We set up a small tent, into which (after vain attempts at procuring food or lodgings in the farm or its outbuildings, all of which were crammed to suffocation with officers and soldiers of all arms and nations) we crept, and rolling ourselves in our wet blankets, huddled close together, in hope, wet as we were, and wet as the ground was, of keeping each other warm. I know not how my bedfellows got on, as we all

lay for a long while perfectly still and silent—
the old Peninsular hands disdaining to complain
before their Johnny Newcome comrades, and these
fearing to do so lest they should provoke some
such remarks, as " Lord have mercy on your poor
tender carcass! what would such as you have
done in the Pyrenees?" or "Oho, my boy! this
is but child's play to what *we* saw in Spain." So
all who did not sleep (I believe the majority)
pretended to do so, and bore their suffering with
admirable heroism. For my part, I once or twice,
from sheer fatigue, got into something like a doze;
yet it would not do. There was no possibility of
sleeping, for besides being already so wet, the tent
proved no shelter, the water pouring through the
canvas in streams; so up I got, and, to my infinite joy, found that some of the men had managed
to make a couple of fires, round which they were
sitting smoking their short pipes in something
like comfort. The hint was a good one, and at
that moment my second captain joining me, we
borrowed from them a few sticks, and choosing
the best spot under the hedge, proceeded to make
a fire for ourselves. In a short time we succeeded in raising a cheerful blaze, which materially
bettered our situation. My companion had an
umbrella (which, by the way, had afforded some

merriment to our people on the march); this we planted against the sloping bank of the hedge, and seating ourselves under it, he on one side of the stick, me on the other, we lighted cigars and became — comfortable. Dear weed! what comfort, what consolation dost thou not impart to the wretched!—with thee a hovel becomes a palace. What a stock of patience is there not enveloped in one of thy brown leaves! And thus we sat enjoying ourselves, puffing forth into the damp night air streams of fragrant smoke, being able now deliberately to converse on what had been, and probably would be. All this time a most infernal clatter of musketry was going on, which, but for the many quiet dark figures seated round the innumerable fires all along the position, might have been construed into a night-attack. But as these gentlemen were between us and the enemy, we felt assured of timely warning, and ere long learned that all this proceeded as before from the infantry discharging and cleaning their pieces. Our conversation naturally turned on our present position; and after discussing all the pros. and cons., we made up our minds to recommence the retreat with to-morrow's sun; but when that retreat was to terminate, baffled all our powers of conjecture.

Whilst so employed, a rustling in the hedge behind attracted our attention, and in a few minutes a poor fellow belonging to some Hanoverian regiment, wet through like everybody else, and shivering with cold, made his appearance, and modestly begged permission to remain a short time and warm himself by our fire. He had somehow or other wandered from his colours, and had passed the greater part of the night searching for them, but in vain. At first he appeared quite exhausted, but the warmth reinvigorating him, he pulled out his pipe and began to smoke. Having finished his modicum, and carefully disposed of the ashes, he rose from his wet seat to renew his search, hoping to find his corps before daylight, he said, lest it should be engaged. Many thanks he offered for our hospitality; but what was our surprise when, after fumbling in his havresack for some time, he pulled out a poor half-starved chicken, presented it to us, and marched off. This was a god-send, in good truth, to people famished as we were; so calling for a camp-kettle, our prize was on the fire in a twinkling. Our comrades in the tent did not sleep so soundly but that they heard what was going on, and the kettle was hardly on the fire ere my gentlemen were assembled round it, a wet and shivering group, but all eager to partake of our good fortune—and so eager that, after various betrayals of impatience, the miserable chicken was at last snatched from the kettle ere it was half-boiled, pulled to pieces, and speedily devoured. I got a leg for my share, but it was not one mouthful, and this was the only food I tasted since the night before.

CHAPTER XIII.

June 18*th*.—Memorable day! Some time before daybreak the bombardier who had been despatched to Langeveldt returned with a supply of ammunition. He reported that he had been much impeded by the confusion on the road, which was everywhere crowded with waggons, &c. Many he had seen overturned, and many plundered, or being plundered; but his account by no means justified those who stated the road to be blocked up in such a manner as to be impassable. Indeed, considering all things, he had performed his journey in sufficiently reasonable time.

With the providence of an old soldier, he had picked up and brought on a considerable quantity of beef, biscuit, and oatmeal, of which there was abundance scattered about everywhere. Casks of rum, &c., there were, and having broached one of these—he and his drivers—every one filled his canteen — a most considerate act, and one for which the whole troop was sincerely thankful. Nor must I omit to remark that, amidst such temptations, his men had behaved with the most perfect regularity, and returned to us *quite sober!*

The rum was divided on the spot; and surely if ardent spirits are ever beneficial, it must be to men situated as ours were; it therefore came most providentially. The oatmeal was converted speedily into stirabout, and afforded our people a hearty meal, after which all hands set to work to prepare the beef, make soup, &c. Unfortunately, we preferred waiting for this, and passed the stirabout, by which piece of folly we were doomed to a very protracted fast, as will be seen. Whilst our soup was cooking, it being now broad daylight, I mounted my horse to reconnoitre our situation. During the night another troop (I think Major Ramsay's) had established itself in our orchard, and just outside the hedge I found Major Bean's, which had also arrived during the night, direct from England. Ascending from the farm towards the ground we had left yesterday evening, the face of the slope, as far as I could see, to the right and left, was covered with troops *en bivouac*—here, I think, principally cavalry. Of these some were cleaning their arms, some cooking, some sitting round fires smoking, and a few, generally officers, walking about, or standing in groups conversing. Many of the latter eagerly inquired where I was going, and appeared very anxious for intelligence, all expecting nothing less than to recommence our retreat. I continued on to the position we had occupied last, and thence clearly saw the French army on the opposite hill, where everything appeared perfectly quiet—people moving about individually, and no formation whatever. Their advanced-posts and vedettes in the valley, just beyond La Haye Sainte, were also quiet. Having satisfied my curiosity, I returned the way I came, communicating my observations to the many eager inquirers I met with. Various were the speculations in consequence. Some thought the French were afraid to attack us, others that they would do so soon, others that the Duke would not wait for it, others that he would, as he certainly would not allow them to go to Brussels; and so they went on speculating, whilst I returned to my people. Here, finding the mess not yet ready, and nothing to be done, I strolled into the garden of the farm, where several Life Guardsmen were very busy digging potatoes—a fortunate discovery, which I determined to profit by. Therefore calling up some of my men, to work we went without loss of time.

Whilst thus employed, I noticed a very heavy firing going on in front, but this did not make us quit our work. Shortly after, to my great astonishment, I observed that all the bivouacs on the hillside were deserted, and that even Ramsay's troop had left the orchard without my being aware of it, and my own was left quite alone, not a soul being visible from where I stood in any direction, the ground they had quitted presenting one unbroken muddy solitude. The firing became heavier and heavier. Alarmed at being thus left alone, when it was evident something serious was going on, I hastened back and ordered the horses to be put to immediately.

Away went our mess untasted. One of the servants was desired to hang the kettle with its contents under an ammunition-waggon. The stupid fellow hung the kettle as desired, but first emptied it. Without orders, and all alone, the battle (for now there was no mistaking it) going on at the other side of the hill, I remained for a few minutes undecided what to do. It appeared to me we had been forgotten. All, except only ourselves, were evidently engaged; and labouring under this delusion, I thought we had better get into the affair at once. As soon, therefore, as the troop was ready, I led them up the hill on the highroad, hoping to meet some one who could give me directions what to do. We had not proceeded a hundred yards, when an artillery officer came furiously galloping down towards us. It was Major M'Lloyd, in a dreadful state of agitation—such, indeed, that he could hardly answer my questions. I learned, however, that the battle was very serious and bloody. Their first attack had been on that part of our position where his battery stood; but now the principal efforts were making against our right. All this was told in so hurried and anxious a manner, that one could hardly understand him. "But where are you going?" he added. I told him my plan. "Have you no orders?" "None whatever; I have not seen a soul." "Then, for God's sake, come and assist me, or I shall be ruined. My brigade is cut to pieces, ammunition expended, and, unless reinforced, we shall be destroyed." He was dreadfully agitated, and when I took his hand and promised to be with him directly, seemed transported with joy; so, bidding me make haste, he darted up the hill again, and went to receive that death-stroke which, ere long, was to terminate his earthly career. I trust before that termination he heard the reason why I never fulfilled that promise; for weeks elapsed ere he died, no doubt—otherwise he must have set me down for a base poltroon. My destiny led me elsewhere. My tutelary spirit was at hand: the eternal Major M'Donald made his appearance, and, giving me a sharp reprimand for having quitted my bivouac, desired me instantly to return to the foot of the hill, and there wait for orders. Sulkily and slowly we descended, and forming in line on the ground opposite the farm of Mont St Jean, with our left to the road, I dismounted the men that they might be a little less liable to be hit by shot and shells which, coming over the hill, were continually plunging into the muddy soil all around us. This was a peculiarly dismal situation—without honour or glory, to be knocked on the head in such a solitude, for not a living being was in sight.

It was while thus standing idle that a fine tall upright old gentleman, in plain clothes, followed by two young ones, came across our front at a gallop from the Brussels road, and continued on towards where we supposed the right of our army to be. I certainly stared at seeing three unarmed civilians pressing forward into so hot a fight. These were the Duke of Richmond and his two sons. How long we had been in this position, I know not, when at length we were relieved from it by our adjutant (Lieutenant Bell), who brought orders for our removal to the right of the second line. Moving, therefore, to our right, along the hollow, we soon began a very gentle ascent, and at the same time became aware of several corps of infantry, which had not been very far from us, but remained invisible, as they were all lying down. Although in this move we may be said to have been always under a heavy fire, from the number of missiles flying over us, yet were we still so fortunate as to arrive in our new position without losing man or horse. In point of seeing, our situation was much improved; but for danger and inactivity, it was much worse, since we were now fired directly at, and positively ordered not to return the compliment—the object in bringing us here being to watch a most formidable-looking line of lancers drawn up opposite to us, and threatening the right flank of our army. A scientific relation of this great struggle, on which the fate of Europe hinged, I pretend not to write. I write neither history, nor 'Memoires pour servir à l'Histoire,' &c. &c., but only pure simple gossip for my own amusement—just what happened to me and mine, and what I *did* see happen to others about me.

Depend upon it, he who pretends to give a general account of a great battle from his own observation deceives you—believe him not. He can see no further (that is, if he be personally engaged in it) than the length of his nose; and how is he to tell what is passing two or three miles off, with hills and trees and buildings intervening, and all enveloped in smoke? Busaco might have been tolerably described, but there are no Busacos in the Pays Bas. The back of the principal ridge on which our army was posted descended by a pretty regular slope in the direction of Waterloo, and but just in rear of its right another shorter and lower ridge ran a little way almost parallel to it. The highroad to Nivelle passed along the hollow between the two. Both ridges terminated in a ravine that enclosed our right flank, running down from the Château de Hougoumont (although it be pretended now that the name is "Goumont," I persist in the orthography which is found in all the old maps of this department) in the direction of Merke Braine; in short, a contracted continuation of the greater valley lying between the two armies and nearly at right angles to it.

The sides of this ravine (much steeper than any other ground near), as far as I can recollect, were partially covered with bushes; and, from the summit of the one opposite to us, the ground ascended by a very gradual slope for about 800 or 1000 yards; and there, on what appeared as the height of the land, there were several small clumps of wood. This slope itself was still covered with fine crops of standing corn. The crest was occupied by the long line of lancers already spoken of, whose movements I was ordered to watch, but on no account to interfere with, unless they attempted to pass the ravine.* Such was our front view.

To the right we looked over a fine open country, covered with crops and interspersed with thickets or small woods. There all was peaceful and smiling, not a living soul being in sight. To our left, the main ridge terminated rather abruptly just over Hougoumont, the back of it towards us being broken ground, with a few old trees on it just where the Nivelle road descended between high banks into the ravine. Thus we were formed *en potence* with the 1st line, from which we (my battery) were separated by some

---

* The light cavalry of the 2d Corps formed in three lines across the causeway from Nivelle, &c., nearly at the height of the first woods at Hougoumont, scouring all the plain by the left, and having main guards near Braine le Leude, and its battery of light artillery on the causeway of Nivelle.—'Memoir of Napoleon,' lib. ix. cap. vi. p. 134; O'Meara's Translation.

hundred yards. In our rear the 14th Regiment of infantry (in square, I think) lay on the ground. In our front were some light dragoons of the German Legion, who from time to time detached small parties across the ravine. These pushed cautiously up the slope towards the line of lancers to reconnoitre. The corn, down to the edge of the ravine nearer the Nivelle road and beyond it, was full of French riflemen; and these were warmly attacked by others* from our side of the ravine, whom we saw crossing and gradually working their way up through the high corn, the French as gradually retiring. On the right of the lancers, two or three batteries kept up a continued fire at our position; but their shot, which could have been only 4-pounders, fell short—many not even reaching across the ravine. Some, however, did reach their destination; and we were particularly plagued by their howitzer shells with long fuses, which were continually falling about us, and lay spitting and sputtering several seconds before they exploded, to the no small annoyance of man and horse. Still, however, nobody was hurt; but a round-shot, striking the ammunition-boxes on the body of one of our waggons, penetrated through both and lodged in the back of the rear

* I believe Jägers of the Hanoverian corps.

one, with nearly half its surface to be seen from without—a singular circumstance! In addition to this front fire, we were exposed to another on our left flank—the shot that passed over the main ridge terminating their career with us. Having little to occupy us here, we had ample leisure to observe what was passing there. We could see some corps at the end near us in squares—dark masses, having guns between them, relieved from a background of grey smoke, which seemed to fill the valley beyond, and rose high in the air above the hill. Every now and then torrents of French cavalry of all arms came sweeping over the ridge, as if carrying all before them. But, after their passage, the squares were still to be seen in the same places; and these gentry, who we feared would next fall on us, would evaporate, nobody could well say how. The firing still increased in intensity, so that we were at a loss to conjecture what all this could mean.

About this time, being impatient of standing idle, and annoyed by the batteries on the Nivelle road, I ventured to commit a folly, for which I should have paid dearly had our Duke chanced to be in our part of the field. I ventured to disobey orders, and open a slow deliberate fire at the battery, thinking with my 9-pounders soon to silence his 4-pounders. My astonishment was great, however, when our very first gun was responded to by at least half-a-dozen gentlemen of very superior calibre, whose presence I had not even suspected, and whose superiority we immediately recognised by their rushing noise and long reach, for they flew far beyond us. I instantly saw my folly, and ceased firing, and they did the same—the 4-pounders alone continuing the cannonade as before. But this was not all. The first man of my troop touched was by one of these confounded long shot. I shall never forget the scream the poor lad gave when struck. It was one of the last they fired, and shattered his left arm to pieces as he stood between the waggons. That scream went to my very soul, for I accused myself as having caused his misfortune. I was, however, obliged to conceal my emotion from the men, who had turned to look at him; so, bidding them "stand to their front," I continued my walk up and down, whilst Hitchins ran to his assistance.

Amidst such stirring scenes, emotions of this kind are but of short duration; what occurred immediately afterwards completely banished Gunner Hunt from my recollection. As a counterbalance to this tragical event, our firing produced

AN ALARMED DOCTOR. 303

one so comic as to excite all our risibility. Two or three officers had lounged up to our guns to see the effect. One of them was a medico, and *he* (a shower having just come on) carried an umbrella overhead. No sooner did the heavy answers begin to arrive amongst us than these gentlemen, fancying they should be safer with their own corps, although only a few yards in the rear, scampered off in double-quick, doctor and all, he still carrying his umbrella aloft. Scarcely, however, had he made two paces when a shot, as he thought, passing rather too close, down he dropped on his hands and knees—or, I should rather say, hand and knees, for the one was employed in holding the silken cover most pertinaciously over him—and away he scrambled like a great baboon, his head turned fearfully over his shoulder, as if watching the coming shot, whilst our fellows made the field resound with their shouts and laughter.

I think I have already mentioned that it was not until some days afterwards that I was able to resume my regular journal, consequently that everything relative to these three days is written from memory. In trying to recollect scenes of this nature, some little confusion is inevitable; and here I confess myself somewhat puzzled to account for certain facts of which I am positive. For instance, I remember perfectly Captain Bolton's brigade of 9-pounders being stationed to the left of us, somewhat in advance, and facing as we did, consequently not far from the Nivelle road. Bolton came and conversed with me some time, and was called hastily away by his battery commencing a heavy fire. Query—Who, and what, was he firing at? That he was himself under a heavy fire there is equally no doubt, for whilst we were not losing a man, we saw many, both of his men and horses, fall, and but a few minutes after leaving me, he was killed himself—this is a puzzle. I have no recollection of any troops attempting to cross the ravine, and yet his fire was in that direction, and I think must have been toward the Nivelle road. A distressing circumstance connected with this (shall I confess it?) made even more impression on my spirits than the misfortune of Gunner Hunt. Bolton's people had not been long engaged when we saw the men of the gun next to us unharness one of the horses and chase it away, wounded, I supposed; yet the beast stood and moved with firmness, going from one carriage to the other, whence I noticed he was always eagerly driven away. At last two or three gunners drove him before them to a considerable distance, and then returned to their guns. I took little notice of this at the time, and was surprised by an exclamation of horror from some of my people in the rear. A sickening sensation came over me, mixed with a deep feeling of pity, when within a few paces of me stood the poor horse in question, side by side with the leaders of one of our ammunition waggons, against which he pressed his panting sides, as though eager to identify himself as of their society—the driver, with horror depicted on every feature, endeavouring by words and gestures (for the kind-hearted lad could not strike) to drive from him so hideous a spectacle. A cannon-shot had completely carried away the lower part of the animal's head, immediately below the eyes. Still he lived, and seemed fully conscious of all around, whilst his full, clear eye seemed to implore us not to chase him from his companions. I ordered the farrier (Price) to put him out of misery, which, in a few minutes, he reported having accomplished, by running his sabre into the animal's heart. Even *he* evinced feeling on this occasion. Meantime the roar of cannon and musketry in the main position never slackened; it was intense, as was the smoke arising from it. Amidst this, from time to time, was to be seen still more dense columns of smoke rising straight into the air like a great pillar, then spreading out a mushroom - head. These arose from the explosions of ammunition waggons, which were continually taking place, although the noise which filled the whole atmosphere was too overpowering to allow them to be heard.

Amongst the multitudes of French cavalry continually pouring over the front ridge, one corps came sweeping down the slope entire, and was directing its course straight for us, when suddenly a regiment of light dragoons (I believe of the German Legion) came up from the ravine at a brisk trot on their flank. The French had barely time to wheel up to the left and push their horses into a gallop, when the two bodies came in collison. They were at a very short distance from us, so that we saw the charge perfectly. There was no check, no hesitation, on either side; both parties seemed to dash on in a most reckless manner, and we fully expected to have seen a horrid crash—no such thing! Each, as if by mutual consent, opened their files on coming near, and passed rapidly through each other, cutting and pointing, much in the same manner one might pass the fingers of the right hand through those of the left. We saw but few fall.

The two corps re-formed afterwards, and in a twinkling both disappeared, I know not how or where. It might have been about two o'clock when Colonel Gould, R.A., came to me, perhaps a little later. Be that as it may, we were conversing on the subject of our situation, which appeared to him rather desperate. He remarked that in the event of a retreat, there was but one road, which no doubt would be instantly choked up, and asked my opinion. My answer was, "It does indeed look very bad; but I trust in the Duke, who, I am sure, will get us out of it somehow or other." Meantime gloomy reflections arose in my mind, for though I did not choose to betray myself (as we spoke before the men), yet I could not help thinking that our affairs *were* rather desperate, and that some unfortunate catastrophe was at hand. In this case I made up my mind to spike my guns and retreat over the fields, draught-horses and all, in the best manner I could, steering well from the highroad and general line of retreat.

We were still talking on this subject, when suddenly a dark mass of cavalry appeared for an instant on the main ridge, and then came sweeping down the slope in swarms, reminding me of an enormous surf bursting over the prostrate hull of a stranded vessel, and then running, hissing and foaming, up the beach. The hollow space became in a twinkling covered with horsemen, crossing, turning, and riding about in all directions, apparently without any object. Sometimes they came pretty near us, then would retire a little. There were lancers amongst them, hussars, and dragoons—it was a complete *mêlée*. On the main ridge no squares were to be seen; the only objects were a few guns standing in a confused manner, with muzzles in the air, and not one artilleryman. After caracoling about for a few minutes, the crowd began to separate and draw together in small bodies, which continually increased; and now we really apprehended being overwhelmed, as the first line had apparently been. For a moment an awful silence pervaded that part of the position to which we anxiously turned our eyes. "I fear all is over," said Colonel Gould, who still remained by me. The thing seemed but too likely, and this time I could not withhold my assent to his remark, for it did indeed appear so. Meantime the 14th, springing from the earth, had formed their square, whilst we, throwing back the guns of our right and left divisions, stood waiting in momentary expectation of being enveloped and attacked. Still they

DANGEROUS MISTAKE. 309

lingered in the hollow, when suddenly loud and repeated shouts (not English hurrahs) drew our attention to the other side. There we saw two dense columns of infantry pushing forward at a quick pace towards us, crossing the fields, as if they had come from Merke Braine. Every one, both of the 14th and ourselves, pronounced them French, yet still we delayed opening fire on them. Shouting, yelling, and singing, on they came, right for us; and being now not above 800 or 1000 yards distant, it seemed folly allowing them to come nearer unmolested. The commanding officer of the 14th, to end our doubts, rode forward and endeavoured to ascertain who they were, but soon returned, assuring us they were French. The order was already given to fire, when, luckily, Colonel Gould recognised them as Belgians. Meantime, whilst my attention was occupied by these people, the cavalry had all vanished, nobody could say how or where.

We breathed again. Such was the agitated state in which we were kept in our second position. A third act was about to commence of a much more stirring and active nature.

It might have been, as nearly as I can recollect, about three P.M., when Sir Augustus Frazer galloped up, crying out, "Left limber up, and as fast as you can." The words were scarcely uttered when my gallant troop stood as desired in column of subdivisions, left in front, pointing towards the main ridge. "At a gallop, march!" and away we flew, as steadily and compactly as if at a review. I rode with Frazer, whose face was as black as a chimney-sweep's from the smoke, and the jacket-sleeve of his right arm torn open by a musket-ball or case-shot, which had merely grazed his flesh. As we went along, he told me that the enemy had assembled an enormous mass of heavy cavalry in front of the point to which he was leading us (about one-third of the distance between Hougoumont and the Charleroi road), and that in all probability we should immediately be charged on gaining our position. "*The Duke's orders, however, are positive,*" he added, "*that in the event of their persevering and charging home, you do not expose your men, but retire with them into the adjacent squares of infantry.*" As he spoke, we were ascending the reverse slope of the main position. We breathed a new atmosphere—the air was suffocatingly hot, resembling that issuing from an oven. We were enveloped in thick smoke, and, *malgré* the incessant roar of cannon and musketry, could distinctly hear around us a mysterious humming noise, like that which one hears of a summer's evening proceeding from myriads of black beetles; cannon-shot, too, ploughed the ground in all directions, and so thick was the hail of balls and bullets that it seemed dangerous to extend the arm lest it should be torn off. In spite of the serious situation in which we were, I could not help being somewhat amused at the astonishment expressed by our kind-hearted surgeon (Hitchins), who heard for the first time this sort of music. He was close to me as we ascended the slope, and, hearing this infernal *carillon* about his ears, began staring round in the wildest and most comic manner imaginable, twisting himself from side to side, exclaiming, " My God, Mercer, what *is* that ? What *is* all this noise ? How curious!—how very curious!" And then when a cannon-shot rushed hissing past, " *There!—there!* What *is* it all ?" It was with great difficulty that I persuaded him to retire : for a time he insisted on remaining near me, and it was only by pointing out how important it was to us, in case of being wounded, that he should keep himself safe to be able to assist us, that I prevailed on him to withdraw. Amidst this storm we gained the summit of the ridge, strange to say, without a casualty; and Sir Augustus, pointing out our position between two squares of Brunswick infantry, left us with injunctions to remember the Duke's order, and to enconomise our ammunition. The Brunswickers were falling fast—the shot every moment making great gaps in their squares, which the officers and sergeants were actively employed in filling up by pushing their men together, and sometimes thumping them ere they could make them move. These were the very boys whom I had but yesterday seen throwing away their arms, and fleeing, panicstricken, from the very sound of our horses' feet. To-day they fled not bodily, to be sure, but spiritually, for their senses seemed to have left them. There they stood, with recovered arms, like so many logs, or rather like the very wooden figures which I had seen them practising at in their cantonments. Every moment I feared they would again throw down their arms and flee; but their officers and sergeants behaved nobly, not only keeping them together, but managing to keep their squares closed in spite of the carnage made amongst them. To have sought refuge amongst men in such a state were madness—the very moment our men ran from their guns, I was convinced, would be the signal for their disbanding.

We had better, then, fall at our posts than in such a situation. Our coming up seemed to re-animate them, and all their eyes were directed to us—indeed, it was providential, for, had we not arrived as we did, I scarcely think there is a doubt of what would have been their fate.* Our first gun had scarcely gained the interval between their squares, when I saw through the smoke the leading squadrons of the advancing column coming on at a brisk trot, and already not more than one hundred yards distant, if so much, for I don't think we could have seen so far. I immediately ordered the line to be formed

---

* One day, on the Marine Parade at Woolwich, a battalion coming up in close column at the double march, Lieutenant-Colonel Brown, who stood near me, remarked, "That puts me in mind of your troop coming up at Waterloo, when you *saved* the Brunswickers." Until this moment I never knew that our having done so had been remarked by anybody; but he assured me it was known to the whole army; and yet the Duke not only withheld that praise which was our due, but refused me the brevet rank of major; and, more than that, actually deprived me of that troop given to me by Lord Mulgrave, the then Master-General, *for* that action, as recommended by my commanding officer, Sir G. Adams Wood.

That the Duke was not ignorant of their danger I have from Captain Baynes, our Brigade-Major, who told me that after Sir Augustus Frazer had been sent for us, his Grace exhibited considerable anxiety for our coming up; and that when he saw us crossing the fields at a gallop, and in so compact a body, he actually cried out, "Ah! that's the way I like to see horse-artillery move." Another proof.

for action—*case-shot!* and the leading gun was unlimbered and commenced firing almost as soon as the word was given: for activity and intelligence our men were unrivalled. The very first round, I saw, brought down several men and horses. They continued, however, to advance. I glanced at the Brunswickers, and that glance told me it would not do; they had opened a fire from their front faces, but both squares appeared too unsteady, and I resolved to say nothing about the Duke's order, and take our chance—a resolve that was strengthened by the effect of the remaining guns as they rapidly succeeded in coming to action, making terrible slaughter, and in an instant covering the ground with men and horses. Still they persevered in approaching us (the first round had brought them to a walk), though slowly, and it did seem they would ride over us. We were a little below the level of the ground on which they moved—having in front of us a bank of about a foot and a-half or two feet high, along the top of which ran a narrow road—and this gave more effect to our case-shot, all of which almost must have taken effect, for the carnage was frightful.* I suppose this state of

* The following extract, from a related account of a conscript, translated from the French and published by Murray, is so true

things occupied but a few seconds, when I observed symptoms of hesitation, and in a twinkling, at the instant I thought it was all over with us, they turned to either flank and filed away rapidly to the rear. Retreat of the mass, however, was not so easy. Many facing about and trying to force their way through the body of the column, that part next to us became a complete mob, into which we kept a steady fire of caseshot from our six pieces. The effect is hardly conceivable, and to paint this scene of slaughter and confusion impossible. Every discharge was followed by the fall of numbers, whilst the survivors struggled with each other, and I actually saw them using the pommels of their swords to fight their way out of the *mêlée*. Some, rendered desperate at finding themselves thus pent up at the muz-

and exact as to need no comment:—" Through the smoke I saw the English gunners abandon their pieces, all but six guns stationed under the road, and almost immediately our cuirassiers were upon the squares, whose fire was drawn in zig-zags. Now, I thought, those gunners would be cut to pieces; but no, the devils kept firing with grape, which mowed them down like grass." It is pleasant, after all, to find we were observed and spoken of as we deserved, though not by those who ought to have done it. I may here mention that Sir James Shaw Kennedy in his book is, I think, mistaken in saying that the Brunswickers were saved by Major Bull's and Captain Mercer's batteries, since after the usual interval on the right of the Brunswick square occurred one of English and then Major Bull's battery, and the front of the French attacking column was only equal to our own.

zles of our guns, as it were, and others carried away by their horses, maddened with wounds, dashed through our intervals—few thinking of using their swords, but pushing furiously onward, intent only on saving themselves. At last the rear of the column, wheeling about, opened a passage, and the whole swept away at a much more rapid pace than they had advanced, nor stopped until the swell of the ground covered them from our fire. We then ceased firing; but as they were still not far off, for we saw the tops of their caps, having reloaded, we stood ready to receive them should they renew the attack.

One of, if not the first man who fell on our side was wounded by his own gun. Gunner Butterworth was one of the greatest pickles in the troop, but, at the same time, a most daring, active soldier; he was No. 7 (the man who sponged, &c.) at his gun. He had just finished ramming down the shot, and was stepping back outside the wheel, when his foot stuck in the miry soil, pulling him forward at the moment the gun was fired. As a man naturally does when falling, he threw out both his arms before him, and they were blown off at the elbows. He raised himself a little on his two stumps, and looked up most piteously in my face. To assist him was impossible—the safety of all, everything, depended upon not slackening our fire, and I was obliged to turn from him. The state of anxious activity in which we were kept all day, and the numbers who fell almost immediately afterwards, caused me to lose sight of poor Butterworth; and I afterwards learned that he had succeeded in rising and was gone to the rear; but on inquiring for him next day, some of my people who had been sent to Waterloo told me that they saw his body lying by the roadside near the farm of Mount St Jean—bled to death! The retreat of the cavalry was succeeded by a shower of shot and shells, which must have annihilated us had not the little bank covered and threw most of them over us. Still some reached us and knocked down men and horses.

At the first charge, the French column was composed of grenadiers à cheval* and cuirassiers, the former in front. I forget whether they had or had not changed this disposition, but think, from the number of cuirasses we afterwards found, that the cuirassiers led the second attack. Be this as it may, their column reassembled. They prepared

* These grenadiers à cheval were very fine troops, clothed in blue uniforms without facings, cuffs, or collars. Broad, very broad buff belts, and huge muff caps, made them appear gigantic fellows.

for a second attempt, sending up a cloud of skirmishers, who galled us terribly by a fire of carbines and pistols at scarcely 40 yards from our front. We were obliged to stand with port-fires lighted, so that it was not without a little difficulty that I succeeded in restraining the people from firing, for they grew impatient under such fatal results. Seeing some exertion beyond words necessary for this purpose, I leaped my horse up the little bank, and began a promenade (by no means agreeable) up and down our front, without even drawing my sword, though these fellows were within speaking distance of me. This quieted my men; but the tall blue gentlemen, seeing me thus dare them, immediately made a target of me, and commenced a very deliberate practice, to show us what very bad shots they were and verify the old artillery proverb, "The nearer the target, the safer you are." One fellow certainly made me flinch, but it was a miss; so I shook my finger at him, and called him *coquin*, &c. The rogue grinned as he reloaded, and again took aim. I certainly felt rather foolish at that moment, but was ashamed, after such bravado, to let him see it, and therefore continued my promenade. As if to prolong my torment, he was a terrible time about it. To me it seemed an age. Whenever I turned, the muzzle of his infernal carbine still followed me. At length bang it went, and whiz came the ball close to the back of my neck, and at the same instant down dropped the leading driver of one of my guns (Miller), into whose forehead the cursed missile had penetrated.

The column now once more mounted the plateau, and these popping gentry wheeled off right and left to clear the ground for their charge. The spectacle was imposing, and if ever the word sublime was appropriately applied, it might surely be to it. On they came in compact squadrons, one behind the other, so numerous that those of the rear were still below the brow when the head of the column was but at some sixty or seventy yards from our guns. Their pace was a slow but steady trot. None of your furious galloping charges was this, but a deliberate advance, at a deliberate pace, as of men resolved to carry their point. They moved in profound silence, and the only sound that could be heard from them amidst the incessant roar of battle was the low thunder-like reverberation of the ground beneath the simultaneous tread of so many horses. On our part was equal deliberation. Every man stood steadily at his post, the guns ready, loaded with a round-shot first and a case over it; the tubes were in the vents; the port-fires glared and sputtered behind the wheels; and my word alone was wanting to hurl destruction on that goodly show of gallant men and noble horses. I delayed this, for experience had given me confidence. The Brunswickers partook of this feeling, and with their squares—much reduced in point of size— well closed, stood firmly, with arms at the recover, and eyes fixed on us, ready to commence their fire with our first discharge. It was indeed a grand and imposing spectacle! The column* was led on this time by an officer in a rich uniform, his breast covered with decorations, whose earnest gesticulations were strangely contrasted with the solemn demeanour of those to whom they were addressed. I thus allowed them to advance unmolested until the head of the column might have been about fifty or sixty yards from us, and then gave the word, "Fire!" The effect was terrible. Nearly the whole leading rank fell at once; and the round-shot, penetrating the column, carried confusion throughout its extent.

---

* Gourgand says :—" Cette division de deux mille grenadiers à cheval, et dragons tous gens d'élite, s'étaient engagés sur le plateau, sans l'ordre de l'Empereur," &c. &c.—P. 88., ed. London. He speaks of the cavalry of reserve of the Guard. Could these be the people?

THE CAVALRY AGAIN REPULSED.

The ground, already encumbered with victims of the first struggle, became now almost impassable. Still, however, these devoted warriors struggled on, intent only on reaching us. The thing was impossible. Our guns were served with astonishing activity, whilst the running fire of the two squares was maintained with spirit. Those who pushed forward over the heaps of carcasses of men and horses gained but a few paces in advance, there to fall in their turn and add to the difficulties of those succeeding them. The discharge of every gun was followed by a fall of men and horses like that of grass before the mower's scythe. When the horse alone was killed, we could see the cuirassiers divesting themselves of the encumbrance and making their escape on foot. Still, for a moment, the confused mass (for all order was at an end) stood before us, vainly trying to urge their horses over the obstacles presented by their fallen comrades, in obedience to the now loud and rapid vociferations of him who had led them on and remained unhurt. As before, many cleared everything and rode through us; many came plunging forward only to fall, man and horse, close to the muzzles of our guns; but the majority again turned at the very moment when, from having less ground to go over, it were safer to advance than retire, and sought a passage to the rear. Of course the same confusion, struggle amongst themselves, and slaughter prevailed as before, until gradually they disappeared over the brow of the hill. We ceased firing, glad to take breath. Their retreat exposed us, as before, to a shower of shot and shells: these last, falling amongst us with very long fuses, kept burning and hissing a long time before they burst, and were a considerable annoyance to man and horse. The bank in front, however, again stood our friend, and sent many over us innocuous.

Lieutenant Breton, who had already lost two horses, and had mounted a troop-horse, was conversing with me during this our leisure moment. As his horse stood at right angles to mine, the poor jaded animal dozingly rested his muzzle on my thigh; whilst I, the better to hear amidst the infernal din, leant forward, resting my arm between his ears. In this attitude a cannon-shot smashed the horse's head to atoms. The headless trunk sank to the ground—Breton looking pale as death, expecting, as he afterwards told me, that I was cut in two. What was passing to the right and left of us I know no more about than the man in the moon—not even what corps were beyond the Brunswickers. The smoke confined our vision to a very small compass, so that my battle was restricted to the two squares and my own battery; and, as long as we maintained our ground, I thought it a matter of course that others did so too. It was just after this accident that our worthy commanding officer of artillery, Sir George Adam Wood, made his appearance through the smoke a little way from our left flank. As I said, we were doing nothing, for the cavalry were under the brow re-forming for a third attack, and we were being pelted by their artillery. " D—n it, Mercer," said the old man, blinking as a man does when facing a gale of wind, " you have hot work of it here." " Yes, sir, pretty hot;" and I was proceeding with an account of the two charges we had already discomfited, and the prospect of a third, when, glancing that way, I perceived their leading squadron already on the plateau. " There they are again !" I exclaimed; and, darting from Sir George *sans cérémonie*, was just in time to meet them with the same destruction as before. This time, indeed, it was child's play. They could not even approach us in any decent order, and we fired most deliberately; it was folly having attempted the thing. I was sitting on my horse near the right of my battery as they turned and began to retire once more. Intoxicated with success, I was singing out, "Beautiful!—beautiful!" and my right arm was flourishing about, when some one from behind, seizing it, said quietly, "Take care, or you'll strike the Duke;" and in effect our noble chief, with a serious air, and apparently much fatigued, passed close by me to the front, without seeming to take the slightest notice of the remnant of the French cavalry still lingering on the ground. This obliged us to cease firing; and at the same moment I, perceiving a line of infantry ascending from the rear, slowly, with ported arms, and uttering a sort of feeble, suppressed hurrah—ankle-deep in a thick tenacious mud, and threading their way amongst or stepping over the numerous corpses covering the ground, out of breath from their exertions, and hardly preserving a line, broken everywhere into large gaps the breadth of several files—could not but meditate on the probable results of the last charge had I, in obedience to the Duke's order, retired my men into the squares and allowed the daring and formidable squadrons a passage to our rear, where they must have gone thundering down on this disjointed line. The summit gained, the line was amended, files closed in, and the whole, including our Brunswickers, advanced down the slope towards the plain.

Although the infantry lost several men as they passed us, yet on the whole the cannonade began to slacken on both sides (why, I know not), and, the smoke clearing away a little, I had now, for the first time, a good view of the field. On the ridge opposite to us dark masses of troops were stationary, or moving down into the intervening plain. Our own advancing infantry were hid from view by the ground. We therefore recommenced firing at the enemies' masses, and the cannonade, spreading, soon became general again along the line. Whilst thus occupied with our front, we suddenly became sensible of a most destructive flanking fire from a battery which had come, the Lord knows how, and established itself on a knoll somewhat higher than the ground we stood on, and only about 400 or 500 yards a little in advance of our left flank. The rapidity and precision of this fire were quite appalling. Every shot almost took effect, and I certainly expected we should all be annihilated. Our horses and limbers, being a little retired down the slope, had hitherto been somewhat under cover from the direct fire in front; but this plunged right amongst them, knocking them down by pairs, and creating horrible confusion. The drivers could hardly extricate themselves from one dead horse ere another fell, or perhaps themselves. The saddle-bags, in many instances, were torn from the horses' backs, and their contents scattered over the field. One shell I saw explode under the two finest wheel-horses in the troop—down they dropped. In some instances the horses of a gun or ammunition-waggon remained, and all their drivers were killed.* The whole livelong day had cost us nothing like this. Our gunners too—the few left fit for duty of them—were so exhausted that they were unable to run the guns up after firing, consequently at every round they retreated nearer to the limbers; and as we had pointed our two left guns towards the people who were annoying us so terribly, they soon came altogether in a confused heap, the trails crossing each other, and the whole dangerously near the limbers and ammunition-waggons, some of which were totally unhorsed, and others in sad confusion from the loss of their drivers and horses, many of them lying dead in their harness attached to their carriages. I sighed for my poor troop—it was already but a wreck.

* "The field was so much covered with blood, that it appeared as if it had been flooded with it," &c.—Simpson's 'Paris after Waterloo,' &c., p. 21.

I had dismounted, and was assisting at one of the guns to encourage my poor exhausted men, when through the smoke a black speck caught my eye, and I instantly knew what it was. The conviction that one never sees a shot coming towards you unless directly in its line flashed across my mind, together with the certainty that my doom was sealed. I had barely time to exclaim " Here it is then!"—much in that gasping sort of way one does when going into very cold water takes away the breath—" whush " it went past my face, striking the point of my pelisse collar, which was lying open, and smash into a horse close behind me. I breathed freely again.

Under such a fire, one may be said to have had a thousand narrow escapes; and, in good truth, I frequently experienced that displacement of air against my face caused by the passing of shot close to me; but the two above recorded, and a third which I shall mention, were remarkable ones, and made me feel in full force the goodness of Him who protected me among so many dangers. Whilst in position on the right of the second line, I had reproved some of my men for lying down when shells fell near them until they burst. Now my turn came. A shell, with a long fuse, came slop into the mud at my feet, and there lay fizzing and flaring, to my infinite discomfiture. After what I had said on the subject, I felt that I must act up to my own words, and, accordingly, there I stood, endeavouring to look quite composed until the cursed thing burst—and, strange to say, without injuring me, though so near. The effect on my men was good. We had scarcely fired many rounds at the enfilading battery when a tall man in the black Brunswick uniform came galloping up to me from the rear, exclaiming, " Ah ! mine Gott!—mine Gott ! vat is it you doos, sare? Dat is your friends de Proosiens ; an you kills dem! Ah, mine Gott!—mine Gott! vill you no stop, sare?—vill you no stop? Ah! mine Gott!—mine Gott! vat for is dis ? De Inglish kills dere friends de Proosiens! Vere is de Dook von Vellington ?—vere is de Dook von Vellington ? Oh, mine Gott!—mine Gott!" &c. &c., and so he went on raving like one demented. I observed that if these were our friends the Prussians they were treating us very uncivilly ; and that it was not without sufficient provocation we had turned our guns on them, pointing out to him at the same time the bloody proofs of my assertion. Apparently not noticing what I said, he continued his lamentations, and, " Vill you no stop, sare, I say ? " Wherefore, thinking he might be right, to pacify him I ordered the whole to cease firing, desiring him to remark the consequences. *Psieu, psieu, psieu,* came our *friends'* shot, one after another; and our friend himself had a narrow escape from one of them. "Now, sir," I said, "you will be convinced; and we will continue our firing, whilst you can ride round the way you came, and tell them they kill their friends the English; the moment their fire ceases, so shall mine." Still he lingered, exclaiming, "Oh, dis is terrecbly to see de Proosien and de Inglish kill vonanoder!" At last darting off I saw no more of him.* The fire continued on both sides, mine becoming slacker and slacker, for we were reduced to the last extremity, and must have been annihilated but for the opportune arrival of a battery of Belgic artillery a little on our left, which, taking the others

* At one time I thought this a French *ruse de guerre*. I remember the man perfectly, with his silver arrow and chain attached to his black shoulder-belt. In Sir John Sinclair's 'Translation of Baron Muffling's Account,' London, 1816, and at p. 29, I find that about 4 P.M., whilst the cuirassiers, after charging through the 1st British line, were roaming over the interval between it and the 2d, "the enemy advanced a battalion on the plain of the platform, at hardly 500 yards' distance from the position, so as, perhaps, to establish his infantry on this side of the little wood of Hougoumont and in La Haye Sainte." Could this have been the one? At p. 35 he says, "The shot from Bulow's artillery reached the British, and the Duke was obliged to send notice of it." Query—Did the Duke observe this himself, or was it communicated to him by my black hussar?

in flank nearly at point blank, soon silenced and drove them off. We were so reduced that all our strength was barely sufficient to load and fire three guns out of our six.

These Belgians were all beastly drunk, and, when they first came up, not at all particular as to which way they fired; and it was only by keeping an eye on them that they were prevented treating us, and even one another. The wretches had probably already done mischief elsewhere—who knows? My recollections of the latter part of this day are rather confused; I was fatigued, and almost deaf. I recollect clearly, however, that we had ceased firing—the plain below being covered with masses of troops, which we could not distinguish from each other. Captain Walcot of the horse-artillery had come to us, and we were all looking out anxiously at the movements below and on the opposite ridge, when he suddenly shouted out, "Victory!—victory! they fly!—they fly!" and sure enough we saw some of the masses dissolving, as it were, and those composing them streaming away in confused crowds over the field, whilst the already desultory fire of their artillery ceased altogether. I shall never forget this joyful moment!—this moment of exultation! On looking round I found we were left almost alone. Cavalry and infantry had all moved forward, and only a few guns here and there were to be seen on the position. A little to our right were the remains of Major M'Donald's troop under Lieutenant Sandilands, which had suffered much, but nothing like us. We were congratulating ourselves on the happy results of the day, when an aide-de-camp rode up, crying "*Forward, sir! —forward! It is of the utmost importance that this movement should be supported by artillery!*" at the same time waving his hat much in the manner of a huntsman laying on his dogs. I smiled at his energy, and, pointing to the remains of my poor troop, quietly asked, "*How, sir?*" A glance was sufficient to show him the impossibility, and away he went.

Our situation was indeed terrible: of 200 fine horses with which we had entered the battle, upwards of 140 lay dead, dying, or severely wounded. Of the men, scarcely two-thirds of those necessary for four guns remained, and these so completely exhausted as to be totally incapable of further exertion. Lieutenant Breton had three horses killed under him; Lieutenant Hincks was wounded in the breast by a spent ball; Lieutenant Leathes on the hip by a splinter; and although untouched myself, my horse had no less than eight wounds, one of which—a graze on the fetlock joint—lamed him for ever. Our guns and carriages were, as before mentioned, altogether in a confused heap, intermingled with dead and wounded horses, which it had not been possible to disengage from them. My poor men, such at least as were untouched, fairly worn out, their clothes, faces, &c., blackened by the smoke and spattered over with mud and blood, had seated themselves on the trails of the carriages, or had thrown themselves on the wet and polluted soil, too fatigued to think of anything but gaining a little rest. Such was our situation when called upon to advance! It was impossible, and we remained where we were. For myself, I was also excessively tired—hoarse, to making speech painful, and deaf from the infernal uproar of the last eleven hours. Moreover, I was devoured by a burning thirst, not a drop of liquid having passed my lips since the evening of the 16th; but although, with the exception of the chicken's leg last night, I may be said to have eaten nothing for two whole days, yet did I not feel the least desire for food.

The evening had become fine, and but for an occasional groan or lament from some poor sufferer, and the repeated piteous neighing of wounded horses, tranquillity might be said to reign over the field. As it got dusk, a large body of Prussian artillery arrived, and formed their bivouac near us. There was not light to see more of them than that their brass guns were kept bright, and that their carriages were encumbered with baggage, and, besides, appeared but clumsy machines when compared with ours. All wore their greatcoats, which apparently they had marched in. As they looked at us rather scowlingly, and did not seem inclined to hold any communication with us, I soon returned to my own people, whom I found preparing to go supperless to bed—the two remaining officers, the non-commissioned officers and men having all got together in a heap, with some painted covers spread under and others drawn over them—at a distance from our guns, &c., the neighbourhood of which, they said, was too horrible to think of sleeping there. For my part, after standing all day amongst all these horrors, I felt no squeamishness about sleeping amongst them; so pulling down the painted cover of a limber over the footboard in the manner of a tent roof, I crept under it, and endeavoured to sleep. The cramped situation in which I lay, and the feverish excitement of my mind, forbade, however, my obtaining that sound and refreshing sleep so much needed—I only dozed. From one of these dozes I awoke about midnight, chilled and cramped to death from the awkward doubled-up position imposed upon me by my short and narrow bed. So up I got to look around and contemplate a battle-field by the pale moonlight. The night was serene and pretty clear; a few light clouds occasionally passing across the moon's disc, and throwing objects into transient obscurity, added considerably to the solemnity of the scene. Oh, it was a thrilling sensation thus to stand in the silent hour of the night and contemplate that field—all day long the theatre of noise and strife, now so calm and still—the actors prostrate on the bloody soil, their pale wan faces upturned to the moon's cold beams, which caps and breastplates, and a thousand other things, reflected back in brilliant pencils of light from as many different points! Here and there some poor wretch, sitting up amidst the countless dead, busied himself in endeavours to stanch the flowing stream with which his life was fast ebbing away. Many whom I saw so employed that night were, when morning dawned, lying stiff and tranquil as those who had departed earlier. From time to time a figure would half raise itself from the ground, and then, with a despairing groan, fall back again. Others, slowly and painfully rising, stronger, or having less deadly hurt, would stagger away with uncertain steps across the field in search of succour. Many of these I followed with my gaze until lost in the obscurity of distance; but many, alas! after staggering a few paces, would sink again on the ground, probably to rise no more. It was heartrending—and yet I gazed! Horses, too, there were to claim our pity—mild, patient, enduring. Some lay on the ground with their entrails hanging out, and yet they lived. These would occasionally attempt to rise, but, like their human bed-fellows, quickly falling back again, would lift their poor heads, and, turning a wistful gaze at their side, lie quietly down again, to repeat the same until strength no longer remained, and then, their eyes gently closing, one short convulsive struggle closed their sufferings. One poor animal excited painful interest—he had lost, I believe, both his hind legs; and there he sat the long night through on his tail, looking about, as if in expectation of coming aid, sending forth, from time to time, long and protracted melancholy neighing. Although I knew that killing him at once would be mercy, I could not muster courage even to give the order. Blood enough I had seen shed during the last six-and-thirty hours, and sickened at the thought of shedding more. There, then, he still sat when we left the ground, neighing after us, as if reproaching our desertion of him in the hour of need.

The Prussian bivouac near at hand offered a far different and more cheering scene. There all was life and movement. Their handsome horses, standing harnessed and tied to the carriages, sent forth neighings of another character. Dark forms moved amongst them; and by the bivouac-fires sat figures that would have furnished studies for a Salvator. Dark, brown, stern visages, rendered still sterner by the long drooping mustache that overshadowed the mouth, from which appended their constant companion, the pipe. Many there were, too, busily occupied with the first great care of all animals—cooking, or eating the mess already cooked. Save these I have mentioned, no living being moved on the moonlit field; and as I cast up my eyes at the lustrous lamp of heaven, I thought on the thousand dear connections far, far away, on whose peaceful dwelling it now looked down, their inmates sleeping in tranquil security, ignorant as yet of the fatal blow which had now for ever severed them from those they loved, whose bodies encumbered the ground around me. And here, even here, what a contrast between this charnel-house and the distant landscape within my ken! Over it the same fair planet shed her mild beams, illuminating its groves and yellow corn-fields, its still and quiet villages, whose modest spires here and there arose from the horizon—emblems of peace, tranquillity, and repose. Long I continued to gaze on this sad and solemn scene; and all this slaughter, I said, to gratify the ambition of one man, and that man—whom?—one who has risen from a station humble as my own, has already devastated Europe, and filled it with blood and mourning—who only recently left behind him 400,000 gallant men, a prey to the sword and the intemperance of a northern clime —fearful holocaust on the altar of that ambition!

At length I again crept into my cell, and again slept by fits and starts, until the first blush of day reddened the eastern sky, and aroused us all to new exertion. As I emerged from under my cover a shudder crept over me, when the stronger light of day enabled me to see the corpse of one of my drivers lying mangled and bloody beneath my lair.

CHAPTER XIV.

19*th*.—The cool air of the morning lasted not long; the rising sun soon burst in all his glory over our bloody bivouac, and all nature arose into renewed life, except the victims of ambition which lay unconscious of his presence. I had not been up many minutes when one of my sergeants came to ask if they might bury Driver Crammond. "And why particularly Driver Crammond?" "Because he looks frightful, sir; many of us have not had a wink of sleep for him." Curious! I walked to the spot where he lay, and certainly a more hideous sight cannot be imagined. A cannon-shot had carried away the whole head except barely the visage, which still remained attached to the torn and bloody neck. The men said they had been prevented sleeping by seeing his eyes fixed on them all night; and thus this one dreadful object had superseded all the other horrors by which they were surrounded. He was of course immediately buried, and as immediately forgotten. Our first care after this was to muster the remaining force, to disentangle our carriages from each other, and from the dead and dying animals with which they were encumbered. Many sound or only slightly-wounded horses, belonging to different corps of both armies, were wandering about the field. Of these we caught several in the course of the morning, and thus collected, with what remained of our own fit for work, sufficient to horse four guns, three ammunition-waggons, and the forge. Of men we had nearly enough for these at reduced numbers, so we set to work equipping ourselves without delay. Although supplies of ammunition had been sent to us during the action, yet little remained. The expenditure had been enormous. A return had been called for yesterday evening just as we were lying down to rest, but, fatigued as we all were, it was impossible to give this correctly. As near as I could ascertain, we must have fired nearly 700 rounds per gun. Our harness, &c., was so cut to pieces, that but for the vast magazines around us from which we could pick and choose, we should never have got off the field. Soon after daybreak an officer came from headquarters to desire me to send all my superfluous carriages to Lillois, where a park was forming, and to inform me that a supply of ammunition would be found in the village of Waterloo. Accordingly the carriages were sent without delay; but this requiring all the horses, they were obliged to make a second trip for the ammunition. Whilst this was doing I had leisure to examine the ground in our immediate vicinity. Books and papers, &c., covered it in all directions. The books at first surprised me, but upon examination the thing was explained. Each French soldier, it appeared, carried a little accompt-book of his pay, clothing, &c. &c. The scene was now far from solitary; for numerous groups of peasants were moving about busily employed stripping the dead, and perhaps finishing those not quite so. Some of these men I met fairly staggering under the enormous load of clothes, &c., they had collected. Some had firearms, swords, &c., and many had large bunches of crosses and decorations; all seemed in high glee, and professed unbounded hatred of the French.

I had fancied we were almost alone on the field, seeing only the remains of Major Bull's troop of horse-artillery not far from us (the Prussians had gone forward about, or a little before, daybreak); but in wandering towards the Charleroi road I stumbled on a whole regiment of British infantry fast asleep, in columns of divisions, wrapped in their blankets, with their knapsacks for pillows. Not a man was awake. There they lay in regular ranks, with the officers and sergeants in their places, just as they would stand when awake. Not far from these, in a little hollow beneath a white thorn, lay two Irish light-infantry men sending forth such howlings and wailings, and oaths and execrations, as were shocking to hear. One of them had his leg shot off, the other a thigh smashed by a cannon-shot. They were certainly pitiable objects, but their vehement exclamations, &c., were so strongly contrasted with the quiet resolute bearing of hundreds, both French and English, around them, that it blunted one's feelings considerably.

I tried in vain to pacify them; so walked away amidst a volley of abuse as a hardhearted wretch who could thus leave two poor fellows to die like dogs. What could I do? All, however, though in more modest terms, craved assistance; and every poor wretch begged most earnestly for water. Some of my men had discovered a good well of uncontaminated water at Hougoumont, and filled their canteens; so I made several of them accompany me and administer to the most craving in our immediate vicinity. Nothing could exceed their gratitude, or the fervent blessings they implored on us for this momentary relief. The French were in general particularly grateful; and those who were strong enough, entered into conversation with us on the events of yesterday, and the probable fate awaiting themselves. All the non-commissioned officers and privates agreed in asserting that they had been deceived by their officers and betrayed; and, to my surprise, almost all of them reviled Buonaparte as the cause of their misery. Many begged me to kill them at once, since they would a thousand times rather die by the hand of a soldier than be left at the mercy of those villanous Belgic peasants. Whilst we stood by them, several would appear consoled and become tranquil; but the moment we attempted to leave, they invariably renewed the cry, "Ah, Monsieur, tuez moi donc! Tuez moi, pour l'amour de Dieu!" &c. &c. It was in vain I assured them carts would be sent to pick them all up. Nothing could reconcile them to the idea of being left. They looked on us as brother soldiers, and knew we were too honourable to harm them: "But the moment you go, those vile peasants will first insult, and then cruelly murder us." This, alas! I knew, was but too true. One Frenchman I found in a far different humour—an officer of lancers, and desperately wounded; a strong square-built man, with reddish hair and speckled complexion. When I approached him he appeared suffering horribly—rolling on his back, uttering loud groans. My first impulse was to raise and place him in a sitting posture; but, the moment he was touched, opening his eyes and seeing me, he became perfectly furious. Supposing he mistook my intention, I addressed him in a soothing tone, begging he would allow me to render him what little assistance was in my power. This only seemed to irritate him the more; and on my presenting him the canteen with water, he dashed it from him with such a passionate gesture and emphatic "*Non!*" that I saw there was no use in teasing, and therefore reluctantly left him. Returning towards our position, I was forcibly struck by the immense heap of bodies of men and horses which distinguished it even at a distance; indeed, Sir Augustus Frazer told me the other day, at Nivelles, that in riding over the field, *he could plainly distinguish the position of G troop from the opposite height by the dark mass which, even from that distance, formed a remarkable feature in the field.*" These were his very words. One interesting sufferer I had nearly forgotten. He was a fine young man of the grenadiers à cheval, who had lain groaning near us all night—indeed scarcely five paces from my bed; therefore was the first person I visited as soon as daylight came. He was a most interesting person—tall, handsome, and a perfect gentleman in manners and speech; yet his costume was that of a private soldier. We conversed with him some time, and were exceedingly pleased with his mild and amiable address. Amongst other things he told us that Marshal Ney had led the charges against us. In this, however (if we understood him rightly), he must have been mistaken, since that Marshal is an infantry general. Be that as it may, we all felt deeply interested for our unfortunate prisoner, and did all in our power for him, which consisted in kind words and sending two careful men to lead him to the village—a most painful undertaking, for we now found that, besides one ball in the forehead, he had received another in his right thigh, which, together with his being barefooted, could not but render his journey both tedious and painful.

I now began to feel somewhat the effects of my long fast in a most unpleasant sense of weakness and an inordinate craving for food, which there were no means of satisfying. My joy, then, may be imagined when, returning to our bivouac, I found our people returned from Lillois, and, better still, that they had brought with them a quarter of veal, which they had found in a muddy ditch, of course in appearance then filthy enough. What was this to a parcel of men who had scarcely eaten a morsel for three days? In a trice it was cut up, the mud having been scraped off with a sabre, a fire kindled and fed with lance-shafts and musket-stocks; and old Quartermaster Hall, undertaking the cooking, proceeded to fry the dirty lumps in the lid of a camp-kettle. How we enjoyed the savoury smell! and, having made ourselves seats of cuirasses,* piled upon each other, we soon had that most agreeable of animal gratifications—the filling our empty stomachs. Never was a meal more perfectly military, nor more perfectly enjoyed.

We had not yet finished our meal, when a carriage drove on the ground from Brussels, the inmates of which, alighting, proceeded to examine the field. As they passed near us, it was amusing to see the horror with which they eyed our frightful figures; they all, however, pulled off their hats and made us low bows. One, a

* Here were more cuirasses than men; for the wounded (who could move), divesting themselves of its encumbrance, had made their escape, leaving their armour on the ground where they had fallen.

smartly-dressed middle-aged man, in a high cocked-hat, came to our circle, and entered into conversation with me on the events of yesterday. He approached holding a delicately white perfumed handkerchief to his nose; stepping carefully to avoid the bodies (at which he cast fearful glances *en passant*), to avoid polluting the glossy silken hose that clothed his nether limbs. May I be pardoned for the comparison: Hotspur's description of a fop came forcibly to my mind as we conversed; clean and spruce, as if from a bandbox, redolent of perfume, he stood ever and anon applying the 'kerchief to his nose. I was not leaning on my sword, but I arose to receive him from my seat of armour, my hands and face begrimed and blackened with blood and smoke—clothes too. "I do remember when the fight was done," &c. &c. It came, as I said, forcibly to my mind as I eyed my friend's costume and sniffed the sweet-scented atmosphere that hovered round him. The perfumed handkerchief, in this instance, held the place of Shakespeare's "pouncet-box"—the scene was pleasant to remember! With a world of bows my man took leave, and proceeded, picking his steps with the same care as he followed the route of his companions in the direction of Hougoumont.

Having despatched our meal, and then the ammunition-waggons to Waterloo, and leaving the people employed equipping as best they could, I set off to visit the Chateau likewise; for the struggle that had taken place there yesterday rendered it an object of interest. The same scene of carnage as elsewhere characterised that part of the field over which I now bent my steps. The immediate neighbourhood of Hougoumont was more thickly strewn with corpses than most other parts of the field—the very ditches were full of them. The trees all about were most woefully cut and splintered, both by cannon-shot and musketry. The courts of the Chateau presented a spectacle more terrible even than any I had yet seen. A large barn had been set on fire, and the conflagration had spread to the offices, and even to the main building. Here numbers, both of French and English, had perished in the flames, and their blackened swollen remains lay scattered about in all directions. Amongst this heap of ruins and misery many poor devils yet remained alive, and were sitting up endeavouring to bandage their wounds. Such a scene of horror, and one so sickening, was surely never witnessed.

Two or three German dragoons were wandering among the ruins, and many peasants. One of the former was speaking to me when two of the latter, after rifling the pockets, &c., of a dead Frenchman, seized the body by the shoulders, and, raising it from the ground, dashed it down again with all their force, uttering the grossest abuse, and kicking it about the head and face—revolting spectacle!—doing this, no doubt, to court favour with us. It had a contrary effect, which they soon learned. I had scarcely uttered an exclamation of disgust, when the dragoon's sabre was flashing over the miscreants' heads, and in a moment descended on their backs and shoulders with such vigour that they roared again, and were but too happy to make their escape. I turned from such scenes and entered the garden. How shall I describe the delicious sensation I experienced!

The garden was an ordinary one, but pretty—long straight walks of turf overshadowed by fruit-trees, and between these beds of vegetables, the whole enclosed by a tolerably high brick wall. Is it necessary to define my sensations? Is it possible that I am not understood at once? Listen then. For the last three days I have been in a constant state of excitement—in a perfect fever. My eyes have beheld nought but war in all its

GARDEN OF THE CHATEAU.

horrors—my ears have been assailed by a continued roar of cannon and cracking of musketry, the shouts of multitudes and the lamentations of war's victims. Suddenly and unexpectedly I find myself in solitude, pacing a green avenue, my eyes refreshed by the cool verdure of trees and shrubs; my ear soothed by the melody of feathered songsters—yea, of sweet Philomel herself—and the pleasing hum of insects sporting in the genial sunshine. Is there nothing in this to excite emotion? Nature in repose is always lovely: here, and under such circumstances, she was delicious. Long I rambled in this garden, up one walk, down another, and thought I could dwell here contented for ever. Nothing recalled the presence of war except the loopholed wall and two or three dead Guardsmen;* but the first caused no interruption, and these last lay so concealed amongst the exuberant vegetation of turnips and cabbages, &c., that, after coming from the field of death without, their pale and silent forms but little deteriorated my enjoyment. The leaves

* In some accounts of the battle, and visits to the field, &c., it has been stated that this garden was a scene of slaughter. Totally untrue! As I have stated in the text, I did not see above two or three altogether. There certainly might have been more concealed amongst the vegetation, but they could not have been many.

were green, roses and other flowers bloomed forth in all their sweetness, and the very turf when crushed by my feet smelt fresh and pleasant. There was but little of disorder visible to tell of what had been enacted here. I imagine it must have been assailed by infantry alone; and the havoc amongst the trees without made by our artillery posted on the hill above to cover the approach to it—principally, perhaps, by Bull's howitzer battery.

I had satisfied my curiosity at Hougoumont, and was retracing my steps up the hill, when my attention was called to a group of wounded Frenchmen by the calm, dignified, and soldierlike oration addressed by one of them to the rest. I cannot, like Livy, compose a fine harangue for my hero, and, of course, I could not retain the precise words, but the import of them was to exhort them to bear their sufferings with fortitude; not to repine, like women or children, at what every soldier should have made up his mind to suffer as the fortune of war, but, above all, to remember that they were surrounded by Englishmen, before whom they ought to be doubly careful not to disgrace themselves by displaying such an unsoldierlike want of fortitude. The speaker was sitting on the ground, with his lance stuck upright beside him—an old veteran, with a thick bushy grizly beard, countenance like a lion—a lancer of the Old Guard, and no doubt had fought in many a field. One hand was flourished in the air as he spoke, the other, severed at the wrist, lay on the earth beside him; one ball (case-shot, probably) had entered his body, another had broken his leg. His suffering, after a night of exposure so mangled, must have been great; yet he betrayed it not. His bearing was that of a Roman, or perhaps of an Indian warrior, and I could fancy him concluding appropriately his speech in the words of the Mexican king, "And I too; am I on a bed of roses?" I could not but feel the highest veneration for this brave man, and told him so, at the same time offering him the only consolation in my power—a drink of cold water, and assurances that the waggons would soon be sent round to collect the wounded. He thanked me with a grace peculiar to Frenchmen, and eagerly inquired the fate of their army. On this head I could tell him nothing consolatory, so merely answered that it had retired last night, and turned the conversation to the events of yesterday. This truly brave man spoke in most flattering terms of our troops, but said they had no idea in the French army we should have fought so obstinately, since it was generally understood that the English Government had, for some inexplicable reason, connived at Napoleon's escape from Elba, and therefore had ordered their army only to make a show of resistance. After a very interesting conversation, I begged his lance as a keepsake, observing that it never could be of further use to him. The old man's eyes kindled as I spoke, and he emphatically assured me that it would delight him to see it in the hands of a brave soldier, instead of being torn from him, as he had feared, by those vile peasants. So I took my leave, and walked away with the lance in my hand.* Ever since

* During the remainder of the campaign Milward carried it; and on returning to England I even rode into Canterbury followed by my lancer—a novelty in those days. Whilst in retirement on half-pay, it was suspended in my library; but on going to America in 1823 I deposited it in the Rotunda at Woolwich. On my return in 1829 the lance was gone. In 1823 or 1824 it seems Lieutenant-Colonel Vandaleur, of the 9th Lancers, came to Woolwich to look for a model. Mine pleased him, and he took it to St John's Wood Riding-House, where it was tried against others in presence of the Duke of York, and approved of as a model for arming the British lancers. After a long hunt I at last found it at the Enfield manufactory, spoilt completely, the iron work and thong taken off, and flag gone. It cost me a long correspondence with the Board before I succeeded in getting it restored and put together. When I received it from him who had so long wielded it, the flag was dyed in blood, the blade notched, and also stained with blood; inside the thong was cut Clement, VII., probably the number of his troop. [It is now in the possession of Dr Hall, an old Waterloo man, and sincere friend of my father.—ED.]

my groom (Milward) has been transformed into my lancer-orderly; and I propose, if ever I return to England, consecrating it to the memory of the interesting old hero. In passing Bull's bivouac it was my fate to witness another very interesting scene. A wounded hussar had somehow or another found his way there from another part of the field, and, exhausted by the exertion, had just fainted. Some of those collected round him cried out for water, and a young driver, who, being outside the throng, had not yet seen the sufferer, seized a canteen, and ran away to fill it. Whilst he was absent the hussar so far recovered as to be able to sit up. The driver returned at this moment, and, pushing aside his comrades, knelt down to enable the hussar to drink, holding the canteen to his lips, and in so doing recognised a brother whom he had not seen for years! His emotion was extreme, as may be supposed.

On regaining my own bivouac I found the ammunition arrived, and, what was still more satisfactory, Mr Coates with his whole train of Flemish waggons—our baggage and provisions. He had got intelligence in time of the battle of Quatre Bras and its results, and therefore altered his route to meet us on our retreat. On approaching the Charleroi road he had been swept away by the torrent of fugitives, and actually carried, *malgré lui*, beyond Brussels, some way on the road to Antwerp, before he could succeed in disentangling his train from the rabble rout, which he described as exceeding all imagination. As he brought the wherewithal, &c., of course his joining was hailed with joy by every one.

Since the order to send away my carriages I had received none; but as my diminished troop was completed as far as could be done here, I resolved to move off this horrid place; and accordingly, at three P.M., we joyfully took to the Nivelles road—by instinct, perhaps, for I knew nothing of the movements of the army, nor by what road they had gone forward.* About a mile or so from the field I formed our bivouac for the night in a sweet and wholesome orchard near the road, with a turflike velvet, and perfectly dry. This in itself was a luxury; it was a luxury to breathe pure uncontaminated air; it was a luxury to be out of hearing of groans, cries, and lamentations. This was not all. Mr Coates brought us a ham

---

* Sir George Wood incurred the Duke's extreme displeasure for not securing and parking the French guns immediately after the action, for the Prussians got hold of many of them; and it was only through the indefatigable activity of Sir Augustus Frazer that they were regained—partly by coaxing, partly by blustering. However, they were all recovered.

and a cheese; the neighbouring farmhouse supplied us with eggs, milk, and cider: so that in due time we sat down to an excellent dinner, seasoned with that sauce which no cook, however *scientific*, has yet learned to equal—hunger. Hilarity reigned at our board — if we may so term the fresh turf at the foot of an apple-tree; and over our grog and cigars we managed to pass a most pleasant evening. Previously, I had caused my servant to bring me a bucket of water, and prepared myself for our repast by the enjoyment of that first of luxuries, a thorough wash and clean clothes. This was the first time I had undressed since leaving Strytem—four whole days and three whole nights. It may be imagined with what joy I got rid of my bloody garments. Like the birds, we all retired to rest with the close of day, and the delicious sleep I enjoyed it is impossible to describe.

20th.—Awoke early, and at first could not imagine where I was. The cheerful sunbeams were playing amongst the leaves and branches overhead. The farmer's people were moving out with their cattle to commence their daily labours. All was peace and rural tranquillity. The events of the last four days passed across my recollection, and I could for a moment scarcely believe them other than a troubled dream; but I raised myself on my elbow, and there was the battle-field, still encumbered with the slain. Ah! there it lay, bathed in the full blaze of sunshine. Starting up, I roused our people, and would have immediately recommenced the march, but upon inquiry, found that, although the farriers had worked throughout the night, they had not yet completed the shoeing. It was ten o'clock before they did so; and then we put ourselves in movement on the road to Nivelles, amidst crowds of stragglers, sutlers, &c., all pushing forward to overtake the army. It was like the highroad to some great fair. Every one appeared lighthearted, and it was delight to leave *that* field behind one.

Arrived at the gate of Nivelles, we found such a throng that there were no hopes of passing for at least some hours. I therefore drew up my troop in a pretty meadow by the roadside, where, besides being out of the dust, we could enjoy the cool shelter of the fine umbrageous elms by which it was surrounded, and water and feed our cattle. Mr Coates had preceded us and procured a fat cow, which one of our men slaughtered and cut up; and the meat being distributed, we were provided with the needful wherever we might bivouac.

Up to this point I had no orders, nor did I know anything of the armies—English, Prussian, or French. We knew, to be sure, that the latter had been defeated on the 18th, and retired, followed by the other two; but we had no notion of the extent of the defeat, and therefore expected to find them again in position. Here I expected to get some information when I could get into the town; but the gate still continued so choked with waggons that it was impossible even for an individual to enter except in turn.

An order overtook us here to send back an officer to take charge of the guns and carriages we had left behind, until they could be rehorsed and forwarded to us again. Lieutenant Hincks, who rejoined us yesterday, being far from well, and suffering much from his contusion, I with some difficulty persuaded him to take this duty. On the opposite side of the road was a neat house, standing in a shrubbery, apparently deserted. Some of my men, wandering into the yard, discovered here three privates of the Guards. I forget what account they gave of themselves, but remember they complained of having eaten nothing for three days. We gave them a lump of beef and some bread, not reflecting at the time on the strange circumstance of their being thus left behind. I have since thought they remained here with the intention of deserting as soon as the coast was clear.

At length I effected my own entrance into the town, hoping to gain some information, or even meet some one who could give me orders. The first thing that struck me on passing the gates was the contrast the present aspect of the streets presented to that when we passed through on the evening of the 16th. Then all was sadness, despair, and lamentation; now all joy, confidence, and revel. The countenance of every one you met beamed exultation and triumph, Belgians as well as English. Men came up with frankness, took our hands, and paid us some compliment. The women, by smiles and kind looks, testified their sympathy; whilst the lower orders, in the joy of their hearts, would slap one on the thigh, *en passant*, with an emphatic "Bon!" "Brave garçon!" "Brave Anglais!" "Bon!" Or, if a number were collected at some corner, they would demonstrate their feelings by a cheer of "Vivent les Anglais!" The numerous cafés and cabarets (of which every door and window was open on account of the oppressive heat) were crammed with officers and soldiers of every arm and of every nation, eating, drinking, swearing, singing, and smoking. Music of some sort increased the *bouhara* in most of them. In many private houses, too, of the first appearance, large parties of officers were regaling themselves; and even in the streets many little assemblages of soldiers were to be seen enjoying their pipes and their beer in some shady corner. It was one complete scene of festivity. The streets were, moreover, crowded almost to suffocation with scattered soldiery: columns on their march; long files of country waggons laden with forage or provisions; together with the pretty little, low, light baggage-waggons of the German infantry, with their snow-white tilts. Here quartermasters and their attendants were running about chalking the doors of the houses (the headquarters were here tonight) with the names of those who were to take up their temporary abode in them. " Lieutenant-Colonel ——" on one; " Deputy-Assistant-Adjutant-General" on another ; " 1st company of such a regiment" on another, and so on. Then several commissaries (followed by a swarm of Flemish waggoners) hurry along in search of the Magazin des Fourrages. Further on, officers of the general staff are arranging the march of troops. Suddenly a loud shout announces something extraordinary even on this day of excitement. Every one hurries to the spot, pushing each other, jumping, shouting. "What can it mean?" I inquired. "Monsieur l'Officier, c'est un convoi des prisonniers que vient d'arriver," replied my man, doffing at the same time his *bonnet de nuit* and making a most respectful salaam. I stopped to see the convoy pass. The prisoners, dressed in grey *capôtes* and *bonnets de fourrage*, march steadily on. Some *vieux moustaches* look very grave, and cast about furious glances at the noisy crowd which follows them with the perseverance of a swarm of mosquitoes, *sacréeing* and venting all kind of illiberal abuse on them and their b— of an Emperor. Many, however, younger men, laugh, joke, and return their abuse with interest, whilst the soldiers of the escort (English) march doggedly along, pushing aside the more forward of the throng, and apparently as if only marching round a relief. The crowd passed on, and so did I, until, meeting some of our own people, I learned that Sir Augustus Frazer was here, and soon after found out his billet. To find one's self in a quiet, genteel, well-furnished room, after such scenes of bustle, &c., as had occupied our last few days, is a pleasing change. Exactly such was that in which I found Sir Augustus engaged with his adjutant. He was in his slippers; his writing materials were arranged on the table, and on another were some books and maps. The open windows looked into a little shady garden gay with flowers and flowering shrubs. There was an air of cheerfulness, of home and home's comfort, about the place that was quite refreshing. My visit was necessarily a short one. I learned much more of our battle and its consequences than I had known before, and that I had better push on with the crowd until I got orders, or fell in with Lord Edward Somerset's division. Frazer and Bell told me many flattering things about G troop, and considered it a certainty that I should get the brevet —*nous verrons!*

Quitting them, I plunged again into the crowd and fought my way towards the gate by which I had entered, but was agreeably surprised at meeting my people in the street, Newland having pushed on the moment he observed the crowd at the gate get somewhat thinner. Traversing the town with our carriages proved a tedious operation; for in addition to what I before found to struggle with, we now fell in with an endless column of Belgic infantry marching the same route as ourselves—a most annoying obstruction. The march of these people was a sort of triumphal procession: colours displayed; bands, with their clattering jangling cymbals, making a most martial noise; officers and men prancing along with short quick steps, bended knees, and stamping the pavement as if they wished to break holes in it, swaggering like turkey-cocks, and trying to appear indifferent, which was belied by the frequent upward glances at the fair dames in the windows, who certainly were doing all they could to blow up the vanity of these their brave countrymen by throwing out flowers on them, waving of handkerchiefs, clapping of hands, and faintly crying " Viva !"

We crept along the flank of this column of heroes, unnoticed and unknown, and soon after, clearing the Porte de Binche, got ahead and clear of them. The road was almost as much crowded as the streets of Nivelles, and I found it useless to expect to make rapid progress. For the first few miles the country was prettily wooded and interspersed with villages and neat houses; but then it began to get less wooded, less thickly inhabited, and in every way less interesting. Continued struggling on until towards evening, when our adjutant (Bell) overtook me with a little scrap of paper, on which was an order for me to bivouac either at Rœulx or Binche; but as we could not very well learn where these places were, and no guide was to be procured, and the evening began to close in, I determined on halting on a high and rather exposed piece of ground where we then happened to be. The bivouac was badly chosen —no water near, no house near, no wood near, no shelter of any kind near, and we were somehow all cross and out of humour. Set the men to work, scrubbing and cleaning appointments, this being the first opportunity of so doing. Went to sleep at nightfall. I think the nearest village to us was Haine. Some rustics who came to gape at us from a neighbouring farm told us that the King of Westphalia and another French general had passed the night of the 18th there with a few attendants, but that early on the morning of the 19th they had departed in a great hurry, evidently afraid of being overtaken.

21*st*. — Paraded early, and, considering all things, tolerably clean and neat. Descended to a lower country, equally dismal and uninteresting, without the one advantage which the other possesses—viz., that of commanding a distant prospect, always more or less pleasing. At noon arrived in the neighbourhood of Mons, where we overtook the Greys, Inniskillings, Ross's troop of Horse-Artillery, and several other corps, both of cavalry and infantry. We had, in short, now rejoined the army. The Greys and the Inniskillings were mere wrecks—the former, I think, did not muster 200 men, and the latter, with no greater strength, presented a sad spectacle of disorganisation and bad discipline; they had lost more than half their appointments. Some had helmets, some had none; many had the skullcap, but with the crest cut or broken off; some were on their own large horses, others on little ones they had picked up; belts there were on some; many were without, not only belts, but also canteens and havresacks. The enemy surely had not effected in a single day so complete a disorganisation, and I shrewdly suspect these rollicking Paddies of having mainly *spoilt* themselves. The other corps all looked remarkably well, although they, too, had partaken in the fight. We overtook these corps about a mile from Mons, on a hill, whence that place, with its old fortifications, looked venerable and picturesque. Descending thence, the road crossed a broad, flat, marshy piece of ground, which appeared nearly, if not entirely, to surround the place. Here our further progress was obstructed by a number of trees felled across the road, and forming a sort of abatis, and we were consequently obliged to make a detour through the meadows, and cross a rivulet by (I think the Trouille) a mill-dam, over which the cavalry were obliged to file. This rendered it a very tedious operation; and that part where at the mill we had to pass our guns, &c., over a bridge of planks barely broad enough, was a rather ticklish one. We crossed after the Greys, and came with them on the main road to Maubeuge at the moment a Highland regiment (perhaps the 92d), which had come through Mons, was passing. The moment the Highlanders saw the Greys an electrifying cheer burst spontaneously from the column, which was answered as heartily; and on reaching the road the two columns became blended for a few minutes—the Highlanders running to shake hands with their brave associates in the late battle. This little burst of feeling was delightful—everybody felt it; and although two or three general officers were present, none interfered to prevent or to censure this breach of discipline. A few hundred yards further on I found Lord Edward Somerset, with his brigade, formed in a field of clover by the roadside; and now, for the *first time*, I reported myself to him, and requested orders. These were simply to proceed straight to Malplaquet, and there bivouac for the night. Accordingly I continued my route independent as heretofore of my brigade. Nothing could be more horridly uninteresting than this country. Well cultivated, yet no habitations, or very few—no enclosures, or rather no hedges, there being banks to some of the fields; no trees, and hills just high enough to prevent an extended view, without adding one jot of beauty to the landscape. Most dismal country! To add to our wretchedness, the clouds which had been collecting all the morning began to drop their contents, so, snugging ourselves under our cloaks, on we jogged sulkily enough. We had left the great Chaussée de Maubeuge, and had been marching some time on a cross-road, occasionally confined between bare banks—not such ramparts as one sees in the county of Cork, but low clay banks about knee-high, with the ditch whence the material has been taken. In this way we had reached a point where a greater elevation of the ground allowed some scope of vision; and when emerging from between the banks, we came on something like a heath, bordered on one side by a large wood. Here an assemblage of rustics appeared awaiting us. Their principal object, no doubt, was to gaze at the strangers ; but they gave themselves infinite trouble to make us comprehend that we were about to cross the frontier and enter on the

WE CROSS THE FRONTIER.

soil of France. Drawing a long line in the mud, right across the road, and vociferating altogether, "Ici, monsieur!" "Voila, monsieur!" "Regardez, monsieur!" "C'est ici, monsieur, que vous entrez en la France!" and when we crossed their line, they grinned and jumped about like so many monkeys. I could not divine what pleasure they derived from seeing strangers violate the sacred territory, nor what could induce the energetic "Voici, monsieur, la France, voila la Belgique!" which they roared in chorus. How different would have been the feelings and actions of Englishmen on a similar occasion! Frenchmen, however, draw amusement from everything—even misfortune. But did they look upon our invasion as a misfortune? From what I have seen of these people, it appears very doubtful whether they care a farthing who reigns over them. Be that as it may, we undoubtedly entered France amidst cheers and greetings of the populace.

Soon after this we arrived at Malplaquet without being able to see it—the truth is, that it consists of a number of large farmhouses, &c., all standing isolated, and surrounded by thick orchards. In one of these we established our bivouac. A beggarly-looking old house, built of wattles, plastered with clay (which in many places had fallen off), windows without glass, and doorways without doors, stood in one corner of our orchard, and as this was very cheerless from the heavy rain, we agreed to do comfortable and dine in the *house*. Accordingly, our prog and materials were conveyed thither, and the dame was desired to make a fire in her best *salon*; yet, after all, it was a matter of doubt whether we should not have been more comfortable under the apple-trees, barring the droppings. The place was a perfect picture of misery; rooms disgustingly filthy, and besides, blackened with smoke; floor of earth, broken into all sorts of holes and inequalities; ceiling of loose planks and full of large holes, as were the partitions; furniture — a rickety table, two or three as rickety chairs, and a sort of chest of walnut, serving the place of a chest of drawers, black as ebony from age and dirt. The mistress, a grown-up daughter, and three or four young children, were the only inmates of this wretched mansion we saw—filthy as their dwelling, their clothes all in rags, and without shoe or stocking. These poor creatures were so alarmed at us that they scarcely seemed to know what they were doing. Our dinner, of course, was none of the

OUR FIRST NIGHT IN FRANCE. 369

most comfortable; but some hot grog and cigars afterwards put us all in good-humour, and we passed the evening admirably. In due time we retired to the nests our servants had provided for us in the orchard, and I was soon sound asleep, but was aroused about two o'clock by the sergeant-major, with a lantern in one hand and a paper in the other, which a dragoon had just brought from headquarters. This was an order to march at four A.M. Raining hard.

END OF THE FIRST VOLUME.

PRINTED BY WILLIAM BLACKWOOD AND SONS, EDINBURGH.

www.ingramcontent.com/pod-product-compliance
Lightning Source LLC
Chambersburg PA
CBHW071648160426
43195CB00012B/1397